NRA MEMBERS' WILDGAME COOKBOOK

© 1992 by National Rifle Association of America

Produced by the NRA Hunter Services Division. For information on the Hunter Skills Series, NRA Hunter Clinic Program, or becoming a volunteer hunter clinic instructor, contact the National Rifle Association of America, Hunter Services Division, 1600 Rhode Island Avenue NW, Washington, D.C. 20036-3268. Telephone (202) 828-6029.

Library of Congress Catalog Card Number;
92-064156

Main Entry under title:
NRA Members' Wild Game Cookbook
—NRA Hunter Skills Series—Supplement

ISBN 0-935998-95-0

 Printed using soy ink on recycled paper   HS5N5805 (hardcover)

ACKNOWLEDGEMENTS

Editor
Doug Pifer, Assistant Manager, Materials Development and Production, NRA Hunter Services Division

Recipe Editor
Martha Jo Corn, Recipe Consultant, Metairie, Louisiana

Editorial Assistants
Fritzi Alwin, Secretary, Advanced Hunter Clinics Department, NRA Hunter Services Division

Sandy M. Sexton, Editorial Assistant, Materials Development and Production, NRA Hunter Services Division

Production Manager
Earl W. Hower, Manager, Materials Development and Production, NRA Hunter Services Division

Illustrator
Doug Pifer, Assistant Manager, Materials Development and Production, NRA Hunter Services Division

Co-Authors and Review Committee
Clifford T. Burgess, Jr., Assistant Director, NRA Hunter Services Division

Gyongyver "Kitty" Beuchert, Assistant Director, NRA Women's Issues and Information Division and former Manager, NRA Hunter Information Department

Janice E. Taylor, Manager, Administrative Services, NRA Hunter Services Division

Robert W. Belford, Program Specialist, NRA Hunter/Member Support Services

Karl J. Gunzer, Manager, Rustic Inn, Annapolis, Maryland

Dr. Martin Marchello, Professor of Animal and Range Sciences, North Dakota State University

Jean Anliker, Extension Food and Nutrition Specialist, Cooperative Extension Service, University of Maryland

The National Rifle Association of America is grateful for the contributions made by hundreds of NRA members and their families who donated their favorite wild game recipes.

Photo Credits
Front Cover Photo by **Mary Ann and Joe Workosky**
Back Cover Photo by **Joe Workosky**

NRA Hunter's Code of Ethics

I will consider myself an invited guest of the landowner, seeking his permission, and conduct myself that I may be welcome in the future.

I will obey the rules of safe gun handling and will courteously but firmly insist that others who hunt with me do the same.

I will obey all game laws and regulations, and will insist that my companions do likewise.

I will do my best to acquire marksmanship and hunting skills that assure clean, sportsmanlike kills.

I will support conservation efforts that assure good hunting for future generations of Americans.

I will pass along to younger hunters the attitudes and skills essential to a true outdoor sportsman.

NRA Gun Safety Rules

The fundamental NRA rules for safe gun handling are:

- Always keep the gun pointed in a safe direction.
- Always keep your finger off the trigger until ready to shoot.
- Always keep the gun unloaded until ready to use.

When using or storing a gun always follow these rules:

- Be sure the gun is safe to operate.
- Know how to safely use the gun.
- Use only the correct ammunition for your gun.
- Know your target and what is beyond.
- Wear eye and ear protection as appropriate.
- Never use alcohol or drugs before or while shooting.
- Store guns so they are not accessible to unauthorized persons.

Be aware that certain types of guns and many shooting activities require additional safety precautions.

To learn more about gun safety, enroll in an NRA hunter clinic or state hunter education class, or an NRA safety training or basic marksmanship course.

TODAY'S AMERICAN HUNTER

I f you're a hunter, you're one of 20 million Americans who love the outdoors, have a close tie with traditions, and help conserve our natural resources. You know the thrill and beauty of a duck blind at dawn, a whitetail buck sneaking past your stand, a hot-headed, bugling bull elk. With your friends and forefathers you share the rich traditions of knowing wild places and good hunting dogs. Your woodsmanship and appreciation of nature provide food for body and soul.

And through contributions to hunting licenses and stamps, conservation tax funds, and sportsman clubs, you are partly responsible for the dramatic recovery of wildlife and its habitat. Hunters can take great pride — and satisfaction that only hunters know — in the great increases of deer, turkeys, elk, some waterfowl, and other species over the last century.

Your involvement with the National Rifle Association of America is also important to promote conservation and sportsmanship. In NRA, concerned hunters and shooters work together for laws and programs of benefit to the shooting sports. Most important is the education of sportsmen through programs like the nationwide Hunter Clinic Program operated by the NRA Hunter Services Division. Through the program and the Hunter Skills Series of how-to hunting books, America's already admirable hunters can keep improving their skills, safety, responsibility, and sportsmanship to help ensure our country's rich hunting traditions flourish forever.

CONTENTS

WELCOME TO WILD GAME COOKERY

Preparing and eating wild game is as important to most hunters as any part of the hunt. It's a way of sharing your enjoyment of the hunt with family and friends. In fact, we suspected that lots of hunters are as eager to swap recipes as they are to swap hunting stories. That's why we decided to ask the members of the National Rifle Association of America to share their recipes with us.

We asked for original ways of preparing wild game or fish. It could be a recipe or just a way of preparing or preserving meat, or some accompanying side dish. But we were in for a surprise when over a thousand recipes came in from all over the country. They were as diversified as NRA members themselves. Some were simple, some complicated, some serious and some funny. Most remarkable was the deep sense of family pride and tradition. These recipes are from real people. Many have a story behind them and were passed down through generations.

Basic information on handling meat, field care of game and fish, a word about safety and ethics, and nutritional information have been added, but our main objective was to allow NRA members to share their game and fish recipes with each other. You'll find the usual deer, rabbit, squirrel and duck, but also ways of preparing groundhog, opossum, beaver and armadillo. Among the usual fish recipes you'll also find fish sausage and sturgeon jerky. We hope you'll enjoy them.

Our sincere thanks to you, the NRA members. This is your book. Good hunting and good cooking!

Part I
Field to Table

Chapter 1

Basic Handling of Wild Game Meat

—DOUG PIFER

A mericans have a rich heritage of hunting and eating wild game. Bringing home the results of the hunt and preparing it is an ancient ritual basic to all societies. We inherited hunting from our pioneer forefathers and the various nationalities who emigrated into America.

Supermarket meats are professionally slaughtered, dressed, and butchered. They are presented in uniform condition, and there is seldom a difference in taste. In this world of shrink-wrap, microwave and processed foods, few people besides hunters have any need to learn how to care for and butcher their own meat. Wild game meat is delicious provided it is prepared and handled carefully. When wild game meat comes to the table, its taste depends upon how well the hunter took care of the meat. Game that was handled or dressed improperly, transported under adverse conditions, kept too long or exposed to high temperatures is bound to taste bad, no matter how it is cooked. So here are a few general guidelines on meat care.

Field Dressing

Regardless of size or kind, all game meat must be field dressed immediately. This means to open the body cavity, remove the entrails, and cut away any shot-damaged meat. The sooner this is done, the better the meat will taste and the less likely the entrails or damaged tissue will decompose or spoil the meat.

Before the Hunt

For field dressing, a sharp knife, clean plastic bag, a few lengths of strong cord, and a small belt axe or folding saw are all you'll need for everything but the biggest game. In that case, a pack frame, meat saw, and a small block and tackle are helpful. In addition, some cloth meat bags to protect meat from flies are a good idea, particularly in warm weather during the early big game seasons.

Read the hunting regulations for specific requirements on tagging and dressing game. Many states require game birds to have at least one fully feathered wing intact so the species and sex can be identified. Ignorance of regulations can result in a fine and your game may be confiscated by law enforcement authorities. Be fully aware of all game laws before you go hunting.

Before your hunt, plan ahead of time exactly what you'll do with the meat. Field dressing generally is all you need to do during cool weather to keep meat fresh until you bring it home from the field. But during the early hunting season and in warm climates, make sure you bring along a cooler for small game and take proper precautions to protect your big game meat from heat, insects, or conditions that could spoil the meat.

Small Game

A pocket knife is all you'll need to field dress small game. A pair of plastic or rubber gloves will help protect you from bacterial diseases that are transmittable to humans by contact with the flesh of wild mammals. Most hunters don't take this precaution, but in areas where such epidemics are known to occur, it's a good idea. The meat from infected animals is perfectly safe to eat because bacteria are killed upon cooking.

As soon as the animal is dead, place it on its back, insert the knife blade under a pinch of skin in the belly and open the body cavity from anus to throat. The entrails can easily be scooped out by hand, and a knife is only necessary to remove any connective tissue. Wipe out the body cavity but do not wash it in the field. If the weather is warm and you have a cooler, proceed to skin small game.

Skin a squirrel as follows (Figure A):

Step 1 — Pinch up the skin in the middle of the back and cut with a knife.

Step 2 — Then grab a piece of skin in both hands and pull in both directions, toward the head and the tail.

Step 3 — When you reach the tail, pull the skin away from around its base and cut it off with the skin attached. Place your boot on the tail of the squirrel and pull the skin off to the ankles, then disjoint the feet and cut the skin off at the base of the tail.

Step 4 — Work the skin forward over the squirrel's head and front legs like peeling off a sweater, and detach the skin at the wrist joints and free the rest of the skin by cutting off the head. There will be a few hairs along the ankles and wrists but the squirrel should be clean.

You can peel the tender skin off a rabbit much more easily, but the same basic method works as well for small game up to the size of a raccoon or groundhog.

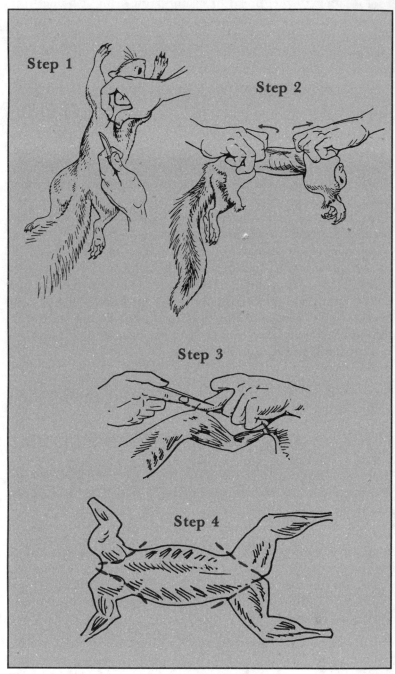

Figure A: **Skinning and Dressing Small Game.**

If you plan to save the fur of a groundhog or raccoon and also eat the meat, make a cut between the two hind legs and around the anus. Carefully skin the entire animal, removing feet, tail and head with the skin, then field dress. Rabbit and squirrel meat are much more delicate, but raccoon and groundhog meat is not usually damaged by delaying field dressing until after skinning. This is recommended if you plan to save the pelt because the cut through the belly skin usually made during field dressing will not be acceptable to fur buyers.

Except for small squirrels, quarter small game before freezing. Cut in half behind the rib cage, then down the middle of the back; or the front and hind legs can be removed at the shoulder and hip joints, and the back can be saved whole or cut in half (Refer to Figure A, Step 4). Be sure to remove all fat and glandular material from all small game. It will affect the taste. Also cut away and discard any shot-damaged meat. To find shot imbedded in meat, hold it up to a light source. The pellets are often visible because meat is translucent. Wash in cold water, pat dry with paper towels, then freeze.

Game Birds

To take the breast meat from a small bird using the following (Figure B):

Step 1 — Hold it breast up in your hand and find where the breast bone ends. Insert the point of a knife under it and then put your thumb under the breast bone and pull back.

Step 2 — The bird will literally break in half; you can then remove the entire breast and cut away the neck, shoulders and skin. With some small birds like doves, this can even be done without a knife.

Field dressing larger birds is begun the same way (Figure C):

Step 1 — Pull away the thick feathers around the point of the breast bone.
Step 2 — At the point of the breast bone make a horizontal cut.

Step 3 — Open the body cavity, reach in with your fingers and scoop out the entrails. Head, wings and feet can be left intact until you get home. Many states require a fully feathered wing and/or head to remain attached to the bird, so be aware of these specific hunting regulations.

Skinning a bird is quick and easy but removes most of the

7

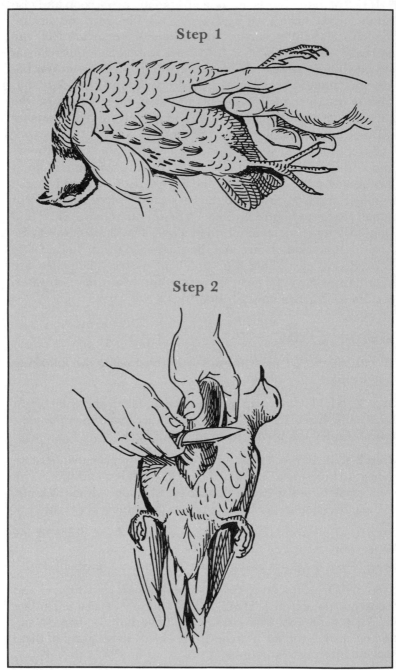

Figure B: Dressing Small Birds.

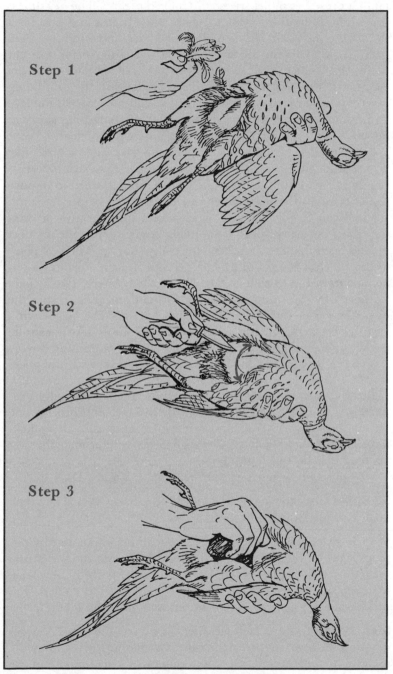

Step 1

Step 2

Step 3

Figure C: **Skinning and Dressing an Upland Bird.**

fat that preserves moisture, so the cooked meat will be dry unless some kind of liquid is added. Begin at the breast and peel back the skin to the neck, cut or disjoint the neck and windpipe, and peel the skin back to the shoulders. If you wish, disjoint or cut the wings off at the back, either at the shoulder joint or at the elbow. Peel the skin back to the tail, and cut off the tail, being careful to remove the oil gland with it. Pull the skin off the legs and disjoint the feet at the "drumstick". The remaining skin can be easily cut or pulled free and the bird will be clean.

Some people save the liver, heart and gizzards of birds like grouse and pheasant. These can be prepared separately or in sauces as an adjunct to the main course. Split gizzard to remove contents and wash heart, liver and gizzard well before freezing.

Birds can be plucked dry, wet, or by using paraffin or wax. Dry plucking works best with quail, grouse, pheasant or most upland birds that have not been too badly shot up. The best place to dry pluck a bird is outdoors, or hold it over a paper bag to help contain the feathers; they will be everywhere. Pluck body feathers a few at a time by pulling straight out. The fresher the bird, the easier the feathers will pull out. For the larger wing and tail feathers you may need a pair of pliers. Use a candle, pocket lighter, or gas burner to singe off any remaining downy feathers. A dry plucked bird looks attractive and the natural juices can be preserved while cooking.

Birds that have cooled down or whose feathers are tight require wet plucking. Hold the bird by the feet and dip for one minute in scalding water and remove feathers as in dry plucking. This method will be somewhat neater because the wet feathers will be easier to contain.

Dry plucking waterfowl can be simple (Figure D):

Step 1—Ducks and geese should first be field dressed. Then melt a stick of paraffin in the boiling water.

Step 2—Meanwhile remove as many feathers as possible by dry plucking. Holding the bird by its feet, dip it into the water and melted paraffin. Allow to cool so a coating of paraffin develops, then repeat. After a heavy coating of paraffin has cooled, you will be able to peel it off the bird along with the feathers.

Step 3—Remove the large feathers as in dry plucking. Any remaining feathers can be singed off. Instead of throwing away the paraffin and water boil it again, strain out the feathers, and use it for the next bird.

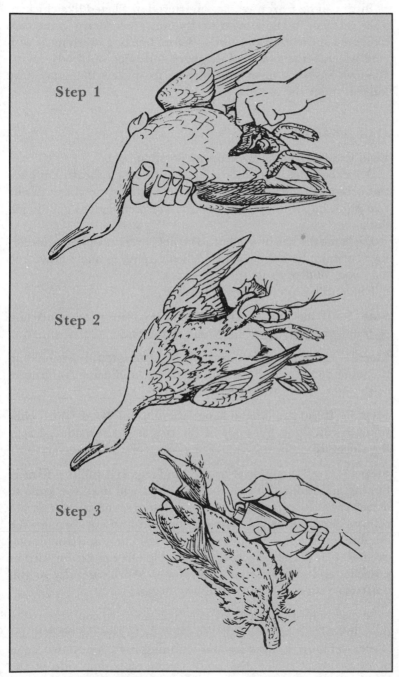

Step 1

Step 2

Step 3

Figure D: **Dressing Waterfowl.**

Birds can be frozen whole, quartered or filleted like chicken. Take care not to allow meat to dry out, particularly in the case of filleted or breasted-out birds. Before freezing, wash meat with cold water, remove any pinfeathers and wipe out body cavity. Remove any shot meat and inspect for pellets that may have lodged under the skin.

Big Game

Field dress big game as soon as possible.

A lockback folding knife is not as good as a sheath knife for this because of the increased chance of cutting your finger. Knife size is not important so long as it is sharp enough to get the job done.

Big game the size of a deer can be field dressed without quartering. Position the animal with its head uphill to allow gravity to help you, and prop it up on its back.

Follow these procedures (Figure E):

Step 1—If the animal is a male, cut around the penis and scrotum and pull them back out of the way.

Step 2—Then open the body cavity from anus to rib cage holding the knife point away from you, blade up, and using two fingers of the other hand to guide the blade.

Step 3—If the game head is not going to the taxidermist, continue to cut along the ends of the ribs to the throad and split the sternum.

Step 4—Grab the animal by the hind legs and roll it sideways, tipping and pulling the entrails out. You will need the knife to detach connective tissues. The liver, intestines, and paunch should roll out fairly easily. Now reach forward and cut through the diaphragm, the thin tissue separating the chest and abdominal cavities. Cut the esophagus and windpipe free as far forward as possible, and pull out heart and lungs. Work carefully so you don't cut yourself or puncture any organs.

At this point put the heart and liver aside to cool, then save them in a plastic bag. Now is also the time to save the tenderloins (Refer to Figure F, Cooling and Skinning Big Game), two strips of prime meat inside the body cavity on either side of the backbone.

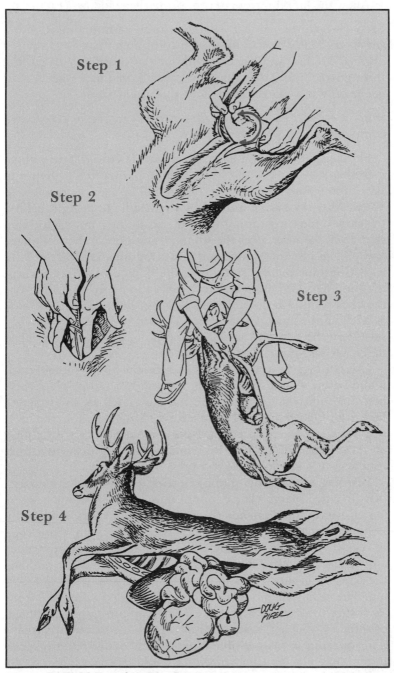

Figure E: **Field Dressing Big Game.**

Allow the hindquarters to cool properly as follows (Figure F):

Step 1—Split the pelvis by using a knife and tapping it with a small ax. This will also allow you to pull and cut away the sex organs, urethra and rectum without the possibility of cutting through them and tainting the meat with body wastes. Cut generously around the anus and pull them free.

Step 2—Prop up or hang the carcass to let it cool down completely.

Skin big game as soon as it is practical. It's easier if the animal is freshly killed. Because of the insulating qualities of hair and skin, it is mandatory to skin the animal as soon as possible in hot weather. Hang the animal by the head, cut around behind the ears to the cut running from throat to the chest cavity. Peel skin down the neck, over the shoulders and down the front legs. Saw off legs just above knee and pull remaining skin off the front legs. Continue pulling skin down the body of the deer and cut the hind legs off below the heel (hock) joint. In skinning, use the knife as little as possible and use your hands to pull the hide away from the meat. Cut the tail off with the skin. If you wish, salt down the skin and save it for tanning, after scraping off as much fat and meat as you can.

Quarter bigger game such as elk or moose after you field dress it and before skinning. Not only will quartering speed up cooling, but transporting quartered meat is much easier (Refer to Figure G, Quartering and Butchering). After skinning, the meat will be exposed to the air and develop a hard protective coating or glaze. This will need to be trimmed off at butchering time, resulting in some loss of good meat.

Dressing out very big game is easier with the help of a partner. To turn a large elk or moose onto its back, use a pole or log as a lever, then anchor the front and hind legs in place by lashing them to small trees or rocks, if available, with strong rope to keep them out of your way while field dressing. Many guides and hunters prefer to skin an elk or moose where it lies and use the skin as a ground cover to keep the meat clean while quartering. The meat is then transported in game bags to protect it from exposure to weather, flies and dirt. If you are hunting in back country by yourself, transporting meat back to camp is easier if the quarters or manageable sized pieces are tied to a backpack frame after placing them in game bags.

Butchering big game at home is easier if you use the boning

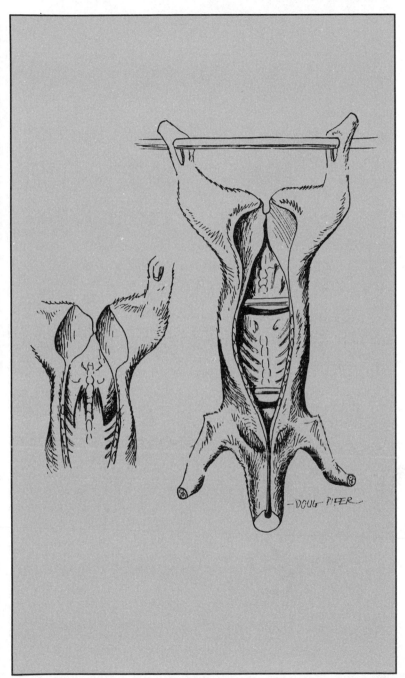

Figure F: **Cooling and Skinning Big Game.**

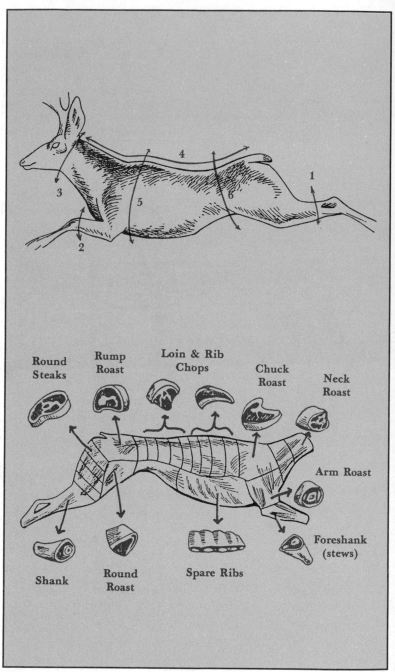

Figure G: **Quartering and Butchering Big Game.**

method. Start with the biggest masses of meat in the hindquarters, cut them into serving size pieces and wrap and freeze them as you go. This makes short work of a deer and avoids sawing through bone which could contaminate the meat. As you butcher, trim every piece of fat away. It turns rancid quickly, is usually tallowy and gives the meat an unpleasant taste.

Save meat scraps that remain and grind them up with beef fat for burger (see recipes for various ground meat combinations). Use the above illustration to help you make various cuts of meat. Double wrap all meat to keep it from drying out in the freezer, and mark it with the cut of meat and the date.

Canning Wild Game

Wild game meat , properly cleaned and cooled, can be canned as an alternative to freezing. To insure safety and protect against food poisoning, all jars or cans must be processed in a pressure canner to get a high enough temperature for a long enough time to kill all bacteria.

To can meat, remove all fat and soak for one hour in water with 1 tablespoon salt per quart. Remove all bones. Meat may be canned raw or cooked:

- Raw Pack—Add 1 tablespoon salt per quart. Fill jars with raw meat pieces, leaving 1 inch headspace. Do not add liquid. Adjust lids and process according to table below.
- Hot Pack—Precook meat by baking, boiling or steaming until about two-thirds done (rare). Add 2 tablespoons salt per quart. Fill jars with cooked meat pieces, add boiling broth, meat drippings, water or tomato juice, leaving 1 inch headspace. Process as on Table 1.

17

TABLE 1
Canning Time Table for Game

Pack	Jar Size	Time Min.	Dial Gauge 0-2000 feet*	Dial Gauge 2001-4000 feet	Weighted Gauge 0-1000 feet	Weighted Gauge Above 1000 ft.
Without Bone	Pt.	75	11	12	10	15
Hot or Raw	Qt.	90	11	12	10	15
With Bone	Pt.	65	11	12	10	15
Hot or Raw	Qt.	75	11	12	10	15

*Local Altitude Above Sea Level

Corning Wild Game

You can corn wild game using the same methods as for beef. Corning changes the flavor of wild game and tenderizes the meat, so that many people who will not eat wild game may like it corned. Use the following recipe to make six gallons of corning liquid.

Corning Liquid

  3 **pounds (6¾ cup) salt**
10 **ounces (1⅜ cup) sugar**
  2 **ounces sodium nitrate**
 ½ **ounce sodium nitrite**
  3 **level teaspoons black pepper**
  6 **bay leaves**
12 **level teaspoons mixed pickling spice**

For onion or garlic flavor, add one medium sized minced onion or 4 cloves of minced garlic. Place ingredients into a crock or glass jar, add water to make a total of 6 gallons, and cover. The best cuts of meat for corning are round steaks, but less desirable cuts such as brisket can also be corned.

The ideal temperature for corning meat is about 38 degrees Fahrenheit. During the spring or fall this is not hard to do, but if the temperature is too warm, add one-third more salt for every 15 degrees above 38 degrees. At 83 degrees add 3 pounds more salt, making a total of six pounds of salt.

Place the meat into the liquid, and put a heavy plate on the meat. Weight the plate if necessary to keep the meat below the pickle brine. Leave the meat in the corning liquid 15 days. On days five and 10, stir well, remove the meat and put the bottom piece on top. After the fifteenth day remove the meat. Use what you want immediately and put the balance in a cool place refrigerated at 38 degrees Fahrenheit. Corned meat at this stage is grayish pink in color. When cooked, it becomes bright pink, the normal color of a cured meat.

To cook corned meat, place in a covered pan, add cold water to cover. Bring to a boil and remove the film from the water. Reduce heat and simmer 5 hours or until tender, season to taste and serve as a main meat dish.

Fish

Fish meat is delicate and spoils quickly. To keep fish alive until they are cleaned, most sportsmen use stringers. Fish keep better if strung through the lips rather than the gills, but this is not always possible with soft-mouthed fish such as crappie. The live well of a boat or a large wire fish basket works much better when available. It is better to put fish on ice as soon as you catch them than to let them die on the stringer in warm weather, since bacteria work very rapidly and could spoil the meat.

To dress a fish, start by killing it with a sharp blow to the head. Run the knife blade from vent to throat and scoop out the entrails, being sure to scrape away the kidney tissue along the backbone with the tip of the knife or your fingernail. Cut into the flesh on either side of the fins and pull the fins out. Remove scales by starting at the tail and scraping towards the head with a blunt knife.

Filleting fish takes practice but the result is a piece of meat with no skin or bones (Figure H).

Step 1 — Lay the dead fish on its side and grip the head firmly. Hold a sharp, double edged filleting knife at an angle just behind the gills, and cut straight down to the backbone but not through it.

Step 2 — Turn the blade flat against the backbone and with a light sawing motion run the knife toward the fish's tail, cutting through

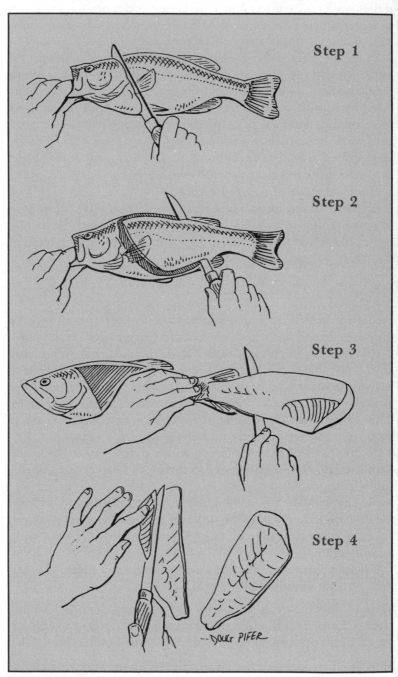

Figure H: Filleting a Fish.

the ribs. Continue toward the tail, but stop before cutting through the skin at the base of the tail fin.

Step 3—Turn the fillet over and insert the knife between skin and meat where you left the skin attached to the tail. Holding the blade nearly flat against the skin, run the knife along the entire filet while pulling on the skin with your other hand. This keeps the skin taut and makes it easier to peel away from the meat.

Step 4—Cut around the ribs and remove them in one piece. Turn the fish over and repeat the process. Rinse the fillets in cold water and they are ready to cook or freeze. As with game meat, double wrap fish or freeze it in a block of ice to preserve its delicate flavor.

Skin catfish as follows (Figure I):

Step 1—Catfish may be skinned by hanging them by the head using a strong hook and sturdy cord. Make a circular cut through the skin just behind the bony part of the head.

Step 2—Grasp the tough, slippery skin on either side with a pair of pliers and pull downwards to the base of the tail.

Step 3—Trim fillets as you would any other fish.

Fish that live along shorelines with heavy residential or industrial development tend to accumulate residues of chemical pollutants in their fatty tissues. If your fish comes from waters known to have high levels of such contaminants, protect yourself by trimming away the fatty tissue. Refer to Figure J, Fatty Areas on Fish.

Also discard the skin, liver and entrails. Cook the fish so the remaining fat can drain away. Broiling is best—do not pan fry. If you poach or deep fat fry, discard all water or fat after cooking.

Canning Fish

Although it is easier to freeze fish, canning is an alternative, but you must use a pressure canner. Fish to be canned must be properly dressed and cooled, but frozen fish that has been thawed in the refrigerator may also be canned if done promptly. Fish may be canned with the bones. They add to the flavor and nutritional value but are only recommended if you use pint containers or smaller.

Carefully clean and dress fish, and cut into pieces about 1 inch

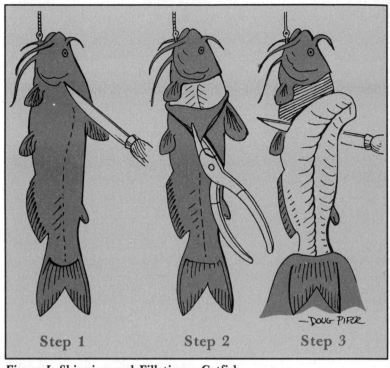

Figure I: Skinning and Filleting a Catfish.

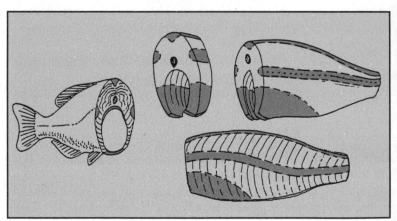

Figure J: Fatty Areas on Fish.

shorter than the height of the jars you intend to use. Soak fish for an hour in cold water containing one cup salt to one gallon water. Place clean plate on fish to keep under brine. Do not reuse salt water. Drain fish for ten minutes, then pack into jars, skin side next to glass. If fish are small, alternate head and tail ends. Leave one inch headspace. Do not add liquids or oil. Process according to Table 2.

TABLE 2
Canning Time Table for Fish

			Pounds Pressure			
			Dial Gauge		Weighted Gauge	
Pack	Jar Size	Time Min.	0-2000 feet*	2001-4000 feet	0-1000 feet	Above 1000 ft.
Raw	½ Pt. or Pt.	100	11	12	10	15

*Local Altitude Above Sea Level

DOUG PIFER

CHAPTER 2
NUTRITIONAL VALUES OF WILD GAME MEAT

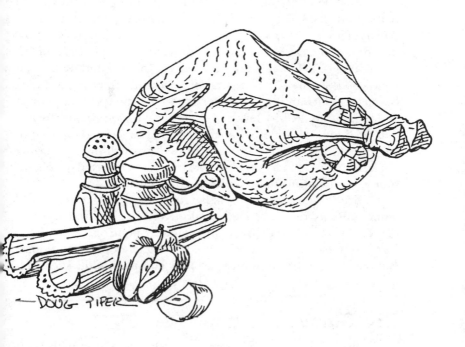

— DOUG PIPER

Americans are becoming aware that a diet low in cholesterol and saturated fats can offset tendencies towards heart disease, obesity and certain types of cancer. The amount of cholesterol that accumulates in your bloodstream is affected by the type of fat you eat. Generally saturated fats in your diet raise your blood cholesterol level, while unsaturated fats lower it.

Cholesterol is a fatty substance contained in red meat, fish, poultry, and also in wild game. Saturated fats, those that tend to become solid at room temperature, are found in meat and dairy products. Unsaturated fats stay liquid at room temperature and are either polyunsaturated (such as those found in vegetable oils) or monounsaturated (such as those found in plants, animals and seafood). While fats are necessary in the diet and make food taste good, eating too much fat of any kind is not a good idea because all fats are high in calories (45 calories per teaspoon).

To maintain healthy levels of cholesterol in your bloodstream, you need to be aware of what kind of fats you eat and cook with. In general, using oils with unsaturated fats will help lower the cholesterol levels in your bloodstream, particularly if you combine careful eating habits with regular exercise.

Naturally more lean and active than domestic animals, wild game animals' diets are free of additives to color their meat or develop fat. Wild game meat also contains none of the synthetic hormones used to increase the growth rate of domestic animals. But how does wild game meat actually compare to the meat you get at the grocery store or butcher shop?

Big Game

As might be expected, big game animals, compared with beef, are lower in fat. But as for number of calories, big game and domestic beef are about the same. Cholesterol content varies widely among different big game animals. For example, moose and bison have slightly less cholesterol than beef, but venison and antelope have more.

A typical venison steak or chop will provide you with a total of 149 calories per 100 grams of raw meat. Other big game animals are similar. Bison and antelope are considered highly nutritious because of the proportion of protein, fat, minerals and fatty acids compared to the number of calories they contain. Compared to lean beef, they have less fat and have more iron and a higher proportion of polyunsaturated fatty acids. Protein levels in wild game are about equal to that in beef.

Table 3 compares samples of the same cut of raw loin from various game animals and USDA quality standard grade beef, which is the most lean.

If you're following a low fat diet, you may be interested in comparing the fat contests of wild game and domestic meat. Table 4 compares the fat content in beef to that of various game animals and breaks the fats down into saturated, mono- and polyunsaturated.

TABLE 3
Nutritional Comparison of Wild Game and Domestic Meat

Animals	No. of Samples	Protein gm/100gm	Fat gm/100gm	Calories kCal/100gm	Cholesterol mg/100gm
Beef	20	22.7	2.7	158	69
Pork	10	22.3	4.9	165	71
Whitetail Deer	21	23.6	1.4	149	116
Mule Deer	29	23.7	1.3	145	107
Elk	16	22.9	0.9	137	67
Moose	33	22.1	0.5	130	71
Antelope	24	22.5	0.9	144	121
Bison	30	21.7	1.9	138	62
Squirrel	15	21.4	3.2	149	83
Cottontail	26	21.8	2.4	144	77
Jackrabbit	8	21.9	2.5	153	131

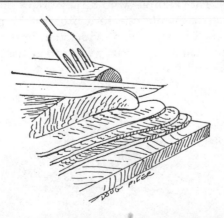

TABLE 4
The Relative Percentage of the Types of Fat Within the Muscle Tissue of Various Mammalian Species

Animals	Percent of Fatty Acids		
	Saturated	Monounsaturated	Polyunsaturated
Beef	46.3	45.5	8.2
Buffalo	43.2	45.0	11.8
Mule Deer	48.0	31.8	20.2
Whitetail Deer	45.6	30.6	23.9
Elk	48.4	26.6	24.9
Antelope	41.2	27.1	31.6
Moose	36.6	24.3	39.1

Game Birds

Nutritionally, while meat from upland game birds (including wild turkey) is quite similar, cholesterol content varies greatly from one species to another. Sharp-tailed and sage grouse have the most cholesterol. Their meat provides less energy because their meat has more moisture and less protein.

Protein and mineral content are similar except for ruffed grouse, which contains less fat and more sodium and calcium than other upland birds. Fat within the breast muscle appears to differ between species, but like mineral content it may also depend upon the bird's age and diet.

Because they prefer running to flying, turkeys and pheasants have proportionately less breast and more leg and thigh muscle development. For example, wild turkey breast makes up 34 percent of the carcass while pheasant breast is 37 percent. Nutritionally, turkey breast meat provides the most energy because it is high in both fat and protein. Wild turkey has proportionately more protein and less fat than domestic turkey.

TABLE 5
Nutritional Comparison of Wild and Domestic Fowl
(Skinned Breast Muscle Analyzed)

Animals	No. of Samples	Protein gm/100gm	Fat gm/100gm	Calories kCal/100gm	Cholesterol mg/100gm
Chicken	10	23.6	0.7	135	60
Turkey (Domestic)	24	23.5	1.5	146	60
Pheasant	27	25.7	0.6	148	52
Sharp-tailed Grouse	28	23.8	0.7	142	105
Sage Grouse	23	23.7	1.1	140	101
Wild Turkey	16	25.8	1.1	163	55
Sandhill Crane	27	21.9	2.7	156	133
Snow/Blue Goose	25	22.7	3.6	171	124
Canada (Lesser)	7	22.7	3.9	171	105
Mallard	15	23.2	2.0	154	143
Dove	9	22.9	1.8	145	94

Fish

Nutritional experts are increasingly expressing the positive health benefits of fish. Low in fat and cholesterol, fish has often been called the food of the 90s.

Fats in fish are highly unsaturated and have been shown to significantly lower levels of fat in the human bloodstream. These fats are called blood lipids, and when present in high levels have been linked to increased risk of heart disease. Another health benefit of fish is the presence of linoleic acid, referred to as the essential fatty acid. This acid is responsible for keeping the body healthy through its maintenance of the immune system. When present in high enough levels it has been shown to fend off such diseases as allergies and cancer.

Fish are also low in cholesterol, in fact, the lowest of all meats available for human consumption. Combining the low levels of cholesterol and fat present in fish, there is not a meat that can match this protein source for healthy nutrition.

If you are now practicing a healthy lifestyle, exercising and following a low fat diet, fish can be a large portion of your diet. Table 6 compares the nutritional content of a number of freshwater fish, saltwater fish and shellfish.

TABLE 6
Nutritional Contents of Fish
(Based on 100 Grams Raw Edible Portion)

Animals	Calories mg	Protein mg	Fat mg	Cholesterol mg	Sodium mg	Iron mg
Saltwater Fish						
Bluefish	124	20.04	4.24	59	60	0.48
Croaker	104	17.78	3.17	61	56	0.37
Eel (mixed species)	184	18.44	11.66	126	51	0.60
Flounder	91	18.84	1.19	48	81	0.36
Rockfish (mixed)	94	18.75	1.57	35	60	0.41
Chinook Salmon	180	20.06	10.44	66	47	0.71
Pink Salmon	116	19.94	3.45	52	67	0.77
Sea Bass (mixed)	97	18.43	2.00	41	68	0.29
Sea Trout (mixed)	104	16.74	3.61	83	58	0.27
Striped Bass	97	17.73	2.33	80	69	0.84
Bluefin Tuna	144	23.33	4.90	38	39	1.02
Freshwater Fish						
Carp	127	17.83	5.60	66	49	1.24
Channel Catfish	116	18.18	4.26	58	63	0.97
Lake Trout	148	20.77	6.61	58	52	1.50
Northern Pike	88	19.26	0.69	39	39	0.55
Walleye	93	19.14	1.22	86	51	1.30
Rainbow Trout	118	20.55	3.36	57	27	1.90
Shellfish						
Clams (raw, mixed)	74	12.77	0.97	34	56	13.98
Blue Crab	87	18.06	1.08	78	293	0.74
King Crab	84	18.29	0.60	42	836	0.59
Crayfish	89	18.66	1.06	139	53	2.45
Northern Lobster	90	18.80	0.90	95	N/A	N/A
Eastern and Gulf Oysters	69	7.06	2.47	55	112	6.70
Pacific Oysters	81	9.45	2.30	N/A	106	5.11
Shrimp (mixed)	106	20.31	1.73	152	148	2.41

Source: NOAA Technical Memorandum NMFS F/SEC-11, U.S. Department of Commerce (1981) and USDA Handbook Eight (1987).

Meat Yield

In addition to nutrient composition, many sportsmen are interested in just how much meat they can obtain from the animals they bring home. Table 7 will give you some idea of how much meat various big game animals provide, given their whole body weight (dead but not field dressed).

TABLE 7

Average Weight of Various Game Animals by Stages of Processing

Animals	Pounds		
	Whole Body[1]	Field Dressed[2]	Carcass[3]
Whitetail Deer	148	115	96
Mule Deer	137	107	89
Elk	555	384	312
Moose	914	666	498
Antelope	96	74	60
Pheasant	2.6	2.2	1.6
Hungarian Partridge	0.85	0.74	0.53
Sharp-tailed Grouse	1.8	1.4	1.0
Sage Grouse	3.4	2.8	2.1
Mallard	2.4	2.2	1.3
Gadwall	1.7	1.3	0.75
Blue-winged Teal	0.89	0.71	0.38
Snow/Blue Goose	5.1	4.00	2.3
Canada Goose	6.0	4.8	3.0
Sandhill Crane	8.5	6.7	4.8

[1] Whole Body is the weight of the entire animal minus blood lost during harvest. Example: If a whitetail deer weighed 200 pounds then 200 x 51.7% = 103.4 pounds of edible lean boneless tissue.

[2] Field Dressed is the whole body weight minus the entrails. Example: If a whitetail deer field dressed 150 pounds then 150 x 61.1% = 91.6 pounds of edible lean boneless tissue.

[3] Carcass is the field dressed weight minus the head, legs and hide (skin and feathers). Example: If a whitetail carcass weighed 100 pounds then 100 x 71.6% = 71.6 pounds of edible lean boneless tissue.

Table 8 shows how much boneless meat you can expect from a field dressed carcass. For example a field dressed deer will yield approximately 58% boneless meat for the freezer while the skinned and dressed carcass will yield 72%. In other words if your deer weighed 120 pounds field dressed and wasn't shot up severely, you could expect to get 70 pounds of boneless meat to put into the freezer as roasts, chops, steaks and sausage trim.

TABLE 8

Average Yield of Lean Edible Tissue of Game Animals by Various Stages of Processing

	Percent		
Animals	Whole Body[1]	Field Dressed[2]	Carcass[3]
Whitetail Deer	51.7	61.1	71.6
Mule Deer	42.7	54.2	64.9
Elk	40.1	54.1	65.7
Moose	36.5	50.3	67.0
Antelope	42.6	55.2	68.4
Pheasant	45.6	51.3	70.8
Hungarian Partridge	42.8	49.3	67.8
Sharp-tailed Grouse	41.3	54.3	69.0
Sage Grouse	41.5	50.4	68.7
Mallard	34.0	35.9	65.4
Gadwall	25.4	33.8	61.6
Blue-winged Teal	26.7	34.3	59.4
Snow/Blue Goose	30.9	38.7	67.2
Canada Goose	32.6	40.3	62.5
Sandhill Crane	35.0	45.1	60.9

[1] Whole Body is the weight of the entire animal minus blood lost during harvest. Example: If a whitetail deer weighed 200 pounds then 200 × 51.7% = 103.4 pounds of edible lean boneless tissue.

[2] Field Dressed is the whole body weight minus the entrails. Example: If a whitetail deer field dressed 150 pounds then 150 × 61.1% = 91.6 pounds of edible lean boneless tissue.

[3] Carcass is the field dressed weight minus the head, legs and hide (skin and feathers). Example: If a whitetail carcass weighed 100 pounds then 100 × 71.6% = 71.6 pounds of edible lean boneless tissue.

Wild game is highly nutritious, compares favorably to domestic red meat and its harvest provides healthy exercise. So what are you waiting for? Get out there and get fresh air and exercise as well as food for body and soul. Go hunting!

Part II
Wild Game Recipes

—DOUG PIFER

CHAPTER 3
SMALL GAME RECIPES

Rabbit

Roast Rabbit with Sage Stuffing

  1 (5 pound) dressed rabbit
1½ teaspoons salt
  ¼ teaspoon pepper
  6 slices bacon, cut in half

Sage Stuffing:
  6 cups bread crumbs
1½ cups onion, finely diced
  1 cup celery, leaves and stalk, finely diced
  ¾ tablespoons sage
1½ teaspoons salt
  ½ teaspoon pepper
  ¾ cup melted butter or margarine

Mix bread crumbs, onion, celery and seasoning. Add melted butter or margarine slowly, tossing mixture lightly with a fork.

Wash rabbit in lukewarm water, drain and dry. Remove one third of fat from inside rabbit. Sprinkle inside rabbit with one teaspoon salt and stuff with sage stuffing. Skewer vent by inserting several toothpicks through skin from side to side. Lace with string, tying end securely. Fasten both fore and hind legs with toothpicks and string. Make several small slits in the less fat parts of the rabbit and insert small pieces of bacon. Sprinkle outside with one half teaspoon salt and one fourth teaspoon pepper. Place on side on a greased rack in a shallow baking pan and roast at 375 degrees for 25 minutes per pound. Turn rabbit when it is half done.

David F. Lucas
Smithfield, RI

Rabbit Cacciatore — Nana Lia Style

1 rabbit, quartered
1 stalk celery, cut-up
1 tablespoon capers
1 tablespoon raisins
12 green olives with pimentos
1 medium onion, diced
1 clove garlic, minced
¼ teaspoon oregano
1 can whole tomatoes
¼ cup sherry
vegetable oil

Cover bottom of a dutch oven or small roasting pan with vegetable oil. Put in rabbit, celery, capers, olives, raisins, onions, garlic, and oregano. Squeeze whole tomatoes over the top, add sherry, cover and bake in a preheated oven 350 degrees for about one hour, or until rabbit is tender.

Tom Arcuri
Tampa, FL

Nana Lia's Sweet and Sour Rabbit

1 rabbit, quartered
plain bread crumbs
½ pound raw ham, diced
1 chorizo (Spanish sausage), diced
½ stalk celery, diced
1 medium onion, diced
1 tablespoon sugar
¼ cup vinegar
½ cup water
12 green olives with pimentos
4 ounces capers
1 tablespoon raisins
small pinch saffron powder

Coat rabbit with bread crumbs. Place rabbit in a large casserole dish, and add all remaining ingredients. Note: dissolve sugar in vinegar prior to putting in casserole dish. Bake, covered, in 375 degree oven for approximately one hour or until rabbit is tender.

Tom Arcuri
Tampa, FL

Hare — Gourmet Style

2 ½ pound hare
  2 cups red wine
  1 bay leaf
    sprig of thyme
    rind of ½ orange
  6 tablespoons lard or butter
  2 cloves garlic, chopped
    sprig rosemary
    salt and pepper

Puncture hare with a fork and marinate in a mixture of red wine, bay leaf, thyme, orange rind, salt and pepper for six to seven hours, turning once in a while.

Melt lard or butter in a frying pan with chopped garlic and rosemary. Remove hare from marinade, season with salt and pepper, put in a roasting pan and brush with melted lard, and bake in a preheated oven for one hour at 375 degrees, turning it occasionally and basting it with pan juices.

Remove from oven, pour off pan juices and replace them with marinade, then return to oven and continue roasting for 45 additional minutes or until fork tender. Remove from roasting pan, cut into pieces and place on a serving platter. Strain marinade and pour over rabbit.

Yield: serves four

Luigi Farina
Brooklyn, NY

Fruited Rabbit Pie

  1 pound cubed rabbit (de-boned)
  1 tablespoon oil
  1 teaspoon salt
  ⅛ teaspoon ground pepper
  1 tablespoon fresh lemon juice
  1 tablespoon water
  ½ cup chopped onion
  ½ cup thinly sliced celery
  1 tablespoon margarine
  ¾ cup chopped, peeled apple
  1 cup whole cranberry sauce*
  2 tablespoons chili sauce
  1 teaspoon prepared mustard
  ⅛ teaspoon ground ginger
  1 (9 inch) unbaked pie crust

Heat oil in heavy skillet and brown rabbit cubes over medium heat. Sprinkle rabbit with salt and pepper, add lemon juice and water. Cover tightly and simmer 20 to 30 minutes or until tender. Remove rabbit from skillet. In same skillet sauté onion and celery in margarine for three minutes. Add chopped apple and sauté another three minutes. Combine cranberry sauce, chili sauce, mustard and ginger and stir into vegetable-apple mixture. Combine with meat and heat through. Pour into empty nine inch pie plate. Cover with crust rolled to one fourth inch thickness, turn under edges and flute. Cut steam holes in the top. Bake in preheated 450 degree oven for 10 minutes. Reduce heat to 375 and bake until top is golden brown, about 15 minutes. Serve immediately.

*Cranberry sauce may be frozen to be used later for another pie.

Ginger Esworthy
Akron, OH

Rabbit in Creamy Dill Sauce

1 pound cubed rabbit (de-boned)
1 tablespoon oil
1 large garlic clove, minced
1 medium onion, sliced
½ cup apple juice
½ cup chicken stock
1 (12 ounce) can evaporated milk
1 tablespoon margarine
3 tablespoons all purpose flour
1 teaspoon dried dill weed
⅛ teaspoon pepper
2 tablespoons dry white wine

Heat oil in heavy skillet, add rabbit and brown over medium heat. Add garlic and onions and sauté a few minutes longer. Add apple juice and chicken stock, cover and simmer for 30 minutes or until rabbit is tender. Remove cover, increase heat and gently boil for 10 minutes to slightly reduce liquid. Remove rabbit from pan. Add margarine and flour to remaining liquid in pan, whisking until smooth. Gradually add evaporated milk, cooking until mixture thickens and boils. Add dill weed, pepper, the reserved cooked rabbit and wine, stirring well. Heat over low heat until warmed through. Serve with buttered noodles.

Ginger Esworth
Akron, OH

39

Rabbit Sauce Piquant

      2 small rabbits, cut in pieces
    ¼ cup cooking oil
      2 cups chopped onions
  1 ½ cups chopped celery
      1 cup chopped bell pepper
      4 garlic pods, chopped fine
    ½ cup parsley, chopped
      1 teaspoon sugar
      2 (8 ounce) cans tomato sauce
      1 (6 ounce) can tomato paste
      1 large can whole tomatoes
      1 (4 ounce) can mushrooms
      7 cups water, approximately
        salt and red pepper to taste

Cook rabbit in oil on medium heat until well browned. Remove rabbit and set aside. In same oil brown onions, celery, and bell pepper until wilted. Add tomato paste to greens and brown lightly. Add tomato sauce, whole tomatoes and six cups water and cook until oil floats to the top. Skim, add browned rabbit, mushrooms, garlic and sugar and cook until rabbit is tender and sauce is desired thickness.

Serve over cooked white rice. Sprinkle with parsley and enjoy.

Al Trosclair
Lockport, LA

Cottontail Rabbit

      2 cottontail rabbits
    ½ cup butter
        salt
        pepper
      1 cup worcestershire sauce
      1 tablespoon onion flakes
        water
        cinnamon

Cut rabbits into five pieces, front quarters, hind quarters and back.

Place rabbits in a glass pan and add one half cup melted butter, 1 cup worcestershire sauce, salt and pepper and one tablespoon onion flakes. Cover and bake at 350 degrees for 35 minutes.

After 35 minutes take out, add one cup water and sprinkle cinnamon lightly over rabbits. Bake another 35 minutes or until meat is tender. You won't believe it's rabbit!

Yield: serves four

Mark Hayes
Genoa, CO

Glutton Rabbit with Madeira

2 ½ **pounds rabbit**
    pinch of cinnamon
    pinch of chopped fresh rosemary
  1 **bay leaf**
  2 **tablespoons red wine vinegar**
 ¼ **cup olive oil**
  2 **tablespoons butter**
  1 **cup dry madeira wine**
    chicken broth
    salt and pepper

Cut rabbit into serving size pieces, then wash, dry and put into large bowl. Marinate for 12 to 24 hours in refrigerator in a mixture of cinnamon, rosemary, bay leaf, salt and pepper, vinegar, and half the oil. Turn occasionally.

Drain and brown rabbit in butter and remaining oil in a frying pan. Add madeira wine and simmer over low heat until tender, about one and a half hours, adding broth as needed. Remove rabbit pieces to a platter and keep warm. Skim off fat from juices, reheat juices, simmer to half the volume and spoon over rabbit pieces.

Yield: serves four

Luigi Farina
Brooklyn, NY

—DOUG PIFER

Rabbit—Hunter's Style

1 rabbit
1 cup olive oil
1 cup diced garlic
1 cup all purpose flour
2 tablespoons dry mustard
1 teaspoon curry powder
1 teaspoon powdered thyme
2 tablespoons salt
½ teaspoon pepper
1 cup light cream

Cut rabbit into pieces, rub all over with olive oil and leave in a cool place overnight. The next day, rub each piece with garlic. Put flour in a bag, add mustard, curry powder, thyme, salt and pepper. Shake rabbit pieces in bag until coated, then fry in olive oil or salad oil until golden brown. Reduce heat to simmer, cover and let simmer for one hour or until tender. Pour cream over rabbit and serve hot.

Peggy Dyson
Columbia, AL

Chinese Rabbit Cake

1 rabbit, boned
2 egg whites, beaten well
½ cup water
1½ tablespoons corn starch
¾ teaspoon salt
oil for deep frying
flour or more corn starch for coating

Sauce:
2 pickled red chilies
3 cloves garlic, peeled
3 green onions
3 slices fresh ginger
½ cup chicken stock
1½ tablespoons brown vinegar
1 tablespoon sugar
1 tablespoon light sauce
1½ teaspoons corn starch
salt and pepper to taste

Mince or grind meat very fine and add egg whites, water, corn starch and salt. Mix thoroughly until paste is smooth. Spread mixture in a lightly oiled heat proof dish and place it in a steamer, steam for about 15 minutes or until cake is firm. Remove from steamer and let cool. Cut into thick slices about two inches long and coat thickly with corn starch.

Finely grind or mince chilies, garlic, green onions and ginger, mix all sauce ingredients together and set aside. Heat oil in a wok or frying pan until it starts to smoke, fry rabbit cakes until golden brown, set cakes on paper towel to drain well. In a clean wok or frying pan heat a little oil and sauté sauce ingredients until they are fragrant. Add rabbit cakes, mix evenly, then add other pre-mixed sauce ingredients and bring to a boil. Stir carefully and serve.

Mr. Marion A. Koszewski
Brecksville, OH

Sweet and Sour Rabbit

1 rabbit, cut in one inch pieces
1 can bamboo shoots
1 can water chestnuts
1 can pineapple chunks (drain and save syrup)
1 can mushrooms
4 green onions
1 green pepper, cut into strips
2 chicken bouillon cubes
¼ cup brown sugar
1 tablespoon soy sauce
2 tablespoons corn starch
¼ cup vinegar
½ teaspoon salt
1 cup Drakes Mix
½ cup milk
1 egg
1 inch oil in a pan

Mix milk and egg, dip rabbit in mixture then into Drakes Mix. Stir fry in hot oil for one minute or until brown. Set aside. Simmer one cup water, bouillon and one and one half teaspoon salt for a few minutes. Add and stir fry bamboo shoots, water chestnuts, green peppers, green onions and mushrooms. In a

separate pan combine brown sugar and corn starch, add pineapple juice, vinegar, soy sauce and salt. Mix until bubbly and
serve over rice.

Sweet and sour rabbit is a special recipe to us. We had a great
beagle who loved bunny hunting. I dedicate this to you, Sally.

Mrs. Don Sherman
Evart, MI

Rabbit Sauce Piquant
South Louisiana Style

4 swamp rabbits
2 (15 ounce) cans tomato sauce
1 (12 ounce) can rotel tomatoes
1 (6 ounce) can tomato paste
1 (15 ounce) can chopped mushrooms
1 bell pepper
1 clove garlic
2 bay leaves
1 bunch green onions
½ cup chopped parsley
½ cup chopped celery
   salt, black pepper, cayenne pepper
   Louisiana hot sauce
1 cup Italian dressing
5 tablespoons flour
   olive oil
½ lemon, quartered
   water

Cut up rabbits and marinate overnight, refrigerated, in Italian
dressing, Louisiana hot sauce, salt, pepper and cayenne pepper.

In a large pot add about one eighth inch olive oil and fry rabbits until brown, then put aside. Sauté garlic, bell pepper, and
the white part of the green onions until they are wilted. Add approximately one and a half quarts water, tomato sauce, rotel
tomatoes, tomato paste, mushrooms, the green part of the onions,
parsley, celery, lemon quarters and bay leaves. Cook on medium
heat, stirring constantly until it comes to a boil. To make roux,
add olive oil to cover the bottom of a small skillet, add flour, and
stir constantly over medium heat until light brown. Add roux
to sauce, lower fire and let cook approximately one half hour.

Add fried rabbits to sauce, lower heat, cover and cook until rabbit is tender, about two and one half hours, stirring about every 15 minutes. Adjust salt and pepper to taste. Serve over rice or spaghetti.

Eldon C. Clement
Thibodaux, LA

Rabbit or Squirrel Creole Bake

    3 rabbits or 4 squirrels, cut into serving pieces
    2 envelopes dry onion soup mix
 2 ¼ cups boiling water
    1 (16 ounce) can whole tomatoes, drained and chopped
    1 (7 ounce) can whole kernel corn, drained
 1 ½ cups uncooked regular rice
    1 green pepper, chopped
      salt and pepper to taste

In a baking dish place rabbit or squirrel pieces in a single layer. In medium bowl blend onion soup mix, water, tomatoes, corn, rice and green pepper and pour into baking dish and cover. Bake in 350 degree oven for one and a half to two hours, or until meat is tender.

Mike Davich, Jr.
Hammond, IN

Rabbit Salad

    3 cups boiled rabbit, boned
    ¾ cup sweet cucumber chips, chopped fine
 4-5 ribs only, Chinese cabbage, chopped fine
    3 boiled eggs, chopped
    2 tablespoons catalina dressing
    3 tablespoons mayonnaise
    1 teaspoon celery seed
    1 tablespoon prepared mustard

Cut rabbit into pieces, place in a pan covered with water, add salt, parsley flakes and garlic powder to taste. Bring to a boil and simmer until tender and meat falls from bones. Bone rabbit and place in refrigerator to cool. Combine remaining ingredients and add to rabbit. Serve on a bed of lettuce or a split tomato.

Anita C. Jones
Punta Gorda, FL

45

Old Fashioned Hasenpfeffer with Spaetzles

Hasenpfeffer:

1 small rabbit (2½ pounds), cut into serving pieces
½ cup vinegar
2 cups water
2 teaspoons salt
¼ teaspoon pepper
½ cup sugar
2 tablespoons whole pickling spice wrapped and tied in a cheese-cloth
1 medium onion, sliced
½ cup flour
4 tablespoons cooking oil
½ pint sour cream

Spaetzles:

2½ cups all purpose flour
2 teaspoons salt
1 egg slightly beaten
1 cup water
boiling salted water

Combine vinegar, water, salt, pepper, sugar, pickling spice and sliced onion in a bowl. Stir sugar until dissolved. Add pieces of rabbit and cover. Let stand in refrigerator six to ten hours, turning and marinating rabbit occasionally so meat will absorb flavors.

Remove rabbit, save liquid, onions and pickling mixture. Fill dutch oven with two inches water. Place rabbit in water and bring to a slow boil. Boil for five minutes in a rapid boil, pour off water and rinse rabbit well. Repeat this procedure. Put rabbit back into dutch oven with marinating mixture of vinegar water, pickling spice and onions that you have saved from the marinating process and bring rabbit back to a gentle boil.

Remove rabbit, save liquid and onions, but discard pickling mixture.

Place four tablespoons cooking oil in a fry pan on medium heat. Roll rabbit in flour until well coated, shake off excess flour and brown evenly.

Place rabbit in a casserole dish with pickling liquid and onions saved from the last boiling. Stir in sour cream. Cover and place in oven. Bake at 375 degrees for two and a half hours.

To make spaetzles, combine flour, salt, egg and water. Beat until smooth. Heat teaspoon in boiling water (will help the dough come off the spoon easier), drop by one half teaspoon into salted boiling water. Cook 10 minutes. Rinse with cool water and drain. Add to hasenpfeffer 30 minutes before serving.

Karen C. Kiefer
Hiram, OH

Lapin St. Jacques

   wild rabbits, boned
 1 cup dry white wine
 1 bay leaf
 ½ pound fresh mushrooms, sliced
 ½ cup sliced green onions
 ¾ cup chopped tomatoes
 4 tablespoons margarine or butter
 2 teaspoons black pepper
 1 teaspoon dill
 ½ teaspoon salt
 ¼ teaspoon nutmeg
 ½ cup flour
 1 cup whole milk

Cube rabbit and soak in salted water for one hour. Thoroughly rinse meat in fresh water. Poach in white wine with bay leaf. Strain meat from broth and retain both.

Sauté mushrooms and onions in butter. Add tomatoes and sauté two more minutes. Remove from heat and add seasonings and flour. Mix well into a thick paste. Return to heat and add broth, mix well, add milk while stirring and simmer until thick. Add rabbit and stir.

Pour into a baking dish and bake at 350 degrees for one half hour.

Ron North
San Diego, CA

Rabbit ala Mac Dei Glaze

3–4 large rabbits
  2 tablespoons each, basil, oregano, salt and pepper
  1 tablespoon each, celery salt, chopped chives,
    chopped parsley

Sauce:
  1 gallon rabbit stock
  ¾ pound butter
  3 ounces pimentos
  ½ teaspoon nutmeg
  2 tablespoons fresh parsley
2¼ cups flour
3½ cups marsala wine

Cut rabbit into pieces, place on a sheet pan. Season with basil, oregano, salt, pepper, celery salt, chopped chives and chopped parsley. Bake at 350 degrees for 35 to 40 minutes or until golden brown. Drain stock from the sheet and save, keep warm. Melt butter in a one and a half gallon saucepan, add flour and cook roux for five minutes. Add warm rabbit stock, a little at a time. Add marsala wine, pimentos, nutmeg and parsley and cook until thickened, stirring constantly.

Put rabbit in serving bowl, cover with roux, garnish with chopped parsley and serve.

Scott Macri
Middletown, CT

Marsala Hare

  2 rabbits, cut up
  ½ cup flour
  2 tablespoons butter
  1 teaspoon Chinese 5 spices blend
  ¼ teaspoon MSG
  ¼ teaspoon salt
    dash paprika
  ½ teaspoon pepper
  1 tablespoon chopped onion
  1 ounce marsala wine
  1 can cream of mushroom soup
  ½ teaspoon Kitchen Bouquet

Mix all spices with flour in a bag and shake several pieces of rabbit at a time. Brown rabbit in butter over medium heat. Reduce heat, add onion, marsala wine and soup. Simmer for one half hour. For gravy add Kitchen Bouquet.

John R. Zeig
Dell Rapids, SD

Rabbit or Squirrel Dumplings

2 rabbits or squirrels (will have enough extra meat to make a salad)
2 large cans of biscuits (not flaky), or your home made dumplings
broth
flour
salt and pepper
poultry seasoning, optional

Boil or pressure cook rabbit or squirrel until very tender, cool, strain broth into eight quart kettle and set aside. De-bone meat and add one cup meat to broth and heat to very hot. Reserve remaining meat for a rabbit salad. Cut two cans of biscuits into fourths and coat with flour, drop into hot broth slowly and stir lightly. Turn heat down and cook for 10 to 15 minutes. Thicken broth with flour or corn starch. Salt and pepper to taste.

Rabbit Salad:

2 cups cooked, chopped rabbit
1 cup celery, chopped
⅓ – ½ cup sweet pickle relish
2 hard boiled eggs, chopped, optional
½ cup chopped pecans, optional
½ cup mayonnaise or salad dressing
salt and pepper to taste

Mix rabbit and salad dressing in a bowl and let stand, covered, in refrigerator for one hour (or longer). Add remaining ingredients, mix well. Serve on lettuce or stuff into a tomato.

Betty King
Berry, KY

—DOUG PIFER—

49

Squirrel

Squirrel and Eggplant Stew

1 fox or 2 gray squirrels or a six pack of red
    squirrels or a dozen chipmunks
1 eggplant, peeled and diced
1 large green pepper, sliced
1 sweet red pepper, sliced (optional)
1 large onion, sliced
2 cloves garlic, minced
3 stalks celery, sliced
1-2 medium tomatoes, wedged (1 red and
    1 orange for color)
    grated parmesan or romano cheese
    basil
3-4 tablespoons olive oil
½-1 cup white wine

Squirrels are tough suckers. Pre-cook them by simmering them in a covered pot for at least 45 minutes, while you cut up the other ingredients. Cook onion, celery and garlic, covered, in olive oil. Use a large frying pan. When they are mostly cooked add and fry peppers and basil. Add cubed eggplant on top after about five minutes.

The eggplant will soak up a lot of oil, at that point add wine, and simmer. Meanwhile drain and rinse squirrels in cold water.

Arrange tomato wedges on top. Sprinkle generously with grated cheese, cover, and let simmer over low heat for another five minutes. Bon appetit.

Yield: serves four people

Tom H. Nagel
Columbus, OH

Squirrel or Rabbit Creole

4 squirrels or 2 rabbits
   salt and pepper to taste
2 tablespoons vegetable oil
1 cup brown rice, uncooked
1 clove garlic, minced
2 (14½ ounce) cans tomatoes, chopped
1 green pepper, chopped
1 medium onion, chopped
⅛ teaspoon cayenne pepper

Season meat pieces with salt and pepper, lightly brown in oil. Combine remaining ingredients and mix well. Spoon into large casserole, arranging meat pieces on top. Cover and bake at 325 degrees oven for one and one-fourth to one and a half hours, or until meat is tender enough to easily remove from bone.

Yield: serves four to six

Mrs. Raymond (Minnie) Carr
Harrisonburg, VA

Squirrel or Rabbit Bake Pot Pie

1 pie crust, top and bottom
1 rabbit
2 cups peas, fresh, frozen or canned
2 carrots, chopped finely
2 potatoes, chopped
½ cup chopped onion
1 cup broth
1 teaspoon margarine, melted
1 egg, beaten
½ teaspoon salt
¼ teaspoon pepper

Cook rabbit until tender in one quart water. Take meat from bones and dice. Line bottom of black iron skillet or casserole dish with pie crust. Spread meat and vegetables in crust. Cover with second pie crust, seal edges, vent, and bake at 350 degrees for 45 minutes or until crust is brown.

Yield: serves four to six people

Mrs. Raymond (Minnie) Carr
Harrisonburg, VA

Splendid Blended Squirrel Quiche

½ large or 1 whole small to medium fresh
    dressed squirrel*
1 cup coarsely chopped broccoli
2 carrots, shredded
¼ cup green pepper, diced
½ cup onion, diced
2 tablespoons water
1 (9 inch) pie shell, baked
1 cup shredded swiss cheese
¼ cup grated parmesan cheese
4-5 eggs, depending on size
¼ teaspoon black pepper
⅜ teaspoon salt
1 cup heavy cream

*As with chicken, squirrel skin is very flavorful. Those wishing to enjoy the full wild squirrel flavor should not remove skin from squirrel meat, remove only fur from meat and use one of the following methods, after which rinse thoroughly in clear water.

Method 1. (Preferred method, but powerful exhaust vent over gas or propane stove, or outside grill, required.) Quickly pass squirrel meat back and forth over flame, fur side down, being careful not to inhale smoke or set fire to nearby objects.

Method 2. Immerse in boiling hot water for five minutes, then carefully pick off fur.

In a quart bowl, combine broccoli, carrots, green pepper, onion and water. Cover with plastic and microwave on high six to seven minutes (stir twice). Sprinkle vegetables into pie shell and set aside. In blender, combine all other ingredients and blend on low for 45 seconds (leaving tiny squirrel meat shreds). Mix squirrel, cheese, egg and cream blend and pour over ingredients in pie shell. Microwave on medium for 17 minutes, then let stand 15 minutes. Garnish as desired.

    Yield: one to eight depending on appetite

Robert M. T. Wilson
Silver Spring, MD

Squirrel and Dumplings

5-6 squirrels or 3 rabbits
    4 cups water (for meat)
    1 large onion, sliced
    1 cup chopped celery with leaves
    1 medium carrot, scraped and sliced
    2 teaspoons salt
    ¼ teaspoon pepper
    ½ cup cold water (for gravy)
    6 tablespoons flour

Combine meat, water, vegetables, salt and pepper in a large kettle with tight cover. Cover, heat to a boil and simmer until meat is tender (one to one and a half hours). Remove meat from broth and pick out bones. Strain broth and mash vegetables through strainer into broth. Add water to make five cups. Return to heat and boil.

Stir one half cup cold water into six tablespoons flour to make gravy, stirring constantly until gravy thickens and boils (about one minute). Season to taste. Return meat to gravy, heat slowly to boiling while making dumplings.

Dumplings:
    2 cups sifted flour
    3 teaspoons baking powder
    1 teaspoon salt
    2 tablespoons shortening
    ¼ cup parsley, optional
    1 cup water, approximately

Mix flour, baking powder and salt in a bowl. Cut in shortening until crumbly, stir in parsley and enough water to moisten flour. Dough should be soft.

Drop dumpling batter into steaming kettle in 12 or more mounds, cover and cook 20 minutes with no peeking! Serve on heated platter with gravy separate.

Jean Ledford
Atlanta, GA

53

Squirrel Cacciatore

2 gray squirrels
½ cup oil
¼ cup butter or margarine
1 medium onion
2 cloves garlic, chopped
   rosemary
   parsley
   black pepper
   salt
1 (16 ounce) can tomatoes
1 tablespoon tomato paste

Cut squirrel into five sections, consisting of four legs and the back. Combine oil and butter in a good sized pot. Add onions and brown slowly. Add squirrel and brown. Sprinkle garlic, rosemary and parsley together with salt and pepper. Stir well, add tomatoes and paste. Cook slowly for about one and a half hours until done. Do not overcook. This squirrel is delicious with fresh cooked linguini on the same plate with sauce spooned over all.

Dave Hyder
Ansonia, CT

Succulent Squirrel

4 tender squirrels (dressed whole)
1 (16 ounce) bottle Italian dressing
8 small potatoes
4 carrots
2 medium onions
4 tablespoons barbecue sauce
¼ cup salt
   black pepper
   pinch of celery seed, paprika and sage
   2 tablespoons bacon bits

Soak dressed squirrels overnight in the refrigerator in a large bowl of fresh water with one fourth cup salt added to water.

The next day, rinse squirrels off with fresh water and place on their backs in a cake pan. Pour Italian dressing over meat and place back in refrigerator for four to six hours.

On a sheet of aluminum foil (large enough to wrap one

squirrel) place a layer of sliced onions and potatoes in the center. Place one Italian dressing-doused squirrel on vegetable layer upon its back. Pepper squirrel, add paprika, celery seed and ground sage (takes very little spice). Sprinkle bacon bits inside body cavity.

Stuff cavity full of carrots sliced thin and long. Pour barbecue sauce over to taste. Place another layer of onions and thin sliced potatoes on top.

Wrap complete entreé in sheet of aluminum foil, careful not to puncture it. Wrap once more with foil, sealing on all sides. Repeat with other squirrels.

Place four servings on double-burner gas grill for 45 minutes with lid closed. Set on low temperature and turn every 10 to 15 minutes.

Rev. Kenneth R. White
Brandensburg, KY

Sage Squirrel

3 squirrels, leg parts only
1 cup flour
1 teaspoon each: salt, paprika and sage
¼ teaspoon black pepper
½ teaspoon white pepper
2 slices bacon, diced
½ cup olive oil
3 medium carrots, sliced
1 medium onion, sliced
1 tablespoon lemon juice
1 teaspoon sugar
2 tablespoons dried parsley
1 (13¾ ounce) can chicken broth

Heat oil in a dutch oven, add bacon and brown lightly. Remove bacon and save. Combine flour, salt, paprika, sage and peppers in a plastic bag, add squirrel pieces and shake to coat thoroughly. Reserve excess flour mixture. Brown squirrel in oil and remove. Stir reserved flour mixture and sugar into pot drippings and add chicken broth. Cook over a medium heat and stir constantly until a thick sauce forms. Add lemon juice, carrots, onion and parsley. Mix. Return squirrel and bacon bits to pot, cover and simmer 45 to 60 minutes or until meat is tender. Stir occasionally during cooking.

William B. Walton
Chesterton, IN

Austin's Squirrel and Rice

1 squirrel per person is usually enough
lemon pepper
red pepper, just a sprinkle
1 teaspoon garlic powder
½ teaspoon salt per squirrel

Cover squirrels with water, add salt and boil until tender, save water for the rice. Cook until meat falls from bone. In a large skillet make enough gravy to cover squirrels. Add garlic powder and lemon and red pepper to taste. Simmer for 30 to 45 minutes. Cook rice with water from the squirrel boil.

Bruce Austin, Jr.
Houston, TX

Crockpot Brunswick Stew

2 squirrels, cleaned
2-3 celery stalks, cut to fit into crockpot
2-3 carrots, cut to fit into crockpot
1 large onion, quartered

Place squirrels and vegetables into crockpot. Add water to fill crockpot. Cook on low setting 8 to 12 hours. Discard vegetables, retaining liquid stock. Remove meat from squirrels, discarding bones.

squirrel meat
liquid stock
⅛ teaspoon cayenne pepper
1 teaspoon salt
½ teaspoon black pepper
1 large onion, chopped
2 carrots, sliced
2 celery stalks, sliced
2-3 potatoes, diced
1 (16 ounce) can whole tomatoes
1 (10 ounce) package frozen corn
¾ -1 (18 ounce) bottle Kraft Thick 'n' Spicy Hickory
    Smoke barbecue sauce

Place all ingredients into crock pot. Add retained liquid stock. Cook six hours on low setting.

Yield: serves four to six

Dave Richardson
Augusta, GA

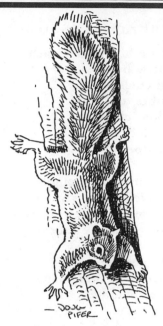

Squirrel Stew

2 squirrels, dressed and cut into bite size pieces
2 cups dried lima beans, soaked overnight
   flour, salt and pepper for coating squirrels
½ pound bacon
1 tablespoon sugar
1 cup okra
4 potatoes, diced
2 (16 ounce) cans stewed tomatoes
1 bay leaf
   dash of thyme, savory and parsley
2 stalks celery, chopped
2 cups frozen corn
2 onions, sliced
1 teaspoon crushed red pepper

Fry bacon and remove. Brown meat in bacon drippings, then cover meat, bacon, beans, onions and celery with boiling water. Simmer for two hours. Add remaining ingredients and simmer for one hour longer. Thicken with flour or cornstarch.
   Yield: serves six

Winnie Alphonse
Forked River, NJ

Brunswick Stew

2 squirrels or 1 rabbit, or one each
2 pounds lean stew beef
2 pounds boned chicken
1 pound veal cubes, optional
1 very large onion, chopped
1 cup chopped celery
2 large cans tomatoes
½ cup catsup
2 (16 ounce) cans mixed vegetables
1 (16 ounce) can yellow or white corn
1 (16 ounce) can small butter beans
1 tablespoon worcestershire sauce
2 teaspoons salt
½ teaspoon black pepper
3 tablespoons butter or margarine
1 cup diced white potatoes

Optional:

¼ cup chopped okra
1 teaspoon Texas Pete or other hot sauce
½ teaspoon hot dried red peppers

Boil squirrels and/or rabbit until tender, let cool and remove all bones. Combine squirrel, rabbit, beef, chicken and veal in a large stew pot and cover with water. Bring to a boil. Turn heat down and let water and meat stew gently. After 20 to 25 minutes add onion, celery, tomatoes, salt, pepper, worcestershire sauce, hot sauce, okra and sugar. Continue to simmer, stirring occasionally. When meat begins to fall apart, add remaining ingredients, stir well, and continue to simmer and stir every 10 to 15 minutes until mixture reaches thick consistency of stew. Add more salt, pepper to taste if desired. Stew may be frozen in one quart containers for later consumption after cooling.

Wayne G. Hatch, Sr.
Orlando, FL

Succulent Squirrel

6 squirrels, cut into legs and saddle (back) pieces
2 tablespoons cooking oil
2 large onions, finely chopped
3 cloves garlic, finely chopped
6 stalks celery, chopped
½ cup sweet vermouth
2 cans Campbell's cream of mushroom soup (add one
    can water)
1 cup fresh sliced mushrooms
1 teaspoon salt
1 teaspoon black pepper

Thoroughly brown squirrel in oil or butter over high heat, turning regularly until all sides are dark brown. Remove squirrel from pan and add onions, mushrooms, garlic and celery. Lightly brown these ingredients. Replace squirrel meat in pan and add mushroom soup, vermouth and water. Make sure all meat is covered with liquid. Simmer on low heat until squirrel begins to fall off bones, one to three hours, depending on age of the squirrels. Serve with mashed potatoes so the wonderful gravy has a home.

   Yield: serves six to eight.

Philip C. Whitford
Montello, WI

— DOUG PIFER

Furbearers

Oven Roasted Coon

2 young raccoons, cleaned

Remove all visible fat and cut carcass into serving pieces.

Marinade:
1 cup vinegar
2 tablespoons salt
1 large onion, sliced
5 cloves garlic, crushed
2 tablespoons pickling spices

Mix and heat. Pour over meat and add cold water, cover and marinate for 24 hours.

Strain, saving onions, etc. Pre-heat oven to 350 degrees. Arrange pieces in baking dish or roaster. Pour onions and spices over meat and add:

3–4 bay leaves
4–6 fresh garlic cloves
2 teaspoons black pepper
2 more teaspoons pickling spice
water to make 1 inch liquid in pan

Bake for approximately 90 minutes, covered. After 45 minutes turn all pieces and baste. When done, remove meat to serving platter, strain liquid into another pan. Use liquid to make dumplings (your favorite recipe or use Bisquick). Remove dumplings and serve with meat, using the thick broth to make gravy. Serve with any vegetable—very good!

Felicia J. Swisher
Delhi, NY

Beaver Barbecue

Pre-heat oven to 350 degrees.

1 small or medium beaver
1-2 cans Manwich sauce
3-4 tablespoons baking soda

Cut up beaver still on bone, so that it can be boiled in a pan. Add baking soda, to help remove all fat from meat (fat has a bitter taste). Boil 15 to 20 minutes, then rinse meat thoroughly. Place it in a pan in oven, covered with lid or foil. Bake until meat flakes from bone. Add a can or two of Manwich. Serve hot on a bun! The larger the beaver the more Manwich you might want to add.

Thelma Pueppel
Washington Courthouse, OH

Opossum and Sweet Potatoes

1 opossum, cleaned and skinned
1 large onion, quartered
1 large apple, quartered
1 tablespoon sage
salt and pepper
sweet potatoes

Trim all possible fat from opossum. Sprinkle inside and out with sage, place onion and apple inside, and lightly salt and pepper. Place in a large roasting pan, add water to pan, cover and bake in a 300 degree oven for one hour. Add sweet potatoes around opossum, cover and bake until sweet potatoes are tender. Uncover to brown possum.

Jerry Ponder
Fairdealing, MO

Baked Raccoon

1 raccoon
2 strips bacon or salt pork
1 apple
2 bay leaves
  salt and pepper

Trim all fat from raccoon and parboil in salted water for 30 minutes. Drain, (save two cups water for later), place meat in a roasting pan, rub salt and pepper generously inside and out. Quarter apple and place inside cavity, lay bacon or salt pork strips over the top. Add two cups of the water used for parboiling, place in the preheated oven for one and a half hours, baste occasionally.

Jerry Ponder
Fairdealing, MO

Baked Coon

1 raccoon (skinned and cleaned, remove scent glands)
½ cup pepper relish
5 large sweet potatoes, baked and peeled
1 teaspoon salt

In a large pot cover coon with water and bring to a boil for about 20 minutes. Remove from heat, pour out water, do not save! Repeat parboiling process twice more, each time beginning with fresh water. After the third boiling, place coon in a roasting pan with a lid. Season meat with salt and then generously baste coon with pepper relish. Place peeled sweet potatoes around meat in pan. Seal pan up tight with a lid or foil. Bake at 350 degrees for three hours.

This is one of my very favorite dishes.

Dixie Snyder
Gatesville, TX

62

DOUG PIFER

Barbecue Raccoon

1 raccoon
barbecue sauce

Cut up raccoon and bake at 350 degrees with salt, pepper and onions until tender, one half to one hour. When tender add barbecue sauce and put back into a low temperature oven, basting with sauce, for a while longer. Extremely tender and delicious.

Barbecue sauce:

1 onion
½ cup ketchup
2 tablespoons brown sugar
2 tablespoons vinegar
2 teaspoons prepared mustard
2 teaspoons worcestershire sauce
1 teaspoon salt

Depending on animal's size, you may need to double or triple barbecue sauce ingredients.

Karen Kathleen Roffman
Monona, IA

Summer Sausage from Beaver Burger

As did early trappers, some of today's wilderness trappers rely heavily on beaver meat as a staple ration, and for a good reason. It's tasty! The following recipe makes excellent cold cuts for sandwiches or a spicy addition to any snack of cheese and crackers.

2 pounds ground beaver meat (a couple slices of fatty bacon with each pound of beaver meat, especially if young/lean beaver, will be a good addition)
2 scant tablespoons Morton's Tender Quick salt
1 teaspoon liquid smoke
½ teaspoon garlic powder
2 tablespoons course ground black pepper
2 teaspoons mustard seed
1 cup water (or as needed)

Mix ingredients thoroughly in a large mixing bowl. Form two meat rolls, about two inches in diameter, wrap in plastic wrap, and place in refrigerator for 24 hours. Remove meat rolls from refrigerator and unwrap, place rolls in a large baking pan and cook in a pre-heated oven at 300 degrees for 90 minutes. Remove from pan and if rolls have been resting in juices, drain on paper towel and several layers of newspaper. Let cool and wrap in foil to store in refrigerator or freezer. This summer sausage freezes very well, and it seems the spiciness is accentuated with freezing. To serve, slice thin sections off roll and be prepared for fine eating. This recipe would undoubtedly work equally well with ground venison. Bon appetit.

Donald D. Smith
Independence, MO

Creamed Hog

- 1 medium groundhog, quartered
- 4 medium potatoes, quartered
- 2 large carrots, diced
- 1 large onion, sliced
- 1 cup celery, chopped
- 1 can cream of mushroom soup
  salt and pepper to taste

Boil groundhog until meat has fallen off bone, and liquid and meat is of a gravy-like consistency. This will clean the meat. Place meat and vegetables in a baking dish. Add cream of mushroom soup diluted with 1 soup can milk. Salt and pepper to taste. Cover dish and bake at 350 degrees for one and one half hours or until meat falls off bones at the touch of a fork.

This recipe can also be used for rabbit, squirrel, muskrat and deer. Works wonders on older animals.

Yield: serves four to six

Michael M. Petronio
Pittsburgh, PA

—DOUG PIFER

Roast Coon

1 raccoon
4 carrots, cut into spears
4 stalks celery, cut into pieces
1 large onion, cut into rings
1 large green pepper, cut into strips
1 apple, cut into eighths or thin slices
2 oranges with peel, cut into eighths
1 tablespoon worcestershire sauce
  corn starch
  salt and pepper
  water

Clean coon thoroughly. Cut away all fat and be sure to remove glands in forelegs. Wash and cool. Soak in salt water for two hours. Rinse and freeze or prepare immediately. Place coon in roaster whole or cut into pieces by quartering and cutting back into three pieces. Place coon in roaster with carrots, celery, onion, green pepper, and apple. Add salt and pepper to personal taste.

Roast at 350 degrees for three hours in covered pan or until tender and meat starts to release from bone.

Remove from pan, discard fruit and vegetables. Use liquid to make gravy. Add worcestershire sauce and corn starch to thicken. Remove and grind any meat left on bone and mix with gravy.

Bob Hillermann
Washington, MO

Pasture Casserole

1-1½ cups cleaned, cooked and cut up groundhog
  ½ cup water
  1 can beef broth
2½ cups noodles
  1 tablespoon corn starch
  1 tablespoon butter
  ½ cup chopped onion
  1 cup frozen peas
  1 teaspoon salt
  1 teaspoon pepper

Combine water and beef broth in a two quart saucepan. Add noodles and cook until tender. To cooked noodles add salt, pepper and butter. Use corn starch to thicken mixture. Combine

65

peas and onion, cook until tender and drain. In a one and a half to two quart casserole dish combine noodle mixture, peas/onions and groundhog. Can be topped with buttered bread crumbs, or onion rings or left plain.

Can be heated through in an oven at 350 degrees for 20 to 30 minutes or in microwave for three to four minutes on high setting. Keep covered.

We have enjoyed this original recipe many times. It is also good with squirrel.

Patricia A. Sigman
New Providence, PA

Beaver Pot Roast

   2 pounds boned beaver
   ¼ pound salt pork, diced
1 ½ cups boiling water
   4 carrots
   4 small white turnips
   4 potatoes
   2 large onions
   1 tablespoon salt
   ½ teaspoon pepper
   1 bay leaf
   1 teaspoon worcestershire sauce

Cut beaver into two inch squares and roll in flour mixed with salt and pepper. Fry salt pork in a dutch oven or heavy frying pan and sear beaver cubes in drippings. Add boiling water, cover and cook at low heat until meat is almost tender (about one hour). Place vegetables around meat, cover and cook until meat and vegetables are done (about 45 minutes). Place meat on a platter and arrange vegetables around meat. If you wish, thicken the liquid and make into a gravy and serve hot with meat.

David F. Lucas
Smithfield, RI

Chapter 4
Game Bird Recipes

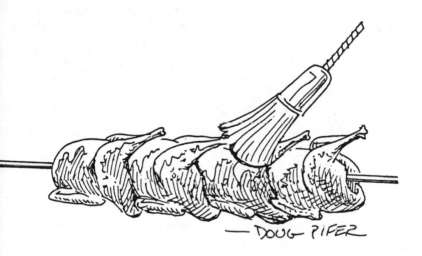

— DOUG PIFER

67

Wild Turkey

Wild Turkey Roast

Clean and dress bird. Wash thoroughly and pat dry. Preheat oven to 325 degrees. Stuff turkey with your favorite stuffing. Brush entire bird with melted butter. Sprinkle with salt and pepper. Place bird on rack in adequate size roasting pan. Roast, allowing 22 to 25 minutes per pound. Baste turkey often with equal parts melted butter and a dry white wine. Wild turkeys have very little fat and will be dry without extra liquid. Low heat will also protect turkey from drying out. Wine will enhance the flavor of game. Serve with traditional accompaniments.

Sugar Ferris
Arlington, TX

Wild Turkey Roast

1 wild turkey, put in brine for 24 hours, completely immersed.

Brine:

> 5 quarts water
> ½ cup salt
> ¼ cup brown sugar
> 1 tablespoon worcestershire sauce
> 1 tablespoon soy sauce

Drain turkey. Wipe dry as thoroughly as possible with paper towel, let set out one hour longer to dry. Rub inside and out with lemon juice. Smoke six hours in smoker.

Stuff with your favorite stuffing or the following:

> ¼ cup butter
> ⅓ teaspoon salt
> ¼ teaspoon pepper
> 1 cup chopped onion
> ½ cup chopped celery
> 1 teaspoon poultry seasoning
> 4-6 slices bacon
> ¾ teaspoon rosemary
> ⅛ teaspoon crushed thyme
> 5 cups day old bread, cubed
> ½ cup milk
> 1 egg, beaten

Melt butter, add onion and celery. Cook until tender. Mix together with seasoning, bread, milk and eggs, spoon loosely into cavity. Mix together:

1 cup melter butter
⅛ teaspoon peper
1 teaspoon salt

Rub turkey inside and out.

Cover breast with bacon slices and cheese cloth soaked in melted butter or bacon fat. Place turkey breast side up on a rack in roasting pan. Bake in 325 degree oven until leg and second joints move loosely.

Baste with:
¼ cup butter
⅓ cup white wine

Guard against overcooking. Cook turkey giblets and neck for stock. Use with pan drippings for gravy.

Smoked turkey is good served hot or cold.

Mrs. Raymond (Minnie) Carr
Harrisonburg, VA

Wild Turkey Fingers

1 wild turkey breast
flour
lemon pepper
salt and pepper
vegetable oil
Cavenders seasoning

Remove wild turkey breast and de-bone. Slice turkey breast into long strips, approximately one inch wide and one half inch thick. Place flour, salt and pepper, Cavenders seasoning and lemon pepper in a paper bag and shake vigorously to coat thoroughly. Heat vegetable oil and drop turkey fingers into oil and cook until golden brown.

Dan Dobbins
Columbia, SC

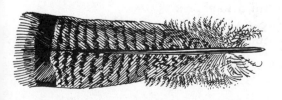

69

Upland Birds

Roast Quail

4 whole quail with skin
2 tablespoons butter
1 tablespoon Kitchen Bouquet
   your favorite stuffing

Add stuffing to cavities of quail and place them breast side down
in a roasting pan. Turn legs toward inside of pan so they don't
cook too fast. Mix melted butter and Kitchen Bouquet, brush
half the mixture on quail. Cover with wax paper and microwave
on high for 12 minutes. Turn birds over. Brush on the rest of
sauce. Microwave another 12 minutes until legs move freely; this
is a way to check for doneness. Watch legs and wings carefully
and shield with pieces of parchment paper if they start to dry out.
   Yield: serves two

Lowell Linsley
Hamilton, OH

Rice Stuffed Quail

Pre-heat oven to 325 degrees.

10 quail breasts, cleaned
1 ½ cups cooked white rice or ¾ cup white and ¾ cup
     wild rice
 ½ cup green peas
 ½ cup diced apple
10 strips bacon
 2 large pinches of rosemary
 2 pinches salt
   black pepper

Prepare stuffing by adding peas and apples to cooked rice. Stir
in rosemary and salt. Fill each quail breast with as much stuffing as it will hold. Wrap each quail breast with a strip of bacon,
securing loose end with a toothpick.
   Lay all 10 quail breasts in a lightly greased 9x13 inch glass
baking dish, leaving some space between each breast and around
sides.

Pack remaining stuffing around quail, sprinkle lightly with pepper, cover with foil and bake at 325 degrees for one half hour. Remove foil and bake uncovered an additional 5 minutes or until rice is lightly browned.

Serve promptly with steamed artichokes.

Yield: serves four country folk or six city slickers

Kirk R. Warburton
Oklahoma City, OK

Quail and Rice Delight

12 quail breasts
12 pair quail legs
 1 cup brown rice, uncooked
 1 cup cream of mushroom soup
 1 cup water
 1 teaspoon paprika
½ teaspoon oregano
¼ teaspoon garlic
½ teaspoon parsley
½ teaspoon dried chopped onion
 1 pound bacon

Line inside of a glass dish, approximately 14x9x2 inches, with bacon slices. Spread uncooked rice over bacon slices. Salt and pepper quail pieces and place them on bed of rice. Combine liquid and dry ingredients then pour over layers of bacon, rice and quail. Cover dish with foil and cook for three hours in a 300 degree oven.

Elvin C. Verett
Ransom Canyon, TX

Joe Turner's Braised Quail

16 whole quail
2 cups white onions, chopped
1 tablespoon garlic, chopped
½ cup olive oil
½ cup red wine vinegar
2 cups chicken stock
  salt to taste
  black pepper to taste, fresh ground

Rinse and dry quail. Tuck wings under back. Make small slits just under the edge of breast bone, toward the back of breast, and insert leg bone ends in slits. This keeps birds from spreading during cooking.

Heat olive oil in a large dutch oven and add onions and garlic. Cook on medium heat for about five minutes, to soften onions. Do not brown onions.

Lay quail on onions and cook for five minutes at medium heat. Turn quail and cook other side another five minutes. Add a little water or white wine if necessary. Arrange quail breast side up, bring up heat and pour vinegar over birds. Continue to cook until vinegar smell is gone.

Add chicken stock, salt, pepper and other spices to taste, cover and cook for 40 minutes over medium heat.

Serve with rice or an egg dish. This is a Spanish recipe. A salad of greens, orange slices, avocado, sliced onions and pimentos with a wine dressing is a good accompaniment.

Joe M. Turner
Vista, CA

Stuffed in a Can Quail and Dove

2 dressed quail or dove, quail should be skinned and
    split down the back
  stuffing made with chunks of apple, orange slices,
    onion and celery
  butter
  aluminum foil
  tomato can with one end cut out
  hot bed of coals

Stuff body cavity with available ingredients and one inch cube of butter; wrap in foil with body cavities together. Stuff into tomato tin and bury in hot coals 8 to 10 minutes.

P. H. Kramer
Houston, TX

Quail Texas Style

12 quail, plucked (whole, not breasted)
1 large onion
3 medium jalapeño peppers, fresh or canned
12 strips of thick bacon
1 (16 ounce) bottle Italian dressing, oil variety
12 round tooth picks

Wash quail thoroughly in cold water, making sure all feathers are removed and body cavity is clean.

Cut onion in half lengthwise, then slice onion lengthwise into slices one fourth to three eighths inch thick. Slice jalapeño peppers lengthwise into quarters and remove stems and seeds.

Stuff each quail with a slice of onion and a slice of jalapeño pepper. After all quail are stuffed, wrap each one around the middle with a slice of bacon (try to cover as much of bird as possible), then pin it in place with a tooth pick (works best with tooth pick completely through bird).

Place all stuffed wrapped quail in a large mixing bowl and pour Italian dressing over them. Mix birds with dressing, making sure that each bird gets covered by dressing. Let quail marinate for two to three hours in your refrigerator, stirring birds in dressing about once each hour. Remove quail from marinade and grill over an open fire (hickory or mesquite is great) for 30 to 45 minutes (can also be cooked in a smoker type grill, but allow birds to cook about three times longer). Make sure quail are completely cooked, then serve immediately.

All you have to do now is remove toothpicks and enjoy some great eating. This goes great with some roasted ears of corn and a tossed salad.

Bob J. Cippele, Jr.
Longview, TX

Quail Supreme

    6 quail
    1 can chicken broth
    2 cups rice, uncooked
    1 medium onion, chopped
    1 cup mushrooms, sliced
    1 carrot, shaved
    2 tablespoons butter
    3 tablespoons flour
    ½ cup milk

In a crock pot add chicken broth and quail. Add water to cover. Simmer on low for four to six hours until meat is tender and completely cooked. Remove quail and half the broth. Add rice, onion, carrot and mushroom to crock pot and cook 30 minutes or until rice is tender.

Meanwhile, de-bone quail. In a medium-sized pan melt butter over medium heat. Stir in flour, cook one minute. Add remaining broth. Stir and cook until smooth. Add milk. Cook until gravy is thickened. Spoon out rice mixture and top with quail, cover with gravy.

Deborah Lackey
Leeds, AL

Glazed Quail with Pecans and Marmalade

    4–6 quail
    1 cup shelled pecans
       pinch of poultry seasoning
       pinch of black ground pepper
       pinch of onion salt
    3 tablespoons butter
    1 tablespoon corn starch
    ½ cup bread crumbs
    ½ orange
    ½ lemon
    5 tablespoons flour
    2 eggs
    1 small can chicken broth
    ¼ cup marmalade

Crush pecans well and roll to powder. Or use food processor in pulse mode, cutting up until very fine.

Wash quail well and leave slightly damp. Put quail in bag with flour, seasoned with a pinch of poultry seasoning, onion salt, and ground black pepper, shake well and remove.

Make egg wash by beating two eggs, then add one half cup milk and beat until well mixed. Then dip quail into egg wash.

Roll quail in three-fourths cup pulverized pecans mixed well with one fourth cup bread crumbs (can use well crushed and rolled soda crackers in place of bread crumbs).

In a nine inch skillet, sauté quail in two or three tablespoons melted butter. After turning once, squeeze one half orange and one half lemon over quail while in saucepan. After browning, add one cup chicken broth mixed with one fourth cup marmalade.

When quail are almost done remove them and keep them warm.

Dissolve one tablespoon corn starch in one fourth cup remaining chicken broth to thicken, heat slowly and add remaining butter and chicken broth. Pour over quail.

Place in covered dish and put into oven. Bake until done (for about 15 to 20 minutes) in preheated 350 degree oven. Remove and garnish with chopped parsley, use remaining sauce in pan for gravy.

Joseph E. Vollmar, Jr.
St. Louis, MO

—DOUG PIFER

Quail Quinn

4-8 quail
4-8 slices country ham
   white wine (enough to make gravy
     sufficient to cover quail)
   stick butter
   salt
   pepper

Cover quail in white wine and simmer. When almost done, remove quail. Line the bottom of a deep pan or casserole dish with ham slices and place quail on top of ham.

Dissolve six tablespoons flour in one cup cold water. Bring wine to a boil and slowly add dissolved flour and whisk to make a thick gravy. (Be sure to make enough gravy to completely cover quail). Pour gravy over quail, cover tightly and bake at 350 degrees for 30 to 45 minutes until done.

Dan Dobbins
Columbia, SC

Divine Deep Dish Ptarmigan

4 ptarmigan, including legs, breasts, and giblets
2 cups wild rice
2 oranges, sliced
1 teaspoon garlic powder
½ teaspoon sage
1 teaspoon salt
1 quart orange juice
½ pound bacon
1 large onion, sliced
  pepper

Oil the bottom of a large covered roasting pan or dutch oven. Line the bottom of pan with wild rice. Layer ptarmigan legs and breasts (plus giblets if you like them) over wild rice. Sprinkle with salt, garlic, and sage. Layer onion and then orange over ptarmingan. Pour three of the four cups orange juice over bird. Dash on a few shakes of pepper. Cover tightly and place in a 325 degree oven for two hours. Check frequently to be sure liquid is not cooked off, adding remaining orange juice as necessary. (If more liquid is necessary, add water). After two hours remove pan from oven and layer surface of dish with one half pound of bacon. Make sure there is still enough fluid to just cover rice. Re-cover and return to oven. Lower temperature to 300 degrees and cook for one hour. Remove and serve. The trick is to be careful that liquid does not cook out too soon.

Donna Braondel
Chickafoon, AK

Roast Partridges

 4 partridges, dressed
½ cup chopped walnuts
½ cup chopped mushrooms
1 cup plain bread crumbs
1 teaspoon ground coriander
1 teaspoon nutmeg
⅛ teaspoon black pepper
½ cup currants
½ cup blackberry brandy
½ cup blackberries
½ teaspoon sage
1 teaspoon lemon juice
1 teaspoon corn starch

Clean birds well. Mix walnuts, mushrooms, bread crumbs, currants and one half teaspoon each of the following: ground coriander, nutmeg, and black pepper. Stuff birds and place in baking dish, cover with foil and bake 425 degrees for approximately 45 minutes. Remove foil during last fifteen minutes. While birds are baking, mix cornstarch in a little cold water and add brandy, blackberries, nutmeg, lemon juice and one teaspoon each (or remaining) nutmeg, coriander, and sage and heat until thickened. Pour heated mixture over birds. Serve with wild rice.

Yield: serves two

Bob Dunn
New Hyde Park, NY

Crock Pot Grouse

2 grouse, cleaned, washed and cut up
seasoned flour
oleo

Gravy:
1 can cream of mushroom soup
1 can cream of celery soup
1 package dry onion soup
⅓ cup diced green pepper
½ teaspoon oregano

Dip grouse pieces in seasoned four. Brown in oleo.

Put browned birds into crock pot. Mix gravy and pour over birds before turning on pot, and cook on low setting for 8 to 10 hours.

Yvonne Carlson
Roanoke, IL

Grouse Bake

4 breasted birds, soaked overnight in salt water
½ stick butter
1 teaspoon salt
½ teaspoon pepper
⅓ cup Italian dressing
½ cup Holland House Tom Collins drink mixer

Pre-heat oven to 450 degrees.

Arrange birds in a casserole dish. Blend above ingredients and baste birds. Cover and bake 50 to 60 minutes or until done, basting often. Serve with white or wild rice.

Donald Ford McFetridge
Pleasantville, PA

Flighty Eggs

The delicate taste of blue grouse has rarely been better than with this recipe.

1 breast of blue grouse, sliced very thin
6 eggs
¼ cup cream or milk
1 small scallion or ½ teaspoon chopped onion
2 tablespoons butter

Sauté grouse in a small amount of oil, drain, set aside and keep warm. Heat melted butter and cream, add onions, then beat in eggs. As eggs start to firm up, add grouse and cook until eggs are scrambled and done. Serve with buttered toast and discover the taste of grouse like you've never had before.

Robert Moffatt
Denver, CO

Roast Pheasant

2 dressed pheasants
¼ teaspoon cinnamon
½ teaspoon nutmeg
½ teaspoon crushed rosemary
⅛ teaspoon black pepper
¼ cup Courvoisier brandy
½ teaspoon sugar
1 can dark sweet cherries in heavy syrup
2 teaspoons cornstarch
¼ teaspoon savory
¼ cup Kipschuasser

Stuffing:
2 pears, chopped
4 ounces walnuts, chopped
Frangelico liqueur

Clean birds well and sprinkle with seasonings. Place birds in baking pan along with stuffing. Cover with foil and bake at 425 degrees for approximately one hour. Mix cornstarch in a little cold water, add cherries, brandy, sugar and Kipschuasser and heat. Pour heated mixture over birds and flame with Frangelico if desired. Serve with corn, squash and wild rice.

Yield: serves two to four

Bob Dunn
New Hyde Park, NY

Pheasant in Plum Sauce

2 pheasants
1 large can plums, pitted and pureed
¼ cup butter
1 onion, finely chopped
¼ cup lemon juice
¼ cup brown sugar
2 tablespoons chili sauce
1 teaspoon worcestershire sauce
½ teaspoon ground ginger
apples, enough to fill cavity

Sauté onion in butter, add rest of ingredients except apples, let cook 10 minutes. Place birds in pan, fill cavity with apples and sautéd ingredients. Season birds with salt, pepper and garlic powder, cover with bacon strips and bake at 360 degrees for two and a quarter hours. Just before they are done, baste with sauce and bird juices.

Susan Geyer
Fontana, CA

Pheasant Gravy with Mushrooms over Toast

1 pheasant, cleaned
¼ cup mushrooms, sliced
1 (10½ ounce) can condensed cream of mushroom soup
1 (10½ ounce) can condensed cream of chicken soup
½ cup milk
½ cup water
toast

Cook pheasant in pot of water, covered, until meat is tender, about one to one and a half hours. Remove pheasant from pot to cool, then de-bone meat and set aside. Sauté mushrooms in a little butter, put pheasant meat and mushrooms in a two and a half quart covered saucepan. Add in both cans soup, milk and water. Stir and heat through over low heat. Add salt and pepper to taste. Serve over toast.

Joan M. Rosengrant
Windsor, PA

Plum Good Pheasant

1-2 pheasants, cut in serving pieces
 1 jar plum preserves
 ½ stick margarine or butter
   salt
   pepper
   thyme

Melt margarine in frying pan and brown pheasants. Turn heat down, add a few tablespoons water, cover and cook pheasants until done. Sprinkle with salt, pepper and thyme. Just before serving, add plum preserves and cover until heated through. Serve with drippings. Delicious!

Jo Havel
Monticello, MN

Pheasant a la Mike

 1 pheasant, cut in half (chicken may be substituted)
 3 large yellow onions, sliced thick
 1 garlic bulb, peeled, or two small bulbs
 1 orange, peeled and cut in half
 ⅛ teaspoon Angostura bitters
 ⅛ teaspoon Tabasco
 ¾ teaspoon each: white wine and worcestershire
 1 teaspoon lemon juice
 ¼ teaspoon Wright's Liquid Smoke hickory seasoning
 3 ounces Kimlan teriyaki sauce
   Schillings garlic season-all
   olive oil
 1 bottle semi-sweet white wine (Rhine wine is best)
 1 aluminum roasting pan, approximately 11x9x2 inches

Coat bird lightly on all sides with olive oil, sprinkle liberally with garlic seasoning. Place one half, skin side down in roasting pan. Put orange halves on top and then place the other half bird, skin side up (as if you have formed a whole bird). Add onion and whole garlic cloves around bird. In a small mixing bowl, stir together bitters, Tabasco, worcestershire sauce, lemon juice and Liquid Smoke. Pour mixture around bird (not on top) and sprinkle teriyaki sauce over bird and onions. Fill pan three fourths full with wine. Cover pan with heavy duty foil and place in lighted barbecue and close cover. (We use a Weber.) Cook 20 minutes, then remove foil. Cook for 10 minutes more, then flip "whole" bird. Remove orange halves at this time or leave them for added orange flavor. Cook for 30 minutes longer, uncovered, until bird is done. This will vary slightly, depending on size of bird. The onions and garlic should be quite soft. Remove pheasant to a serving dish and save sauce in pan for gravy. Excellent over rice or mashed potatoes.

Yield: serving for two or three people

Mike Sala
Oakdale, CA

Pheasant Muscatel

3 (1 ½ pounds) pheasants, split in half, or 6 breasts
⅓ cup butter, softened
1 cup white raisins
⅓ cup muscatel
½ lemon
3 oranges, halved
1 teaspoon grated lemon peel
1 cup chicken broth
    salt and pepper to taste

Rinse pheasants with warm water, drain well. Rub inside with lemon, season with salt and pepper. Place skin side down in baking dish. Spread with butter. Squeeze juice from oranges, reserving shells for cups. Combine orange juice with remaining ingredients, pour into baking dish and bake at 350 degrees for 45 minutes. Baste with pan juices at 10 minute intervals.

Fill orange cups with cooked rice. Remove cooked pheasant to platter and surround with filled orange cups and fresh parsley springs. Drizzle rice with a couple tablespoons pheasant juices and serve.

Sugar Ferris
Arlington, TX

Pheasant Diablo

2 pheasants, legs and whole breasts (reserve backs for
   soup)
1 large red onion, diced
4 stalks celery, diced
6 slices bacon, cut into 4 inch strips
⅓ cup red wine
⅓ cup Escoffier Diablo sauce
   wild rice mix
   water
   poultry seasoning

For sauce, mix red wine and Escoffier with enough water to make
one cup sauce.

Place diced vegetables in baking dish. Place pheasants, bone
down, on vegetables. Poke some holes in pheasants with two prong
carving fork. Pour sauce over birds, add salt and pepper, shake
on poultry seasoning and cover with bacon strips.

Bake one hour in covered dish at 375 degrees. At the end of
30 minutes baste pheasant and remove cover from baking dish.

Remove bones from pheasants, place over a bed of wild rice
mixed with vegetables and gravy from baking dish.

Gerald Navaretta
Kingwood, TX

Pheasant Casserole

3 cups cooked pheasant
2 cups celery, chopped
2 cups long grain and wild rice mix (cooked without
    seasonings)
¾ cup mayonnaise
1 tablespoon onion, chopped
1 teaspoon lemon juice
1 can cream of chicken soup
1 cup water chestnuts, sliced
3 hard boiled eggs, chopped
1 stick butter
1 cup corn flakes, crushed
½ cup sliced almonds

Combine all ingredients except butter, corn flakes and almonds
in a large casserole dish. Melt butter and combine with crushed
corn flakes and almonds. Spread over casserole and bake at 350
degrees 10 to 15 minutes or until heated through.

Kathleen Pestinger
Beloit, KS

Warrior Pheasant

2 pheasant, legs and whole breasts (reserve backs for
    soup)
1 large green apple, cut up
1 large green pepper, cut up
6 slices of bacon
½ white sweet wine
⅓ cup water
⅓ cup Dijon mustard
    poultry seasoning
    margarine
    yellow rice mix

For sauce, mix one half cup sweet white wine, one third cup water
and one-third cup Dijon mustard to make one cup sauce.

    Place cut apple and green pepper in baking dish. Place pheas-
ant bone down on fruit. Poke some holes in pheasant with two
prong carving fork. Pour sauce over pheasant and season with
salt, pepper and poultry blend. Cover with bacon slices.

Cover and bake one hour in covered dish at 375 degrees. The last 30 minutes, remove cover.

Melt one half stick margarine and add three spoons cracked peppercorns.

Mix yellow rice with vegetables and gravy from baking dish, remove bones from pheasant and place meat over rice mixture. Just prior to serving, coat pheasant with peppercorn and margarine mix.

Yield: serves four

Gerald Navaretta
Kingwood, TX

Pheasant Italian

1 pheasant breast, skinned and boned
1 thin slice ham
1 slice mozzarella cheese
mayonnaise
Italian bread crumbs
parmesan cheese

Flatten breast with mallet and spread lightly with mayonnaise. Cover with a thin slice of ham and mozzarella cheese. Roll up and secure with a toothpick. Coat roll lightly with mayonnaise. Mix bread crumbs with a small amount of Parmesan cheese, coat pheasant roll with bread mixture. Bake uncovered in slow 275 degree oven approximately two hours.

Serves one or two persons, depending on the size of the breast. Increase as needed. Serve with pasta and a good Marinara sauce or purchased spaghetti.

Variation: After preparing pheasant rolls, fry in melted butter. Place in baking dish, cover with marinara sauce and bake as directed.

Kathleen Pestinger
Beloit, KS

85

Favorite Pheasant

1 pheasant, cut in serving size pieces
4 medium onions, sliced
  seasoned flour
  salt and pepper to taste
  butter or oil
1 cup cream or half-and-half

Dredge pheasant in seasoned flour and sauté in butter. Place in large baking dish in single layer. Cover with sliced onions, pour enough cream over the top to almost cover pheasant pieces. Cover and bake in 300 degree oven for one and a half to two hours.

Kathleen Pestinger
Beloit, KS

Chinese Pheasant

1 pheasant, boned, skinned, cut in bite sized pieces
2 tablespoons cooking oil
⅔ cup sliced celery
½ cup sliced green onion
1 (8 ounce) can sliced water chestnuts
6 ounces snow peas
6 ounces pineapple chunks
½ cup chicken broth
¼ cup sugar
1 tablespoon cornstarch
½ teaspoon powdered ginger
2 tablespoons vinegar
2 tablespoons soy sauce

Add oil to hot wok or large iron skillet. Add pheasant and stir fry for five minutes. Add celery, onion, water chestnuts and stir fry two more minutes. Add pea pods, pineapple chunks and broth, stir fry for two more minutes. In a small bowl, mix sugar, cornstarch, ginger, vinegar and soy sauce and pour over pheasant and vegetable mix. Reduce heat, stir and simmer until sauce thickens, about two minutes.

Serve mixture over rice.

Don Gasaway
Mount Prospect, IL

Curry and Fowl

2 pheasants, cut up
⅓ cup oil
1 can tomato soup
1 can beer, stale is okay
1 onion, chopped
  salt and pepper
  curry

Heat oil in a heavy frying pan, lightly salt and pepper pheasant, brown pieces lightly, a few pieces at a time. Place side by side in a flat 13x9x2 inch pan. Drain excess oil from frying pan and sauté onions until soft, (not brown), pour in soup, beer and curry, bring to a slow boil for a few minutes and pour over birds. Bake, covered with foil, at 350 degrees for about one and a half to two hours. Check for doneness about halfway through cooking, as some birds cook faster than others. Remove foil to cover two thirds of the pan for the last part of cooking. This recipe is good on quail and chicken. Cooking time may be adjusted.

Ida Pryor
Newhall, CA

Pheasant Pie

1 pheasant, cooked and cut in pieces (2 pheasants are better and are best for two pies. Double the ingredients and give the extra pie to a special family).
1 deep dish pie crust, plus crust to cover the top
1 large head broccoli, cut up and partially cooked (or a 10 to 16 ounce frozen package. Also equal amounts of asparagus may be substituted).
12-16 ounces sharp cheddar cheese, shredded
16 ounces pheasant stock (if you had the foresight), can use canned chicken stock if necessary. Thickened with about 6 ounces heavy cream and flour.
2 large apples, cored, peeled, cut in pieces
1 large pear, cored, peeled, cut in pieces
3-4 thin slices swiss cheese

Partially cook vegetables and prepare stock. If using prepackaged pie crust, follow the directions. If homemade cook approximately

10 minutes at 425 degrees. Add a layer of pheasant, topped with all vegetables, then cheese, more pheasant and top with apple and pear pieces. Pour stock over the top, top with swiss cheese if desired, cover with remaining crust. Bake at 300 degrees for approximately 35 to 40 minutes.

Please cut me a piece!

Ken Juckett
Pawtucket, RI

Pheasant-Stuffing Bake

2 cups diced, cooked pheasant
1 (12 ounce) can evaporated milk
3 tablespoons butter or margarine
1 (7 ounce) package herb-seasoned stuffing cubes
1 (10–11 ounce) can condensed mushroom soup
2 cups shredded swiss cheese
2 stalks celery, chopped
1 cup cooked broccoli flowerets
½ teaspoon dried thyme leaves, crushed

In a one quart saucepan, over high heat, heat three fourths cup milk and butter to scalding. In a large bowl, pour hot mixture over stuffing, toss to mix well. Pat one half stuffing mixture into a buttered 12x8 baking dish. In a medium bowl, stir soup, remaining milk, pheasant and one cup of cheese, along with celery, broccoli and thyme until well mixed. Spoon evenly over stuffing mixture in baking dish. Top with remaining stuffing mixture. Bake at 350 degrees for 30 minutes. Remove from oven and sprinkle remaining cheese on top, return to oven until cheese is melted.

Any upland game bird can be substituted for pheasant. This is a frequently requested favorite in our family.

Yield: serves six

John Stine
Saginaw, MI

Pheasant a la Hays

pheasants, generously salted and peppered

Inside each bird add:

¼ onion
2 inch long orange peel
1 garlic pod
2 tablespoons wine

Add 1 butter patty to breast and wrap each bird individually and tightly in foil.

Place in dutch oven with water covering three fourths of birds. To water add salt and pepper, onion, orange peel, garlic and wine. Cover dutch oven and cook three and a half hours at 350 degrees.

Robert W. Hays
Apache, OK

David's Pheasant Soup

1 pheasant, skinned and quartered
4 cups water
2 chicken bouillon cubes
6 potatoes, chopped
2 large onions
1 stalk celery, diced
3 carrots, sliced
2 apples, peeled, cored and chopped
1 teaspoon each salt, pepper, garlic salt and celery salt
1 tablespoon each sage and marjoram

Cook pheasant in a pot with four cups water, bouillon cubes, sage, salt and pepper for about 25 to 30 minutes until tender. Pull out pheasant and de-bone, cut into pieces and strain stock. Put potatoes into stock with pheasant and cook on low heat. Add onions, carrots, celery, celery salt and crush marjoram in your hand and sprinkle in. Add apples last and simmer for two hours. Serve with salad and freshly baked bread.

David Wallace
Cleveland, OH

Sugar Cured and Smoked Fowl

I have been using this recipe for about ten years and it works great on every upland bird as well as various cuts of pork. It is not recommended for waterfowl. The below recipe is for 4–6 pheasants or any similar birds. If you are low on game try a 10 pound domestic turkey as a test.

This is a four step process, brining or marinating, smoking, roasting and re-smoking.

Brine:

1½ cups sugar
  1 cup dark brown sugar
  1 cup salt
 20 peppercorns, approximately
2–3 bay leaves
  ½ teaspoon each: chili powder, curry powder and coriander seeds
  2 quarts water
  ½ teaspoon sodium nitrate or commercial cure. If using a commercial product use their directions.

Prepare brine (marinade) by bringing first seven ingredients to a boil. Allow to cool, then stir in sodium nitrite or cure. Prepare fowl by washing thoroughly in cold, strong, salty water. Pierce meat every inch or so with a meat fork to speed penetration of marinade. Rinse fowl in clear water. Place birds in a plastic container large enough to allow complete immersion. I find that a plastic dish pan works great. Add prepared brine and enough cold water so as to insure coverage, usually one to two gallons. Cover container and refrigerate for 24 to 48 hours, stirring occasionally. When brining is complete drain off all liquid and pat meat dry.

Place birds high in smoker and apply a cool smoke (100 degrees) for four hours. I use a mix of oak, hickory, apple and cottonwood, but any other hardwood can be used. Any commercial smoker is suitable for this operation or you can build your own cabinet. The key point in this smoking step is not to get the temperature too high or meat will dry out.

After four hours in smoker remove birds and place in an oven roaster pan, covered grate on bottom. Add two cups water. Roast birds at 375 degrees as follows:

Pheasant:	45 minutes
Quail:	30 minutes
Grouse or Prairie Chicken:	50 minutes
Ten Pound Turkey:	2 hours

Baste with juices frequently. When done roasting, allow birds to cool slightly and coat exterior of bird with vegetable oil. Save cooking juices.

While still warm return birds to smoker for another three to four hours. Periodically baste with juices left from step three. Allow to thoroughly cool. Place in plastic bag and refrigerate for at least 24 hours. Your birds are done.

Lt. Col. (Ret.) Walter Muller
Manhattan, KS

Pheasant ala Toaldo

1 pheasant
1 teaspoon salt
1 teaspoon pepper
1 onion
¼ cup raisins (white or red)
1 cup chicken broth
2 tablespoons oil
   touch of sage
¼ cup pignoli nuts (pine nuts)
½ cup sherry or marsala wine

Use a heavy covered frying pan (stainless steel or iron).

Cut pheasant into eight pieces. Put oil and meat into frying pan. Add salt, pepper, sage, pignoli nuts, raisins and sliced onion to meat. With one half flame brown meat on both sides. The pan should become a little tacky. When meat is browned, add wine and raise flame almost to highest point for about one and a half to two minutes. Using a metal spatula, scrape bottom of pan to keep from sticking. After loosening residue in bottom of pan, pour in chicken broth and let it come to a boil. Place cover on and let simmer for 30 minutes at reduced flame.

Yield: makes four servings

Gino Toaldo
Seaside Park, NJ

Claire's Pheasant

    2 good sized pheasants, cut in half, legs and thighs
        de-jointed
1 ½ cups sliced onion
    4 tablespoons chopped parsley
1 ½ cups chopped celery
    1 clove minced garlic
    1 bay leaf
    6 whole cloves
    1 tablespoon worcestershire sauce
    1 teaspoon Kitchen Bouquet
    1 teaspoon Italian herbs (dried)
    2 tablespoons catsup
3-4 inch sprig fresh or dried rosemary
    2 cups white wine
    1 cup chicken broth
    1 (12 ounce) can tomato juice
    2 cups sliced fresh mushrooms or 1 jar button
        mushrooms
2-3 carrots, sliced
    Wondra flour to thicken
    may add 2 packages Schilling brown gravy mix
        (directions on package)
    salt and pepper to taste

Cover and cook in 350 degree oven 60 minutes or until meat
is good and tender.

Mrs. Anthony White
Napa, CA

Apple Pheasant

    1 pheasant
    2 eggs
    flour (cornmeal or crushed crackers will substitute)
    salt
    pepper
    garlic salt
    1 tablespoon butter
2-3 apples
    milk
    flour

De-bone pheasant and cut into 1 by 2 inch pieces. Beat eggs, dip meat in egg mixture and roll in flour mixed with spices. Fry pheasant in butter quickly until tender and place in oven at 250 degrees. Slice apples into flat pieces and cook briefly in the same butter as the pheasant. Place apples over pheasant in oven. Make up a white gravy by adding milk or cream and flour to butter reside until thick. Serve pheasant and apples with biscuits, potatoes or rice. Add gravy as desired.

Edd Rankin
Colorado Springs, CO

Mike's Modified Pheasant

A cast iron skillet is recommended. You can use a little or more of the ingredients given, it will still turn out just great.

 2-3 pheasant breasts, partially frozen so they can be sliced against the grain into finger size portions.
  2 cups flour
  2 cups Bisquick
  4 tablespoons paprika
  1 teaspoon garlic salt
 1-2 tablespoons Oriental 5 Spice Mix, (most necessary for this dish, Tones Bros., Des Moines, Iowa, 50301)
  1 small can cream of chicken soup (any brand)
  1 finely chopped carrot
  1 finely chopped celery stalk
  3 green onions chopped
  ½ chopped green, red or yellow pepper
 3-4 eggs
 ½-1 cup sherry (I use 1966 vintage, but any sherry will do)
1-2½ cups water
    oil for iron fry pan fill to at least ½ inch (add more later for absorption)
4-10 squirts soy sauce
    pepper to taste

Heat one half of oil (turn up heat at first to get hot, but turn heat down to medium while cooking). Put flour, Bisquick, garlic salt, two of the four teaspoons paprika, and five spice mix in a large plastic bag. Whip up eggs in a separate dish. Dip pheasant in egg, then coat with above mixture. Fry in hot oil. Cook until three quarters done, take out and drain on paper towels. After all pheasant is cooked, drain oil from pan and wipe pan with a paper towel. Set heat on medium low. Throw all vegetables in pan along with soup. Let it boil down, adding water when necessary. As soon as a thick sauce is apparent, add spices, soy sauce, and sherry. Stir, then stir in drained pheasant and cook an additional three to four minutes. Serve over a bed of Texmati rice or a similar brand of premium rice.

Michail Westphal
Waukesha, WI

Dove

Dove ala Relling and Vollmar

5-10 doves
    1 quart buttermilk
    thyme and white pepper
    large pinch basil
    large pinch tarragon
    2 bay leaves
    ¼ garlic clove (use judgment)
    sprinkle paprika
    ½ cup vinaigrette
    2 strips bacon per bird
    2 tablespoons cornstarch, per cup liquid
    1 small bunch parsley
    1 cup rosé wine
    1 cup water

Clean doves and wash to rid of feathers and trash. Soak, covered in buttermilk, for three hours. Remove from milk, season in cavity with a pinch of thyme and white pepper. Wrap each dove in two strips of bacon and anchor bacon with toothpicks.

Place in pan and brown in pre-heated oven at 350 degrees for 30 minutes.

While doves are browning, mix rosé wine, water and vinaigrette. Add bay leaves, a large pinch of tarragon, basil and garlic in a small sauce pan and bring to a boil.

When doves are browned, add wine, water and vinaigrette mixture and let doves cook at 350 degrees for 30 to 45 minutes longer.

Keep doves warm in a covered pan while thickening wine, water and vinaigrette mixture with corn starch. Pour into mixture, heat and stir as it thickens. Strain and use as a sauce for doves. Sprinkle with paprika and garnish with parsley.

Joseph E. Vollmar, Jr.
St. Louis, MO

DJ's Dove Paté

1 bunch green onions, cut into 1 inch pieces
¼ cup butter or margarine
½ pound boneless dove breasts
⅓ cup heavy cream
¼ teaspoon each; salt, dry mustard, ground black
   pepper

Fillet dove breasts from bone by running a sharp knife, carefully, between meat and breast bone, from front to back end.

Place green onions in food processor and chop finely. Melt butter in skillet over medium high heat. Briefly sauté onions, add dove breast and gently cook until no longer red in the center. Allow to cool slightly.

Place contents of skillet in processor with remaining ingredients. Process continuously until smooth. Spoon paté into greased one cup mold and chill until serving.

Unmold and serve with Triscuits, Wheat Thins, Diet Center plain or lightly seasoned crackers.

On Thanksgiving of 1987, I served this paté and it was all but gone before dinner was served. A high school student asked for the recipe to make for her lunches.

Cliff Johnson
Taos, NM

Dove ala Detrick

  whole dove breast (2 or 3 per person)
  Scottish, Irish or English ale
1 (or more) jars pickled grape leaves
  lean bacon, optional
  Italian sausage, as hot as you like it

Partially cook sausage. Fill cavity of each dove breast with rendered sausage. Wrap one slice of bacon around dove breast, pepper lightly and no salt. Wrap entire breast in grape leaf and/or leaves. Skewer with toothpick if needed. Place in appropriately sized casserole dish. Lay on additional layer of grape leaves on top of dove and cover with ale. Marinate at least four hours, preferably overnight in the refrigerator.

Pre-heat oven to 350 degrees. Remove casserole from

refrigerator and let stand at room temperature. Place casserole on middle rack of oven and bake approximately 10 minutes or until top layer of leaves brown and liquid bubbles for at least five minutes. Do not overcook. Discard top layer of leaves and serve.

Enjoy! You may not have made enough!

John T. Detrick
Costa Mesa, CA

Dove a l'Orange

24 doves or 4 pounds dove, cleaned
4 tablespoons each, olive oil, chopped carrot, chopped
    celery and chopped onion
2 teaspoons chopped garlic
1 cup dry sherry
2 teaspoons dry mustard
4 tablespoons currant jelly
1 tablespoon soy sauce
    juice of one orange
1 tablespoon cornstarch, dissolved in 2 tablespoons
    water

Cook garlic, onion, celery and carrot in olive oil in a large casserole. Add doves, then sherry, dissolve mustard in sherry and cook at 225 degrees for one hour. Turn heat up to 325 degrees and cook for one more hour.

Mix currant jelly, soy sauce and orange juice and add to casserole. Stir to mix. Cook 15 more minutes. Pour off liquid and thicken with cornstarch.

Serve with rice.

Susan Flynt Stirn
Arlington, VA

—DOUG PIFER

97

Dove Gumbo

20 dove breasts, steamed 30 minutes and de-boned (save broth)
4 links Italian sausage, fried and cut up
4 green onions, chopped (save tops for garnish)
1 stalk celery, chopped
1 bell pepper, chopped
1 clove garlic
4 teaspoons worcestershire sauce
1 (8 ounce) can okra, cut up
2 bay leaves
2 teaspoons poultry seasoning
1 teaspoon thyme
½ teaspoon ground cinnamon
1 can tomato soup
1 can rotel tomatoes

Roux mix:
2 cups broth from steamed doves
6 tablespoons flour
1 stick margarine

Cook until light brown.

Place all ingredients in crock pot and cook on medium for six hours. Serve over wild rice and top with saved green onion tops.

Yield: four servings

Mike Lewis
Memphis, TN

Dove Pie

6 doves
¼ pound saltines
black pepper to taste
½ - ¾ stick of margarine, chopped into bits
1 (8 ounce) can evaporated milk
2½ butter-me-not biscuits

Soak doves in lightly salted water. Boil until tender. Reserve about one half cup stock. Use a round 9x3 inch pan or casserole dish. Debone birds and cut in small pieces, put in pan along with crushed saltine crackers, margarine and black pepper. Toss, pour in evaporated milk and stock. Let stand for a few minutes to soak up crackers, but you need enough liquid to make pie moist. Roll out two and a half butter-me-not biscuits and put on top as a pie crust. Bake at 400 degrees until crust is golden brown.

Geneve Morse
Pomaria, SC

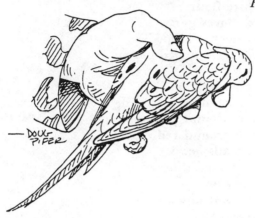

Dove Breast Stroganoff

12-18 dove breasts
   1 medium onion
   1 can cream of celery soup
   1 can mushrooms
  ½ cup sauterne
     oregano
     rosemary
     salt and pepper
     Kitchen Bouquet for color
   1 cup sour cream

Place meat in a large baking dish. Do not crowd breasts. Dice and sauté onion, mix with remaining ingredients except sour cream. Pour over breasts, cover lightly with foil and bake in 325 degree oven for one hour, turning occasionally. Add sour cream, stir. Bake uncovered for another 20 minutes. Serve over combined white and wild rice.

  Yield: serves six to eight

Susan Geyer
Fontana, CA

Dove Gumbo with Sausage

15 dove breasts
1 (10 ½ ounce) can consommé
1 beef bouillon cube
½ cup vegetable oil
½ cup white flour
2 minced cloves garlic
2 stalks celery, chopped
2 cups sliced browned okra
2 bay leaves
½ teaspoon whole basil
¼ teaspoon poultry seasoning
¼ teaspoon ground pepper
½ teaspoon ground red chili
⅛ teaspoon allspice
¾ pound smoked sausage
½ cup red wine
⅛ teaspoon hot sauce
  hot cooked rice

Cover breasts with water and boil about 10 minutes. Cool and remove meat from bones. Save liquid and add water, if necessary to make two and a half cups liquid. Set meat aside.

Add consommé and beef bouillon cube and cook until cube is dissolved. Brown dove in one half cup hot vegetable oil in a large skillet, remove dove and drain well. Pour off all but one fourth cup oil. Add white flour to oil in skillet, cook over medium heat, stirring until mixture is the color of a copper penny, about 10 to 15 minutes.

Gradually add consommé liquid to copper-colored mixture and cook over medium heat while stirring constantly until mixture thickens and bubbles. Stir in minced garlic, celery and browned okra, cook five minutes. Add bay leaves, basil, poultry seasoning, ground pepper, ground red chili and allspice. Brown smoked sausage and drain well. Stir sausage and dove meat into consommé mixture and simmer for one and a half hours. Add red wine and hot sauce, stir well.

Serve gumbo over hot cooked rice
Yield: serves six, one and three quarters quarts

Keith Dennis
Albuquerque, NM

Grilled or Broiled Dove

dove
sliced pineapple
jalapeño peppers
thick sliced bacon
pepper
garlic powder, optional
toothpicks

Pluck doves and use game shears to split up the back. Place one inch or so of pineapple in body cavity along with one half jalapeño pepper. Wrap bacon around dove and secure with a toothpick, then pepper. Cook on outdoor grill or broil indoors. Cook until bacon is crisp and doves are dark brown. Turn at least once to cook each side. Cooking time is about 20 to 30 minutes, total. Figure three doves per person. Serve with Spanish rice and field peas for a crowd pleaser.

David Nee
Crosby, TX

Dove Noodles

20 dove breasts
 3 cans chicken broth
 4 packages flour tortillas
 2 tablespoons oil
   salt and pepper to taste

Brown dove breasts in oil. Heat chicken broth and add dove, bring to a boil. Cut tortillas into strips, drop into soup and boil about 7 to 10 minutes. Serves about four.

Carol Tober
Boerne, TX

Wild Ducks

Duck and Wild Rice Casserole

2–3 large wild ducks, cleaned
  3 ribs celery, cut in 2 inch pieces
  1 onion, chopped
1½ teaspoons salt
  ¼ teaspoon pepper
  6 whole allspice
  1 (16 ounce) package long grain and wild rice mix
  1 (4 ounce) can sliced mushrooms
  ½ cup chopped onions
  ½ cup melted margarine
  ¼ cup chopped pimiento
  1 can chicken-mushroom soup, undiluted
  1 tablespoon chopped parsley
  ½ cup slivered almonds
  1 (8 ounce) carton sour cream

Combine first six ingredients in large dutch oven and cook ducks until tender or pressure cook for 35 minutes. Cool and remove meat from bones, cut into bite size pieces. Cook rice mixture according to directions. Drain mushrooms, sauté onion in mushroom juice, mix all ingredients (except almonds). Spread almonds on top and bake at 350 degree in a two quart greased casserole dish for 30 minutes.

Use any wild game with this recipe.

Marian Barrett
Augusta, GA

Maria Turner's Duck Breasts

12 duck breast halves, boned, skinned
    bacon, thick sliced, one strip per breast
    currant jelly, one jar
    peanut oil
 1 teaspoon cumin
    soy sauce
    black pepper to taste
    salt to taste

Trim duck breast halves well and wrap each breast with a slice of thick sliced bacon. Secure bacon with toothpicks. Place duck breasts in a glass dish, cover with a mixture of one part peanut oil and two parts soy sauce. Marinate in the refrigerator overnight or at least six hours.

Place marinated duck breasts on a flat, foil-covered pan and broil. The bacon should be cooked but duck breasts should be very rare, crisp on the outside and rare inside. Do not overcook! Watch carefully; it can burn and flame. The pan and oven will be a mess unless you take care. With an outdoor grill the flame problem is even worse. Take your time and move the duck breasts around frequently so hot spots do not develop.

Melt currant jelly in a small sauce pan, add cumin, pepper and salt. Stir well. Serve as a sauce for meat. To serve, slice duck breasts as you would filet mignon and serve with currant sauce.

This is the best game recipe we ever had. If you are wondering what to do with the duck legs, try marinating them and cooking them first. They make terrific appetizers!

Joe M. Turner
Vista, CA

Smoked Florida Duck

2 whole ducks, cleaned (Florida mottled ducks or
    wood ducks may also be used)
    seasoning salt
    beer, enough to cover ducks
½ teaspoon rosemary
½ teaspoon thyme
    savory, to taste
2 tablespoons butter

Herb sauce: In a saucepan, bring rosemary, thyme and savory to a quick boil in butter. Set aside.

Sprinkle ducks liberally with seasoning salt, including inside cavities. Place in large pan.

Pour beer over ducks and allow to marinate for approximately two hours. After marinating, pat ducks dry and baste heavily with herb sauce. Place ducks on top rack of smoker. Put remaining marinade and herb sauce in water pan. Smoke for approximately five hours or until ducks are tender.

Peter T. Arcuri
Tampa, FL

Microwave Bluegrass Duck

1 **wild duck**
Allegro marinade or a suitable wild game marinade
2-3 **onions, cut in quarters**
1 **can chicken broth**
½ **teaspoon each: sage, garlic powder and thyme**
salt and pepper to taste
3 **strips bacon**
2 **quart microwave covered dish**

Skin one wild duck and marinate for eight hours, turning occasionally. Remove from marinade. Place one half the onions inside duck and place breast side up in dish. Place the rest of the onions around the outside of duck and add chicken broth. Sprinkle seasoning over meat. Place bacon strips over duck, cover and cook in microwave on high for 21 minutes (turning dish one fourth turn every seven minutes) or until done. Remove, slice and serve with broth as a gravy.

Gene Manley
Versailles, KY

Drunk Duck or Goose

1 goose or 2 ducks, filleted breast meat and leg
    quarters
6 tablespoons currant jelly
1 tablespoon worcestershire sauce
½ pound butter or margarine
1 teaspoon salt
⅔ cup sherry
1⅓ cups bourbon

Melt jelly in heavy frying pan and add worcestershire, butter or margarine, salt and black pepper. When butter is melted add sherry and bourbon. Bring to a boil and add duck meat. Keep sauce barely at a boil, about eight minutes. Turn duck once at mid point of cooking time. Serve at once on rice. Use liquid left in pan for sauce.

James Nash
Leona, TX

Marinated Roast Wild Ducks

2 ducks

Marinade:

1 medium onion
½ pod garlic
3 tablespoons worcestershire sauce
½ cup red table wine
2 bay leaves
2 tablespoons black pepper
2 tablespoons salt
1 tablespoon Tabasco
1 tablespoon celery salt
2 quarts water
1 cup apple cider

Clean ducks well, removing the two small glands along the backbone just in front of the tail. These are often missed by commercial pluckers. Cut onions and garlic into small pieces and mix all ingredients in a pot large enough to hold two ducks. Submerge ducks in marinade and keep chilled for at least 12 hours. Two days will not hurt.

Roast Ducks:

- 1 orange, diced
- 1 apple, diced
- 2 stalks celery, diced
- 1 teaspoon garlic, minced (garlic juice will substitute)
- 1 teaspoon onion juice
- 2 teaspoons red hot sauce (not Tabasco)
- 1 teaspoon all purpose seasoning (salt and pepper will substitute)
- 6 slices bacon
- 2 cups apple cider
- 2 cups saved marinade
- 1 large roaster with elevated rack
- 4 toothpicks
- 1 degreasing cup

Preheat oven to 350 degrees.

Remove ducks from marinade and pat dry with paper towels inside and out. Save two cups marinade.

Sprinkle and rub ducks inside and out with a mixture of red hot sauce, garlic and onion juice. Season with all purpose season or salt and pepper inside and out. Stuff cavities with minced orange, apple and celery. Close cavities with toothpicks and place breast down on an elevated rack in a heavy roaster. Cover ducks with bacon and add two cups cider and two cups saved marinade. The ducks should be elevated on rack above liquid. Cook for approximately one and three fourths hours or until quite tender around breast bone. The weight of the pot affects the time for the inside to reach cooking temperature.

When done, remove cavity contents and halve ducks, one half per person. Degrease pot drippings via a degreasing cup or bulb-type baster and serve oil-free dripping as gravy.

Yield: serves four

Marshall B. Brinkley
Baton Rouge, LA

Old Timer Duck Delight

1 **campfire**
1 **medium size rock**
1 **duck**
1 **piece of foil**
1 **shovel**

Put rock in fire until it gets very hot. Remove insides, feathers, head and feet of duck. Put hot rock inside duck, wrap in foil (the old timers used mud, the foil is neater). Dig hole and bury duck with six inches cover of dirt. Let hot rock cook duck from inside out, about two hours. Dig up duck, remove rock. Bon appetit!

Janet and Jim Kessler
Portland, OR

The Famous Roby Duck/Goose Delicacy

**2 ducks or 1 goose, or can combine one of each, clean-
ed. (Remember the person who shot the game is
the one responsible for picking and gutting. The
cook is to receive the ducks ready to cook!)
carrots, celery and onion
1 bay leaf**

Stuff ducks, salt and pepper to taste.

Put into crock pot, fill crock pot half full with water. Put lid
on and cook on low for eight to ten hours.

When ducks are done, cool slightly and pick meat from bones.
If you want to taste something delicious, sneak a bite of the
tenderloin next to the breast bone. Strain liquid and save broth.
Throw away carrots, celery, onion, bay leaf and carcass. Using
wild rice or rice mixes, follow instruction on box, using broth
instead of water. Rice-A Roni and beef flavored rice mixes are
also good as well as stove-top-stuffing, or your own stuffing recipe.
If using rice, separate meat strands and mix into rice mixture.
If using stuffing, grease 9x13 pan, lay meat on bottom of pan,
put stuffing on top of meat and bake for one hour at 350 degrees.

Hints: For additional flavor, chop some fresh onions, carrots
and celery and add to rice mixture.

Oleo is good to add flavor to stuffing.

Add seasonings that your family likes.

Throw in some garlic and mushrooms.

Add cream of mushroom soup for flavor and to
make rice or stuffing a little more moist.

Serve with homemade rye dinner rolls fresh from the oven, with
butter. I credit my mother-in-law for guiding me into the Roby
family tradition of cooking wild game. The key to any good cooking is liking what you do. My husband likes to hunt, I like to
cook and the whole family likes to eat!

Same method for wild turkey and pheasant.

Dyann Roby
Atalissa, IA

Roast Wild Duck

1 wild duck
2 tablespoons soy sauce
2 tablespoons lemon juice
2 tablespoons honey
6 strips bacon

Skin duck and trim all fat. Split duck in half, down through center of breast and back. Place duck halves "center side down" in a roasting pan or baking dish. Pierce meat with a sharp knife or fork. Sprinkle one tablespoon soy sauce and one tablespoon lemon juice on each duck half. Drip or spread one tablespoon honey on each duck half. Blanket each duck topside with three strips bacon. Put one fourth inch water in bottom of pan. Cover with lid or foil. Cook in 350 degree preheated oven for 60 minutes.

Craig Moon
Fairfield, ME

Ducks in a Garden

2 ducks
2 pound package frozen mixed vegetables
3 apples, cored and quartered
2 stalks celery, cut in 3 inch pieces
1 pound carrots, cut in 4 inch pieces
3 large onions, peeled and quartered
4 slices bacon, cut in half
1 can condensed mushroom soup
2 tablespoons flour
  salt and pepper to taste

Shake two tablespoons flour in Brown-n-Bag and place in 2 inch deep roasting pan. Place vegetables in an even layer on bottom of bag. Salt and pepper to taste. Place ducks breast up on top of vegetables. Place onions, carrots, celery and apples around ducks. Place bacon pieces over ducks and vegetables. Ladle mushroom soup over top of everything. Tie bag firmly and punch four to five holes in top of bag. Place in 350 degree pre-heated oven for one hour and 20 minutes. Enjoy!
  Yield: serves six people

Jimmy Hughes
Bastrop, LA

Wild Roasted Duck

1 large can plums
1 cup honey
½ cup catsup
3 tablespoons soy sauce
1 onion, chopped

Make plum sauce first. Remove pits from a large can of plums, add to blender with juice and the other ingredients.

Bring to a slow boil and simmer for two hours, stirring occasionally.

With game shears or scissors, cut duck down back and wash thoroughly. Salt and pepper duck inside and out. Cut onion in quarters and put 2 quarters inside each bird. Cut 1 slice bacon in half and place 2 pieces side by side on a sheet of foil. Place duck back side down on top of bacon. Cut another slice of bacon in half and place these 2 pieces over duck's breast. Fold foil over duck and close ends tightly. Put in a cake pan or sided cooking sheet to avoid any dripping in oven. Place in a 350 degree preheated oven and bake for three and a half to four hours. After baking time, remove from oven and open foil. With shears or scissors, cut duck in half down middle of breast. Place the one half pieces in a cake pan and pour plum sauce over ducks and return to a 250 degree oven for 10 to 15 minutes.

Ronald Soehl
Hastings, MN

Dovard's Quackers

8 duck breasts, skin removed and deboned
1 pound fresh mushrooms, washed and sliced
4 large onions, peeled and quartered
2 garlic cloves, minced
  lemon pepper
  black pepper, freshly ground
1 box (2 envelopes) Lipton onion soup mix
1 bottle sweet red wine
1 large oven baking bag
  corn starch

Follow directions for baking bag and place in a shallow baking pan. Liberally sprinkle duck breasts with lemon and black pepper. Place in baking bag in a single layer. Sprinkle in minced garlic, sliced mushrooms and onion quarters. Top with soup mix and pour in wine. Seal bag as directed and bake in a pre-heated oven for 2 hours at 325 degrees. Remove from oven, open bag (after it cools, or you will be burned by the steam), remove ducks to serving platter and then pour juices and vegetables into a large sauce pan, thicken with a mixture of corn starch and cold water.

Dovard Mitchell
Greenville, MS

Eider Duck a la Veneziana

fillet of eider duck breast (1 duck = ¾ pound and will serve 2 people)
2 medium onions, sliced
6 tablespoons olive oil
salt and pepper

This variation of the famous international recipe "Fegato a la Veneziana" (venetian liver and onions) is a main course that I came up with several years ago after returning from Italy, and it makes a simple and quick preparation for eiders and other sea ducks.

There are only two tricks for this recipe. The first is the carving of the eider fillet. After removing the two fillets from the eider breast, lay them on a cutting board and slice thin slices across the grain of the breast muscles. The other trick is to not over-cook meat.

Sauté sliced onions in olive oil at medium heat in a skillet until soft (about 10 minutes). Move onions to side of pan and add meat. Sauté eider strips at medium/high heat until browned (2–3 minutes). Add salt and pepper to taste and serve.

I prepared this for lunch to re-check the proportions and it was delicious!

John Gribb
Hallowell, ME

Barbecued Duck

2 ducks
½ pound butter
½ cup sugar
1½ tablespoons lemon juice
1 tablespoon worcestershire sauce
1 teaspoon salt
1 clove garlic
1 small onion
½ teaspoon Tabasco sauce
pepper to taste

In a small pan mix above ingredients and simmer covered for five minutes. Makes sauce for four split duck halves.

Split whole ducks in half. Flatten ducks with a cleaver. Place on rack in flat baking pan. Bake at 375 degrees for one hour. Baste every ten minutes with prepared sauce. Turn and cook other side for one hour. Continue basting.

Mrs. Kevin Echterling
LaGrange, IN

Wild Duck Orange

2 large ducks
3 cups buttermilk
3 tablespoons flour
1 cup water
1 tablespoon sugar
1 teaspoon soy sauce
¼ cup orange marmalade
1 (6 ounce) can frozen orange juice concentrate, thawed
6 slices bacon

Soak ducks overnight in buttermilk in a glass or pottery bowl. Keep in refrigerator until ready to use the next day. When ready to cook, remove ducks, pat dry and place in the bottom of a large casserole dish. Cover with slices of bacon. Mix flour and water in a medium sized bowl until smooth. Add sugar, soy sauce, orange marmalade and orange juice concentrate. Pour over ducks.

Bake, covered at 350 degrees for 45 minutes to one hour, depending upon size of ducks. Serve with brown or wild rice and a salad.

Yield: four servings

Nancy Adams
Hancock, NH

Roast Duck

Pluck breast, back and legs of duck. With poultry shears or sheet metal cutter, cut off head, wings, and legs at first joint. Sear bird with propane torch (lightly). Cut off tail at anal bones. With shears, cut down full length of duck from anus to neck. Break open, and starting at left side, remove entrails, being careful to also get the lungs. Rub inside and outside with a soft brush. Remove any shot with end of sharp knife, inserting into shot holes to clean out and remove any blood spots. Rinse and pat dry. Stuff birds, truss with toothpicks or skewers along back cut. Turn over, salt, pepper and paprika skin.

Duck Stuffing:

    1 package Uncle Ben's original recipe-long grain and wild rice with seasoning package

    3 Steero chicken bouillon cubes or 3 tablespoons powdered bouillon

    2 stalks celery, chopped

    1 medium onion, cut into quarters

    ½ cup walnuts
     water

    1 tablespoon margarine
     oil

In a two quart sauce pan, add water, margarine and bouillon. Bring to a boil. Add rice and seasoning. In a large skillet, add oil and sauté onions, add celery, cook until opaque; do not overcook. Add rice mixture and a small amount of water if needed. Add medium chopped walnuts at last minute and stuff the duck. Stuff the duck with hot dressing.

Place in roasting pan, fill with one fourth to one half water in bottom of roasting pan. Place in 425 degree oven. Cook 15 minutes, then rub with margarine and sprinkle with paprika to enhance cooking. Cook 35 to 50 minutes, basting with margarine one or two more times. Do not overcook.

Mark Richardson
Seattle, WA

Duck Breast Hazelnut

4 medium duck breasts, boneless
½ cup diced onion
½ cup shelled, finely chopped hazelnuts
¾ cup all purpose flour, approximately
¼ cup sweet sherry
1 cup prepared chicken broth
¼ cup cooking oil, approximately
   salt and pepper to taste
2 tablespoons chopped chives or green onions to garnish

Tenderize and flatten duck breasts by gently pounding with kitchen mallet made for this purpose. In a large pan, over medium heat, sauté onions in two to three tablespoons oil. Once onions begin to slightly brown, remove from pan and set aside. Reduce heat to low and add remaining oil.

Flour duck breasts generously. Return heat to medium and sauté floured duck breasts until evenly browned on both sides, two or three minutes per side.

Carefully add chicken broth first and then slowly pour in wine. Do not add any liquid containing alcohol into a hot pan first since alcohol can flame. Adding chicken broth first will prevent this.

Simmer breasts for about five minutes, add onions and hazelnuts and then turn breasts over and continue simmering until liquid is reduced by about half. Season to taste with salt and pepper.

Using a fork, turn out duck breasts on a warm platter. Pour remaining sauce over breasts and garnish with chives or green onions.

Yield: serves four

Brian V. Cannavaro
Kalispell, MT

Rare Breast of Duck in Green Peppercorn Sauce

The following recipe is my attempt to emulate possibly the best duck meal I have personally ever enjoyed. I first sampled this unique recipe at the Deep Cove Chalet Restaurant in Vancouver, British Columbia. It replaces the normal fruit-based sauces used on duck with a green peppercorn sauce that is sublime.

4 ducks of choice, breasted out, leave skin on
3 tablespoons olive oil
3 tablespoons butter
   dash of Herbs de Province, or other seasonings
   flour
   milk

Marinate ducks in marinade of choice for 12–24 hours prior to cooking, then breast out. Heat butter and olive oil in a sauté pan or skillet over high heat (do not burn butter). Dip duck breasts in milk, shake dry and coat with light amount of flour, placing non-skin side down. Sprinkle Herbs de Province on skin surface.

Place in hot oil/butter mixture, skin side down and sauté until blood shows through on meat surface (usually two to three minutes). Turn breasts and cook for additional one to three minutes, depending on your choice of how rare you desire. This recipe is best if breast is red in the center.

Remove breasts, slice thinly on a diagonal, fan onto plates, and serve with peppercorn sauce poured on top.

Green Peppercorn Sauce:

12–14 green peppercorns, lightly cracked
  ½ cup chicken stock
   3 tablespoons butter
   3 teaspoons flour
  ½ cup dry white wine
   salt to taste
   nutmeg
   cream (optional)

Crack peppercorns and make a roux with butter and flour, add peppercorns and chicken stock, reduce to half at high heat, add white wine and reduce again at high heat. Adjust seasonings and salt, add a dash of nutmeg.

Note: Those preferring a thicker sauce may add cream at the end of the second reduction, but do not boil.

Preparation and cooking time is about 30 minutes or less.
Yield: four servings

Larry R. Stewart
Plano, TX

Salami Duck

6 duck breasts (mallard preferred)
¼ pound margarine
8 ounces San Francisco dry salami
   garlic powder, salt and pepper

Stuffing:
   ½ loaf bread or stuffing mix, unseasoned
   ¼ medium yellow onion, chopped fine
   ¾ teaspoon salt
      pepper
3-4 tablespoons summer savory seasoning
   ¼ cup water

Break up bread. Add onion, salt, pepper and summer savory. Mix. Add water and mix until stuffing sticks together.

Slice salami one sixteenth inch thick and set aside. Salt, pepper and garlic powder duck breasts. Grease 9x9x2 inch casserole dish, line the bottom with salami. Top with three or four duck breasts. Apply one inch thick layer of stuffing on top, then put on the second layer of duck breasts and top with salami to cover. Roast in 425 degree oven for 45 minutes or until breasts are pink inside. Bon appetit!

Mark Richardson
Seattle, WA

Duck Delight

Duck Delight is a good way to serve wild ducks when carving at the table would be inconvenient, such as at a buffet. It is served hot, with gravy. Corn and wild rice are excellent side dishes.

4 large puddle ducks (black, mallard, pintail)
1 8x8 inch pan cornbread, cooked
1 can chicken broth concentrate
3 stalks celery
6 green onions
2 oranges, peeled and sliced
1 tablespoon dried celery flakes
   poultry seasoning, salt and pepper

Insert oranges inside ducks. Cover with celery flakes, salt and pepper. Roast all four ducks in a large oven at 500 degrees for

50–60 minutes, or individually in small oven for 30–35 minutes each. While ducks are roasting, break cornbread into small pieces. Add chicken broth concentrate, mix until evenly moistened. Mince celery and onions, add to cornbread, along with celery flakes. Add poultry seasoning, salt and pepper to taste. Set cornbread mixture aside.

When ducks are cooked, pour off drippings and set aside. Remove meat from ducks, dice and add to cornbread mixture. Skim 2 tablespoons fat from drippings and add to cornbread, mix thoroughly. Place in a nine inch round, covered glass dish and bake at 350 degrees for 45 minutes or until cornbread pulls away from side of dish.

While baking, make gravy. Skim remaining fat from drippings, placing three tablespoons in a skillet and discard the rest. Sift 3 tablespoons flour into fat, brown at medium-high heat, stirring constantly. Add water to drippings to make two cups, then pour into skillet. Cook over medium-high heat, stirring constantly, until thickened.

Scott Carson
Gambrills, MD

Baked Wood Duck

4 cleaned and dressed woodies
3 tablespoons powdered garlic
1 tablespoon ginger
3 tablespoons parsley flakes
2 teaspoons thyme
¾ cup soy sauce
¾ cup white wine
¼ cup orange juice
  salt and pepper
2 apples

Put woodies in large Ziploc bags along with marinade made from next seven ingredients. Salt and pepper to taste. Refrigerate for one to two days, turning from time to time.

Preheat oven to 325 degrees. Stuff each duck with two apple quarters. Warm leftover marinade in sauce pan. Place woodies in foil lined roaster and baste with warm marinade. Bake covered about two hours. Baste frequently with warm marinade.

Jim Doescher
Panama City, FL

117

Tenderized Duck or Dove Breasts

6–8 duck or dove breasts
  salt, pepper and flour
½ cup onions
1 cup mushrooms
1½ cups red sweet wine
1 stick margarine

Tenderize each breast with a mallet until pieces are double in size. Salt, pepper and flour on both sides. Heat margarine in a large non-stick skillet (do not burn), add breasts, brown on both sides, uncovered for five to eight minutes. Reduce heat and add onions, mushrooms and wine. Cover and let simmer until tender when stuck with a fork. Water may be added if additional liquid is needed. Makes its own gravy. Serve over hot rice. Cooking time about 45 minutes.

Donald S. Wood
Wheatfield, IN

George's Amaretto Duck

4 duck breasts, fillets
2 ounces Amaretto liqueur
  milk
  flour
  cooking oil
  salt and pepper

Fillet breast meat from skinned ducks (mallard or teal). Thick breast fillets should be split to three fourths inch thickness. Rinse with cold water. Soak for one to two hours in milk and Amaretto. Let drip dry. Flour in paper bag with salt and pepper to taste. Pan fry in cooking oil, just enough to keep from sticking. Turn once. Do not overcook. Serve hot. Makes a good cold sandwich.

G. Bryan Schanze
Prairie Village, KS

Cajun Fried Duck

3 ducks
1 tablespoon salt
1 tablespoon red pepper
⅛ cup worcestershire sauce
1 tablespoon minced garlic
1 large bell pepper
   stalk of celery
2 lemons
2 large onions
   egg
   flour

Use a meat fork or knife to penetrate ducks and allow seasoning to flavor meat. Salt and pepper ducks. Cut up bell pepper, celery, onions and lemons. Stuff duck with half this mixture. Place ducks in a large pot, cover with water and boil on medium heat. Add remaining bell pepper, celery, onions and lemons to water. Add garlic and worcestershire sauce and boil until ducks are tender. Place entire pot in refrigerator for 24 hours. Remove, skin ducks and slice or tear into small pieces. Batter in egg and flour and deep fry until brown. Serve as hors d'oeuvres or as a meal. Delicious with homemade biscuits.
   Yield: eight to ten servings

Karl Taylor
Brandon, MS

Easy Duck Gumbo

Skin several duck breasts, cut into pieces and season well with salt, pepper and garlic salt. Brown in butter with chopped onion and bell pepper. Put into crock pot with one can stewed tomatoes (chopped in small pieces), and one can chicken gumbo. If you need more liquid to cover meat, add a can of chicken and rice soup. Cook on medium heat for two to four hours, depending on how much meat is used, can cook on low all day until the evening meal. Good dish to start at the beginning of a very busy day. Serve over rice.

Ginger Aaron
Fort Greeley, AK

119

Creamed Ducks or Doves

8 (or so) duck breasts cut into small pieces, skinned
2 cans cream of mushroom soup
1 can beef consommé
1 teaspoon worcestershire sauce
1 soup can water
1 teaspoon onion flakes
 garlic, salt, pepper and tenderizer

Season duck pieces and brown in small amount of oil. Drain on paper towels. Add all to a crock pot and heat for two to four hours on high or on low for six to eight hours. Serve over rice, noddles or toast.

Ginger Aaron
Ft Greeley, AK

Geese
Smoked Stuffed Goose

1 cup vinegar
½ cup salt
1 gallon water

Mix the above and soak wild goose for 24 hours. Drain and dry. Rub inside and out with lemon juice. Put into smoker for three hours.

If you do not have a smoker, brush with Liquid Smoke a few times during last hour of baking.

Stuffing:
¼ cup butter or margarine
½ cup sausage
½ cup chopped onion
¼ cup chopped celery
1 cup chopped tart apple
3 cups soft, day-old bread crumbs
½ teaspoon salt
⅛ teaspoon pepper
2 cloves garlic, sliced
1 egg, beaten

Sauce:
¼ cup melted butter
1 teaspoon grated orange rind
¼ cup red wine

Melt butter in heavy skillet, add sausage, onion and celery and cook until tender. Stir in remaining ingredients. Spoon lightly into cavity and close with skewers and string.

Place in roasting pan, uncovered, breast-side up, with a foil tent over bird. Cook in preheated 325 degree oven 20 to 25 minutes per pound or until tender, basting frequently with sauce. Remove foil tent during last hour of cooking. For a nice brown glaze, brush with La Choy brown gravy sauce and bake 15 minutes longer.

Variations: (1) Remove bird from pan, skim off fat, make gravy from drippings, add more water if necessary. (2) Pile sauerkraut around goose before placing in oven. This makes kraut that is rich with goose drippings and very acceptable to those who like rich sauerkraut dishes.

Mrs. Raymond (Minnie) Carr
Harrisonburg, Va

Hunter's Wild Goose Delight

1 wild goose
½ cup teriyaki sauce
½ cup Italian dressing
½ cup white wine
1 tablespoon worcestershire sauce
2 large or 3 small onions
1 can mushroom soup
1 can chicken broth
8 strips bacon
  crushed red pepper
  crushed black pepper
  onion salt
  poultry seasoning
  lemon pepper
  Morton's Nature Seasonings
1 plastic bag
1 Reynolds baking bag
  potatoes, optional

Soak goose in cold water for two hours, changing water frequently, until water is clear.

Remove goose from water and drain. Rub inside with crushed red and black pepper and onion salt. Rub outside of goose with Morton's nature seasonings, lemon pepper or any other spices you prefer.

Prepare marinade of teriyaki sauce, Italian dressing, white wine and worcestershire sauce. Place goose in plastic bag and pour in marinade mixture. Seal and place in refrigerator for 24 hours, turning often.

The next day (save marinade), place onions and undiluted soup in body cavity. Cover goose breast with strips of thick bacon. Put goose in "oven baking bag," pour in marinade with undiluted chicken broth and seal bag.

Place oven baking bag in a baking pan and put in a preheated 325 degree oven. Goose should cook from two and a half to three hours. After two hours, check for tenderness. If starting to get tender, break open top of bag and check every ten minutes, basting with juices. When tender, remove from oven and continuing to ladle juices over goose while cooling. Serve marinade as a sauce.

Serve boiled potatoes on the side and use the sauce as gravy.

Jim Morgan
Carolina Beach, NC

Stuffed Wild Goose

     1 (3 ½ to 4 pounds) dressed wild goose
     ½ teaspoon salt
     ⅛ teaspoon pepper
     6 slices bacon
     1 cup sliced green onion
     ¼ cup chopped green pepper
     1 (8 ounce) package herb-seasoned stuffing mix
  1 ½ cups water
     1 cup chopped dried peaches
     ½ cup chopped pitted dates
     1 egg, slightly beaten

Remove giblets and neck from goose, reserve for other dishes. Rinse goose with water, pat dry, sprinkle salt and pepper inside cavity. Fry bacon in a large skillet until crisp, remove bacon and reserve drippings in skillet. Crumble bacon and set aside. Sauté green onions and green pepper in bacon drippings until crisp and tender. Combine stuffing mix, bacon, green onions, green pepper and remaining ingredients, stirring well; spoon mixture into goose cavity. Close with skewers, turn goose and place breast side up on rack in a roasting pan. Insert meat thermometer in thigh, making sure it does not touch bone. Bake uncovered at 350 degrees for one and three fourths hours or until meat thermometer registers 185 degrees.

Spoon any leftover dressing in a lightly greased baking dish, cover and bake at 350 degrees for 40 minutes or until done.

Yield: four servings

John A. Davis
De Witt, AR

123

Wild Goose in Grape Sauce

        2 geese
          garlic salt
          paprika
          salt pork slices
    1 ½ stalks celery, chopped
        1 carrot, chopped
        1 onion, chopped
          fat sufficient for browning
    2–4 tablespoons flour
      ½ teaspoon rosemary
      ¼ teaspoon thyme
    1 ½ teaspoons salt
    ½ –1 cup grape jelly
          fresh mushrooms

Season geese inside and out with garlic, salt and paprika. Cover with salt pork slices. Place on rack in shallow pan. Roast uncovered one and a half hours until fat has cooked off. Drain fat and use to brown celery, carrots, and onion until soft and golden. Stir in flour, then blend in drippings and seasonings. Add grape jelly and mushrooms. Slice off all meat and immerse in grape gravy. Simmer for one and a half hours.

Edd Rankin
Colorado Springs, CO

Big D's Char-Roasted Goose

      2 geese (cut into halves)
      ½ cup olive oil
      ½ cup Italian salad dressing
          thyme
          lemon pepper
          rosemary
          fresh ground black pepper
          seasoned salt
          worcestershire
     12 slices bacon

Lay geese halves in a large shallow tray, pour olive oil over geese. Using your hands, coat both sides well with oil. Arrange geese in one layer in tray with cavity side down and pour Italian salad dressing over birds. Liberally season with worcestershire. Season to taste with thyme, lemon pepper, rosemary, pepper and salt. Cover with foil and let marinate overnight. Build a low-to-moderate charcoal fire and place geese on grill directly over fire. Cook 45 minutes (15 with cavity down and 30 with skin down). Return to tray, cavity down, and lay bacon slices over geese (three per half). Spoon remaining marinade over geese and cover tightly with foil. Bake in pre-heated 325 degree oven for one and a half hours.

Dovard Mitchell
Greenville, MS

Long Island Goose

1–2 **Canada geese**
3–4 **scallions, chopped**
 ½ **cup dry sherry**
 ¾ **cup soy sauce**
 ½ **cup sugar**
 ½ **cup water**
 4 **pieces ½ inch thick fresh ginger**
   wild or white rice

Fillet all meat off geese and put into covered pot with remaining ingredients. Simmer on medium heat for two to two and a half hours or until tender. Stir every half hour. Serve with rice. The geese can also be cooked whole in oven using a covered pot. Place geese in pan, breast up, and pour in ingredients. Pre-heat oven and roast at 350–375 degrees. Roast for two to two and a half hours. Turn geese over after one hour.

Christopher Schwab
Middle Island, Long Island, NY

125

Wild Goose with Prune and Apple Stuffing

1 goose
1 quart bread crumbs
2 cups chopped prunes
2 cups peeled and chopped apples
  salt
  generous grating of fresh nutmeg
  apple juice to moisten

Stuff goose with above ingredients.

Place goose on rack in roasting pan. Roast in 400 degree oven for 20 minutes. Pour off fat and then proceed to baste with your own choice of basting. Reduce heat to very moderate and continue to roast, allowing 20 minutes per pound.

Robert Blair
West Bend, WI

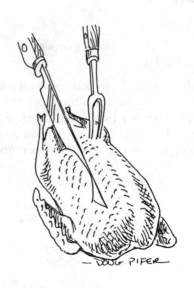

— DOUG PIFER

CHAPTER 5
BIG GAME RECIPES

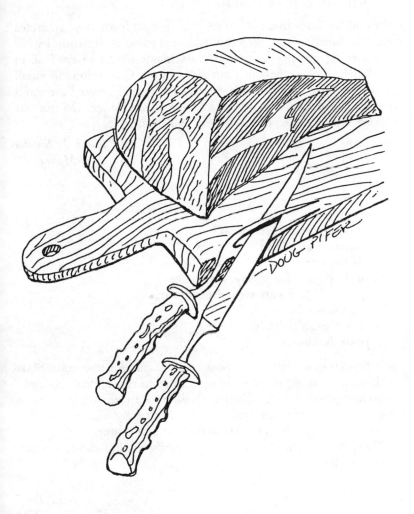

Big Game

Tender Cutlets
Antelope, Bear, Elk, Moose, Deer and even Beef

  round steaks
½ cup whole wheat flour (do not substitute)
3 or more large onions
  salt and pepper to taste

Trim all fat from meat. If meat is strong or from western states trim one fourth of any area that was next to skin. Cut round steak into serving size portions, pound each side to tenderize. Roll in whole wheat flour, brown both sides in oil. Cut onions in small pieces and heap on top of browned steak, simmer covered for about one hour. Add enough water so steak can simmer. Do not stir onions under steak, just let them fall around it.

Joseph P. Senatra
Moline, IL

Smoked Javelina

25 pounds quartered meat
 8 ounces Louisiana hot sauce
 4 tablespoons worcestershire sauce
 4 tablespoons La Choy soy sauce
 1 quart T. J. Swan strawberry wine
 1 gallon water
 1 cup mesquite chips
20 pounds charcoal

Mix liquids in a large bowl. Soak chips in mix for one hour. Start coals while soaking to allow temperature to reach ideal. Remove chips and place on coals. Pour ingredients into smoker pan. Place meat on rack in smoker and cover for five or eight hours. Do not allow pan to dry. Refill with ingredients or water.

Note: You may use this recipe for waterfowl, but substitute peach wine for strawberry.

Susie Bevel
Silver City, NM

Elk Suet Pudding

2 cups finely chopped elk suet
2 cups firmly packed brown sugar
2 cups boiling water
2 cups chopped raisins
2 cups all purpose flour
2 teaspoons baking powder
2 teaspoons each: ground cinnamon, cloves and nutmeg

In a large mixing bowl dissolve brown sugar, spices and baking powder in boiling water. Add suet, raisins and flour, mixing well. Transfer pudding into top half of a double boiler and steam with the lid on for two to five hours. The longer the better!

Serve warm in small bowls with sugar and cream.

Absolutely delicious!

John Martin Sever
Craig, CO

129

Moose Roast

1 medium moose roast, well trimmed
3 large cloves garlic, sliced
  flour
1 teaspoon salt
1 teaspoon cinnamon
1 teaspoon black pepper
½ cup white wine
½ cup cooking oil
1 container cran-raspberry sauce

With a paring knife, cut slits one inch deep into surface of roast, about two inches apart. Insert a slice of garlic in each slit. Turn roast over and repeat process on other side.

Dredge roast thoroughly on all sides with flour. Heat one half cup oil in the bottom of a heavy pan or dutch oven (that can be covered). Brown roast in oil on all sides. Remove from heat.

Mix salt, cinnamon, pepper and one fourth cup white wine. Pour over surface of roast. Put remainder of wine in the bottom of pan. Cover pan tightly and roast in a 350 degree oven for one and one half hours, turning roast occasionally, and adding a little water, if needed, to sauce in pan. After one and one half hours, remove pan from oven and add cran-raspberry sauce, mixing well. Baste roast with sauce before covering and returning it to oven. Roast for 45 minutes longer, turning roast once. Remove from oven and serve.

This sauce may be thickened with flour after adding one half cup water or it may be served as is poured over sliced roast. Also works well with caribou or sheep.

Donna Braendel
Chickaloon, AK

Barbecued Moose Ribs

5 pounds moose ribs, fat trimmed
3 cloves garlic, chopped
2 teaspoons salt
1 quart apple juice
  water
1½ –2 bottles Kraft hickory smoke barbecue sauce

Method #1: Pressure cook moose ribs according to cooker directions. Time is usually one hour for moose ribs, less for smaller game. Put first four ingredients in cooker with as much water

130

as needed to cover. When cooking time is complete and pressure has been bled according to cooker instructions, place ribs in a large flat roasting pan and coat each with barbecue sauce. Roast in a pre-heated 400 degree oven for 20 minutes.

Method #2: If you don't have or don't care to use a pressure cooker, place ribs in a large deep pot with garlic, salt, apple juice and as much water as is needed to cover. Simmer for three and one half hours (or until tender). Remove ribs to roasting pan, cover with barbecue sauce and roast 20 minutes at 400 degrees.

This is especially good for moose, and fine also for caribou, deer and sheep.

Everyone likes moose ribs cooked this way at the lodge.

Donna Braendel
Chickaloon, AK

Game Stroganoff

1-1 ½ **pounds round steak (elk, antelope, or venison)**
  1 **(6 ounce) can sliced mushrooms**
  1 **medium onion, chopped**
  1 **tablespoon worcestershire sauce**
6–8 **drops Tabasco**
  ¼ **teaspoon black pepper**
  1 **clove garlic, chopped**
  1 **can cream of mushroom soup**
  ½ **teaspoon salt**
  1 **(8 ounce) carton sour cream**
    rice

Spray a dutch oven with cooking spray and sauté chopped onion with clove of garlic. Cut meat in one half inch squares and add to dutch oven. Cook until brown and reduce heat back to low. Cook slowly until meat is tender. Add mushrooms with liquid, worcestershire, Tabasco, salt and pepper and mushroom soup and cook slowly for 30 minutes. Just before serving, add sour cream and heat until warm. Serve over cooked rice.

Ann Rawlings
Knoxville, TN

Wild Hog or Venison

heavy duty aluminum foil
10 pound (approximately) ham or shoulder with lower
    leg-bone removed.
1 large sweet onion, cut in small pieces
3-5 pounds potatoes, sliced ¼ inch thick
1 bag carrots, cut in medium size pieces
1 small stalk celery, cut in small pieces, or 2 teaspoons
    celery powder
1 teaspoon hot sauce of your choice, or to taste
¼ cup lemon or lime concentrate
2 tablespoons worcestershire sauce
    black pepper to taste
¾ teaspoon garlic powder or fresh garlic to taste
1 cup hickory style barbecue sauce
    cooking spray

Take enough foil for three layers eight to ten inches longer than the meat you are cooking. Lay two layers down and spray with cooking spray. Lay meat fat side down on foil. Press onions on top of meat. Place potatoes around meat, followed by carrots on top of potatoes and celery over carrots. At this point fold edges of foil up. Mix remaining ingredients, except barbecue sauce, in a medium size container and pour over meat, letting juice settle for a minute or so. Pour barbecue sauce over meat. Place remaining foil on top and seal all edges.

Method #1: Place package in baking pan with short sides. Place in middle of preheated oven at 275 degrees for three to three and one half hours. Turn oven off and leave in oven one half hour. Remove and enjoy.

Method #2: Place in same type pan in preheated 400 degree oven for one hour, turn oven off for one half hour. Turn on to 400 degrees again for one hour and off again for one half hour. Remove and enjoy.

Method #3: For campfire cooking, use two more pieces of foil 10 to 12 inches longer than wrapped meat. Spread hot coals large enough to handle the meat package. Place one piece foil on top of coals, place wrapped meat on top of foil and cover with the other piece of foil. Cover with more hot coals to maintain proper heat. Cook two and one half hours. Remove carefully and enjoy.

William S. Lewis
Homestead, FL

Liver Patties

1 pound deer or elk liver
2 tablespoons dry onion
¼ teaspoon salt
¼ teaspoon pepper
½ teaspoon seasoning salt
2 eggs
2 cups prepared dry bread crumbs

Grind liver, drain off any excess liquid. Stir in eggs, dry onion, salt, pepper, and seasoning salt. Add dry bread crumbs and stir to mix. Shape into patties and fry as you would hamburger patties.
   Yield: ten medium patties

Mrs. Eleanor Davis
Coatesville, IN

Elk Stew Oven Style

3 pounds elk stew meat
3 teaspoons butter
3 (10½ ounce) cans cream of mushroom soup
1 (4 ounce) can sliced mushrooms
1 package Lipton onion soup, dried
1 (¾ ounce) package brown gravy mix, dried
1 cup water
1½ cups Carlo Rossi white wine

Brown meat in a dutch oven with butter. Add other ingredients and stir until well mixed. Cover and bake at 350 degrees for three hours.

   Serve over well prepared rice or noodles. Can and should be cooked in a bed of hot embers in a campfire.

Charles Howard
Centralia, WA

Antelope Stew

1½ pounds antelope meat
1 tablespoon butter
3 medium onions
2 beef bouillon cubes
½ teaspoon Nature's Seasonings or other seasoned salt
1 teaspoon teriyaki sauce
½ teaspoon worcestershire sauce
1 cup red wine
1 bottle beer, use dark for more robust flavor
1 (16 ounce) can stewed tomatoes
1 can Campbell's golden mushroom soup

Cut up antelope meat into bite size pieces. Remove any fat. Brown lightly in melted butter. Chop onions and add to meat while browning. After five minutes add seasoned salt, teriyaki sauce, worcestershire sauce and mix well. Add wine, beer, stewed tomatoes and beef bouillon cubes. Simmer for one hour, stirring occasionally, add golden mushroom soup and simmer until meat is tender.

Yield: four servings

Tom H. Sleeter
Downers Grove, IL

Burick's 5-Pound Elk Salami

5 pounds ground elk (grind twice)
5 rounded teaspoons Morton's Tender Quick salt
2 ½ teaspoons black pepper
⅛ teaspoon garlic powder
2 teaspoons hickory smoke salt
5 teaspoons whole peppercorns (more if you like)

Mix all above ingredients and put into a tightly covered bowl (not aluminum) and refrigerate three days. Remove each day and mix thoroughly, as mixture will become stiff.

After three days, separate mixture into five log rolls and place on un-greased cookie sheet. Cover with foil and return to refrigerator for one more day.

On fourth day remove foil and place on cookie sheet in oven and bake for 12 hours at 125 degrees.

I suggest that salami be made in a 10 pound batch.

R. J. Burick
Los Alamos, NM

Game Burgers

2 pounds elk or deer meat ground up (add a little pork
    sausage if you like)

Mix well with salt and pepper. Make into patties as large as you prefer and broil or cook on outdoor grill. Baste with the following sauce. Mix together the following and simmer for five to ten minutes:

½ cup molasses
½ cup beer
½ cup chili sauce
½ cup minced onions
¼ cup prepared mustard
1 teaspoon worcestershire sauce
    salt and pepper to taste

Brush on generously.

Mrs. Bill Wilson
Aberdeen, WA

Venison Cornbread Cake

1-1½ venison pan sausage or burger*
  2 packages Mexican style cornbread mix
  2 (8 to 8½ ounces) cans sweet cream style corn
2-4 finely chopped fresh garlic pods**
  1 finely chopped medium to large jalapeño pepper**
  1 finely chopped medium onion of your choice**
    grated extra sharp cheddar cheese**

Preheat oven to 350 degrees. Brown meat in skillet. Prepare cornbread batter according to package instructions. Chop garlic, peppers and onion and mix thoroughly into cornbread batter. Add corn to batter and thoroughly mix. Pour one half to two thirds of batter into a well greased glass cake dish, 9x13x2 inch, bake for 15 to 20 minutes or until a light crust forms on the sides, the top should be soft; this is the reason for the glass cake dish. Add an evenly-spread layer of sausage over entire layer of baked cornbread. Add freshly grated or packaged cheese evenly covering layer of meat; adjust thickness of layer to suit taste. Pour remaining cornbread batter over meat and cheese layers. Bake another 15 minutes or until layer is golden and sides are crusty.

Cut in squares and serve with soup, stews, beans or any dish traditionally served with cornbread.

*Elk, hog, javelina work just as well.
**More or less according to taste.

John B. Jacobs
Humble, TX

Elk Doggies

Dough:

4 cups flour
5 teaspoons baking powder
2 teaspoons salt
½ cup shortening
1½ cups milk

Filling:

2 pounds elk roast
4 ounces green chilies
1 medium onion (finely chopped)
  salt and pepper to taste
6 peppercorns
1 tablespoon cumin
½ cup shortening or oil
3 garlic cloves
1 bay leaf
2 tablespoons worcestershire sauce
2 cups water

Rub salt, pepper and one garlic clove over roast. Brown in oil in cast iron skillet. Add worcestershire sauce and peppercorns and cover with foil. Bake at 325 degrees for approximately one hour and 15 minutes. Remove elk and set aside to cool. Keep stock but discard bay leaf. After roast has cooled, separate into shredded mixture by using two forks to pull meat apart. Use one cup stock, remaining crushed garlic, cloves and cumin. Mix with roast and simmer approximately one hour or until meat and spices have been thoroughly cooked.

Make biscuit mix from dough ingredients and knead. Allow dough to stand for 20 minutes at room temperature. Flour rolling pin and surface. Roll out dough one eighth inch thick. Cut with biscuit cutter. Place meat mixture on dough and roll up your "doggie." Bake 15 to 20 minutes or until outside is golden brown. Serve hot with salsa or sour cream dip.

Edd Rankin
Colorado Springs, CO

Elk Fillet with Mushrooms in Wine Sauce

1 ½ pounds fillet or tenderloin tips, cut into half inch strips
1 pound fresh mushrooms, sliced
3 tablespoons butter or margarine
½ cup port or marsala wine
½ teaspoon Dijon mustard
  salt and fresh ground pepper to taste
1 (10 ounce) package Pepperidge Farm frozen puff
  pastry shells, baked according to directions

In a large skillet, sauté meat in one tablespoon butter until pink.
Remove meat and set aside. Heat one tablespoon butter in skillet.
Add shallots and mushrooms. Sauté until golden brown. Add
wine and increase heat and, stirring, reduce to half. Add remaining butter and stir quickly into mixture. Serve immediately.
  Yield: six servings

Edd Rankin
Colorado Springs, CO

Elk Loin Roast in Port Wine Sauce

2 pounds roast from loin
2 tablespoons olive oil
2 tablespoons butter
  salt and pepper to taste
1 teaspoon thyme

Sauce:
⅓ cup port wine
½ cup game stock or beef broth
1 tablespoon cornstarch
1 tablespoon cold water
  salt and pepper to taste

Preheat oven to 450 degrees. Heat oil and butter in a heavy-bottomed frying pan over medium high heat. Season roast with
salt, pepper and thyme and brown on all sides. Put in oven. After
15 minutes, lower oven temperature to 375 degrees. Baste meat
with drippings. Roast for another 20 minutes for medium rare
to medium. Remove meat, set aside on a plate to catch the juices
and keep warm.

  Using the same pan, discard frying oil and set pan back on
stove. De-glaze pan with port and stock and bring to a boil. Mix

cornstarch with water. Using a wire whisk, gradually stir in corn-starch mixture to thicken sauce. Add meat juices to sauce and adjust seasoning with salt and pepper if necessary.

Serving suggestions: Carve roast into thin slices. Pour a little sauce on warmed plates and arrange meat on top. Serve with colorful vegetables and potatoes.

Substitute: All deer family and mountain sheep.

Yield: four to six servings

Edd Rankin
Colorado Springs, CO

Drunken Antelope

¾ **pound antelope backstrap**
½ **teaspoon salt**
½ **teaspoon pepper**
½ **cup flour**
¼ **cup white cooking wine**
1 **tablespoon sugar**
¼ **cup butter**
1 **tablespoon parlsey**

Slice antelope backstrap into one fourth by two inch pieces. Mix flour, salt and pepper. Melt butter in frying pan. Dredge antelope in flour and fry until brown on both sides. Mix wine with sugar and add to antelope. Let simmer until all juice is absorbed. Sprinkle parsley over antelope and serve warm. Serve with but-tered noodles, broccoli with cheese and a combination salad. Allow 45 minutes preparation time.

Yield: three servings

Terri Gauthier
Colorado Springs, CO

Wild Game Hot Dish

2 pounds elk or venison pieces (can use elk or venison
    steak or stew pieces)
1 medium onion
1 medium green pepper
1 small jar mushroom pieces
1 can cream of mushroom soup
1 tablespoon Kitchen Bouquet
    salt and pepper to taste
1 teaspoon worcestershire sauce, optional

Brown meat, onion, green pepper and mushroom pieces. Cover
but stir often. Add mushroom soup and Kitchen Bouquet. Leave
uncovered and simmer for 20 to 25 minutes. Serve over noodles,
rice or mashed potatoes.

Lois Huber
Sparta, WI

Moose and Broccoli

1 pound moose, cut into bite size cubes
1 large onion, cut into bite size pieces
1 pound broccoli, stalks thinly sliced, flowerets cut
    into bite size pieces
¼ cup oil
2 tablespoons soy sauce
3 tablespoons corn starch
1 tablespoon sugar
1 teaspoon each: salt, pepper and garlic powder
1½ cups water

Combine soy sauce, cornstarch, sugar, salt, pepper and garlic
powder in water and set aside. Heat one third oil in skillet, stir
fry broccoli flowerets for two minutes, remove and set aside in
large bowl. Heat one third oil in skillet and stir fry broccoli stalks
and onions about three minutes, remove and add to flowerets.
Heat remaining oil, brown moose on all sides, add seasoning
mixture and simmer until thick. Add broccoli and onions and
heat through thoroughly.

Serve over rice. You can use any wild red meat for this recipe.

Carla Drews
Wausau, WI

Wild Game Bologna/Salami Recipe
from Deer, Elk or Moose

2 pounds ground meat
1 teaspoon each onion salt, garlic salt and mustard
    seed
2 teaspoons celery seed
1 teaspoon seasoned pepper
2 tablespoons Liquid Smoke
3 tablespoons Morton's Tender Quick salt
1 cup water

Mix all together, make into rolls one foot by one and one half inches. Wrap in foil and refrigerate for 24 hours to allow meat to cure. Punch holes through foil with fork. Put foiled-wrapped rolls on flat sheet in oven and bake at 350 degrees for one and half hours. Allow to cool in foil, then enjoy.

Dick E. Redman
Stoutsville, OH

Boneless Rolled Roast

Seasoning:
  1 part garlic powder
  1 part salt
  1 part pepper

Take a boneless, rolled roast and rub seasoning all over surface. Wrap roast in foil and seal very tightly. Place in a roaster with one half inch water and cover. Cook at 275 degrees for one hour per pound of meat. Be sure to save the juice for gravy.

Optional: Sprinkle dry onion soup over roast along with seasoning. Makes an excellent gravy. *OR* add a horseradish sauce to the inside of roast before seasoning. Makes a real tangy and tasty gravy.

Jack W. Marler
Sturgis, SD

Moose Roast

2–4 pounds moose roast

Marinade:
  1 onion, diced
  1 clove garlic, diced
  2 cups sherry cooking wine
  ¼ teaspoon pepper
  ¼ teaspoon thyme
  1 package onion soup mix
    red and green pepper slices

Place meat in glass or earthenware bowl. Add marinade ingredients except soup mix and pepper slices. Let stand in refrigerator 24 hours. Turn meat several times in marinade. Remove meat.

  Sauté roast in shallow, hot fat until brown on both sides. Place in foil-lined roasting pan. Add onion soup mix and pepper slices. Seal foil and bake in 300 degree oven for two to two and one-half hours or until tender.

Jim Norine
Ashburn, VA

Sour Cream Casserole

1½ pounds ground venison or antelope
  2 medium onions, chopped
  1 teaspoon salt
 ¼ teaspoon pepper
  1 tablespoon parsley
  1 cup bread crumbs
  1 envelope onion-mushroom soup mix
  1 cup hot water
  1 can whole kernel corn, drained
  1 (10½ ounce) package frozen mixed vegetables,
     thawed and uncooked
  1 cup sour cream

Crumble meat into skillet and brown in small amount of shortening or butter. Add onions and cook a few minutes more. Drain off any grease. Add salt, pepper, parsley, and soup mix, and mix well. Add water and mix again. Add corn, vegetables, and sour cream. Mix lightly but thoroughly. Spoon into baking dish. At this point, casserole may be refrigerated or frozen. If frozen, thaw before baking. Sprinkle with bread crumbs.

    Bake uncovered for 15 minutes in a 350 degree oven, then cover loosely to prevent over-browning and bake about 30 minutes longer or until bubbly.

    Yield: six servings

Mrs. Thomas Sanders
Hanover, PA

Elk Steak with Green Peppers

1 pound elk steak, trimmed
  soy sauce
2 tablespoons dry cooking sherry
1 tablespoon cornstarch
½ teaspoon sugar
¼ cup vegetable oil
1 medium onion, sliced
1 teaspoon ginger powder
1 large green pepper, cut into strips
2 medium kosher dill pickles, sliced

Cut steak into one eighth inch thick strips, three or four inches long. Sirloin or New York steaks are best, but round steak works well also. Combine three tablespoons soy sauce, wine, cornstarch and sugar. Marinate meat strips in a covered bowl four to six hours in the refrigerator. Longer is better, especially with less choice cuts of meat.

Heat wok or large fry pan to high temperature. Add oil and swirl in pan for a few seconds. Add meat and marinade mixture and stir until three fourths of the meat changes color (about one minute). Remove pot from heat, remove meat from pot and set aside.

Return pot to heat and brown onions and ginger powder for a few seconds. Add green pepper and pickles and stir fry for 30 seconds. Add meat mixture and stir-fry until meat is cooked.

Serve with rice.

Yield: four servings

Bob and Carol Greuter
Los Alamos, NM

Wild Boar Sausage Loaf

1 (10 ounce) package chopped frozen broccoli
2 pounds wild boar sausage (any wild game or
    domestic sausage works well)
½ cup un-sugared corn flakes
¼ teaspoon ground black pepper
1 (4 ounce) can mushroom pieces
⅓ cup catsup
⅓ cup favorite barbecue sauce
3 slices Swiss cheese
3 slices cheddar cheese

Thaw, wash, and drain broccoli in colander. Drain mushrooms well.

Mix sausage, mushrooms, corn flakes, black pepper, catsup and barbecue sauce.

Cover 10x16 inch cookie sheet with aluminum foil. Place sausage mixture on foil and spread evenly to each edge. Spread broccoli on sausage. Pat broccoli lightly into sausage mixture. Next roll sausage into a loaf. To do this, gently lift foil over to begin your first roll. It is easiest to begin rolling from the longer sides, then cut loaf in half for handling and cooking, if needed.

Place loaf on greased or non-stick cookie sheet for baking. Bake at 350 degrees for approximately one and one half hours. Remember that pork must be cooked completely. At last five minutes arrange cheese slices across top of loaf, finish cooking until cheese melts.

If a sauce or gravy is desired, a plain brown gravy works great! Leftovers are great when reheated the next morning for a hearty breakfast before going in the field.

Mark Nethery
Louisville, KY

—DOUG PIFER

Western Game Hash

1 pound ground elk or venison
1 large onion, chopped
1 bell pepper, chopped
1 (16 ounce) can tomatoes
1 can water
½ cup uncooked rice or uncooked macaroni
2 teaspoons salt
1–2 teaspoons chili powder
½ cup black olives
⅛ teaspoon pepper
2½ cups shredded cheese

Heat oven 350 degrees.

In large heavy skillet brown meat, onion and pepper. Drain any fat. Stir in remaining ingredients and bake in a two quart casserole dish for one hour. Cover top with two and one half cups shredded cheese for the last 15 minutes of cooking time. Serve with buttermilk biscuits and fresh fruit salad.

Jannie Vaught
Sheridan, WY

British Columbia's Caribou Mountain Breakfast Moose Liver, Bacon and Eggs with Onions

1 moose liver
2 pounds sliced bacon
3 dozen eggs
6–8 large brown onions
    salt, pepper, flour, butter or margarine

As hunters know, on prolonged hunts far from home, it is impractical to transport organ meat home; it spoils too quickly. We have always used the organs (liver, heart, tongue) in camp. After washing thoroughly, hang liver in cheese cloth sack outside at least eight feet high. Hang for two days and nights in the shade. Prepare a work area such as a table top at least three feet by three feet. Fill a large bowl with water and add one half cup salt for each gallon of water. On a clean surface, spread with wax paper and pour a pile of flour. Cook bacon in large cast iron skillet, removing bacon as it cooks to a flexible tenderness, leaving bacon grease in skillet.

Slice liver into one inch thick steaks. They will be very large, approximately one and a half pounds each. Place liver steak in bowl of salt water and let soak one to two minutes, to draw out remaining blood. The color will quickly change from deep red-brown to light pink. Remove and roll in flour until thickly coated. Sprinkle salt and pepper on both sides and place in hot skillet of bacon grease. Fry several minutes on each side, until golden brown. Test by cutting open to check for doneness. Adjust cooking time to suit taste. Repeat until all liver is cooked. In another large skillet, place one fourth pound butter or margarine. Slice all onions in advance of cooking. Do not dice or cube. Fill skillet with onions, salt lightly and cover. After onions soften, stir and re-cover. Add more butter if needed for thin coating and cooking. When onions, bacon and liver are all cooked, store in oven at "warm" setting (100 to 150 degrees). Onions should be soft. Clean both skillets and cook eggs to order, using butter. Serve with coffee, hot biscuits, jelly.

On large plate, place one liver steak with eggs next to it. At hunter's option, lay strips of bacon across liver then top with a generous pile of onions.

Cooked liver can be stored in cold (40 degree) ice chest for several days.

Yield: serves eight to ten hungry hunters

Gordon K. Holcomb
Garden Grove, CA

Sauteed Moose Heart and Mushrooms in Cognac

  1 moose heart, approximately 5 pounds, thoroughly
      trimmed with tough membranes removed, washed
  2 pounds mushrooms, fresh, thoroughly washed
  2 pounds shallots, fresh, in season, otherwise 3 large
      brown onions
  1 blossom fresh garlic
    salt and pepper
  1 quart cognac (I use cheap El Presidente brand) red
      or white wine can be substituted
  ½ pound margarine or cooking oil (olive oil)

In a large cast iron skillet, place sliced mushrooms and crushed garlic in margarine together with sliced shallots or onions and simmer over low heat, covered.

In separate pot, boil moose heart until tender to fork test. When heart is cooked, remove to cutting board and slice into one inch cubes or bite-size chunks.

Put heart meat in with mushrooms, shallots and garlic. Pour in one quart cognac and simmer lowly until 80% of cognac has evaporated. Lightly salt and pepper.

Serve as appetizers with favorite drink.

Yield: serves eight hungry hunters

Gordon K. Holcomb
Garden Grove, CA

Wild Game Chili

2–3 pounds meat (elk, venison, squirrel, rabbit), ground
1 large chopped onion
4 pieces celery, chopped (almost a cup)
2 tablespoons dried parsley flakes
3 teaspoons garlic powder
2 diced bell peppers (I keep some frozen and I use those)
½ teaspoon cumin (comino)
¼ teaspoon red pepper (more or less to taste)
1 teaspoon paprika
1 (16 ounce) can peeled tomatoes, chopped
1 can Mexican style beans, un-drained
5 tablespoons (more or less) Williams chili mix

Start meat to cooking in large pan with a little water (one cup), add onion, celery and peppers. Then add other ingredients, except beans, add beans in last 30 minutes cooking time. Cook slow for at least two hours, stir to make sure it doesn't stick. May also be cooked in crock pot for a longer period of time. Make sure it has enough liquid; more water may be added.

Rachel Whitney
Tulsa, OK

Arcadia Hunt Club Official Wild Hog

2 pounds wild hog meat, cut into 2 inch cubes
¼ cup flour
1 teaspoon salt
  black pepper to taste
4 tablespoons bacon drippings
1 large onion, cut-up
4 small onions, whole
2 cloves garlic, minced
4 carrots, halved
4 potatoes, halved
4 cups water
1 tablespoon parsley flakes
¼ teaspoon rosemary

Make a mixture of flour, salt and pepper. Coat wild hog meat
with flour mixture. Brown meat in bacon drippings in a dutch
oven or large frying pan, then add cut-up onions and garlic. Cook
for five minutes. Add water, rosemary and parsley flakes, cover
and cook for one to two hours until hog meat is tender. Add
potatoes, carrot and small whole onions. Cook 30 additional
minutes.

Yield: four servings

Tom Arcuri
Tampa, FL

Damet

An acronym for "Don and Marie Armstrong's Elk Treat", as prepared by them from Canon City, Colorado.

> **2 pounds ground lean elk meat (moose or venison both O.K.)**
> **2 medium onions, diced**
> **2 large green peppers, diced**
> **1 medium jar stuffed olives, drained (save juice)**
> **1 small jar capers**
> **½ package seedless raisins**
> **1 large can tomato sauce**
> **½ teaspoon each salt, garlic powder, celery salt**
> **¼ teaspoon each oregano, pepper, paprika**
> **1 tablespoon Pickapeppa sauce or more to taste***
> **2 tablespoons worcestershire sauce**
> **2 tablespoons olive oil**

Sauté onions and peppers in two tablespoons olive oil. Sauté meat in two tablespoons olive oil, stir in seasonings and add worcestershire and Pickapeppa sauce, stir well. Add sauteed onions and peppers and rest of ingredients. Cook about 40 minutes over slow heat, covered. Serve with white, yellow, or wild rice.

This is a most unusual, yet easy to prepare recipe for big game meat. I have prepared this many times and it is enjoyed by almost all my hunting companions from Canada to Texas and from the Rockies to Florida.

*Pickapeppa sauce is a delightful additive from Jamaica. Heinz or A-1 may be substituted.

Don Armstrong
Canon City, CO

Elk and Rice Pilaf

2 cups elk round steak, cut up
1½ cups boiling water
1 (10 ounce) package frozen, chopped spinach (thawed)
¾ cup quick cooking rice
¼ cup green onion, chopped
1 tablespoon butter
1 cube instant chicken bouillon
½ cup shredded mild cheddar cheese

Heat oven to 350 degrees. Dissolve chicken bouillon in boiling water. Melt butter and mix all ingredients (except cheese) in a lightly greased baking dish, 10x6x1¾ inches. Cover and bake one hour. Remove and sprinkle cheese over the top and serve.
Yield: four servings

Cindy Whitley
Arroyo Grande, CA

Caribou Sausage

4 pounds ground caribou, trim all fat
4 teaspoons onion flakes
1 teaspoon garlic powder
1 teaspoon curry
2 teaspoons black pepper
3 teaspoons salt
2 teaspoons cumin
1 teaspoon cayenne
2 teaspoons sage
1 teaspoon thyme
1 teaspoon oregano

Mix with clean hands thoroughly, package and freeze. Thaw in refrigerator and not in the microwave for best results and cook on low temperature in a cast iron pan with cooking spray.

Kathy Braden
Soldotna, AK

Moose Pot Pie

Stew Ingredients:

   3 tablespoons oil
   1 clove garlic (more or less to taste)
   2 pounds moose steak (or any game meat will do)
   2 teaspoons salt
   ¼ teaspoon ground pepper
   1 teaspoon worcestershire sauce
   1 teaspoon lemon juice
   1 bay leaf
   6 cups water
   3 large potatoes, chopped
5–6 large carrots, chopped
   1 large onion, chopped (more or less to taste)
   1 cup frozen peas (or 1 can)
   ¼ cup flour

Pastry Recipe:

   2 cups flour
   1 teaspoon salt
   ⅔ cup shortening
5–7 tablespoons water

Prepare stew in large pot. Cut steak into one and one half inch cubes. Brown meat in oil and garlic. Add three cups water, salt, pepper, worcestershire sauce, lemon juice and bay leaf. Simmer two hours. Add three more cups water and chopped potatoes, carrots and onions. Simmer until almost done, then add peas. Thicken stock with one fourth cup flour diluted with cold water to a runny consistency. Stir constantly while adding flour until stock thickens.

Pastry: Cut shortening into flour and salt. Slowly add water. Roll out two thirds of dough into large circle. Line a 10 inch springform pan with high sides or similar casserole dish. Pour stew into unbaked crust. Roll out remaining dough, place over top, seal edges, and vent. Bake at 400 degrees for one hour or until browned.

My wife once prepared this with the meat of about 24 de-boned dove, a lot of work but most delicious!

Yield: serves eight to ten adults or four hungry hunters

Steve and Susan Roberts
Wasilla, AK

Wild Boar Roast

In Europe wild boar is the best sport and while there a friend of mine gave me this recipe. I had looked for a long time for a recipe for wild boar and I hope you will enjoy this as much as I have. Use this recipe for boar under four or five years old. If animal is older, soak in buttermilk for several days before cooking. You will need the following:

wild boar roast with bone
4–5 small to medium onions
sour cream
beef broth
sage
thyme
marjoram
margarine
rosemary
salt
pepper
cognac

Brown boar roast in heavy iron pot using margarine. When well brown, remove and add fine cut onions, some salt, pepper and brown slightly. Season roast with a small amount of sage and rest of spices to taste. Return roast to pot with onions and add three to four tablespoons beef broth and place covered pot in pre-heated 300 degree oven. Cook one and one half to two hours or until roast is done (meat should start to cook away from bone). Remove meat and strain/press what remains in pot, i.e. onions should be "mashed". Return liquid to pot and over high heat add one half pint sour cream and a small amount of flour to thicken slightly. Just before serving add shot of cognac to sauce. Serve wild boar thinly sliced with side dishes of brussel sprouts and wild rice.

Robert Schmelzlen
APO New York

West Bar Chili

4 pounds elk or venison stew meat
2 medium onions
1 green pepper
1 stalk celery
1 tablespoon jalapeño
4 (28 ounce) cans whole tomatoes
1 (28 ounce) can tomato sauce
1 tablespoon Tabasco
1 teaspoon cumin
1 teaspoon garlic salt
1 teaspoon onion salt
1 teaspoon pepper
1 teaspoon cayenne
3 tablespoons chili powder
1 bay leaf
1 cup zinfandel

Trim all visible fat from meat, cut meat into one inch cubes and brown in olive oil. Reserve meat and pan juices. Coarsely chop onion, green pepper, celery and jalapeño. Sauté vegetables in olive oil until onion is clear and limp. Break tomatoes into chunks. In large stock-pot or soup kettle, combine tomatoes with juice, tomato sauce, meat and pan juices and vegetable mix. Add seasoning and wine. Simmer four to five hours, correcting seasoning after first hour. Serve with cornbread, green salad and cold beer.

Randy Hieronymus
Seattle, WA

Pa-Pa's Wild Pork

3-4 pounds pork loin roast
2 large onions, sliced
1 teaspoon chopped garlic
2 teaspoons salt (to taste)
1 teaspoon pepper (or to taste)
1 quart sauerkraut (drained)
1 tablespoon caraway seed
1 can beef broth
6 potatoes (boiled and mashed)

Using a six quart crock pot put in pork and all ingredients, but not kraut, caraway seeds and potatoes and cook on low for six hours. Then add kraut and caraway seed and cook an additional one to two hours until done. Serve over potatoes that have been boiled and mashed.

Brad Culpepper
Charlotte, NC

Boiled Bear Heart

1 bear heart, quartered
1 teaspoon marjoram
¼ teaspoon nutmeg
  dash pepper
½ teaspoon thyme

Place heart and spices in pot with 3 cups water. Cover and simmer until tender. Let cool in broth, then slice thin and save for sandwich meat.

  Best when put on white bread with real butter.
  Yield: serves 1

Charles Neuendorf
Loyal, WI

Bear Roast

4–5 pound bear roast, trimmed of fat
  1 packet onion soup mix
  1 cup prepared mustard
  4 cups water
  1 tablespoon red pepper
    salt and black pepper to taste

Marinate roast 12 hours in marinade of mustard, onion soup mix, water and red pepper. Turn over continue to marinate for another 12 hours refrigerated.

Roast at 350 degrees for 3 hours, adding water as needed. Salt after cooking and cool. Skim fat from water. Remove roast and partially refreeze. Slice very thin and serve.

Reginald Vaughan
Chicago, IL

Bear Stew

  2 pounds bear meat, cut in 1½ inch cubes, all fat removed
  ¼ cup bacon drippings or vegetable oil
    flour
    salt and pepper
  1 bay leaf
    pinch dried thyme
  3 stalks celery, cut on diagonal
  1 small onion, diced
  2 cloves garlic, minced
  ½ cup dry red wine
  ⅔ cup water
  ½ cup tomato sauce
  1 medium chopped onion
  3 medium carrots, sliced into rounds
  3 stalks celery, cut on diagonal

Coat meat in flour seasoned with salt and pepper. Brown meat on high heat with bacon drippings or oil. Add meat and all remaining ingredients to slow cooker on low setting.

Cook about 6 hours then add chopped onion. Sauté sliced carrots and celery in butter until slightly tender.

Add to pot and cook approximately 2 more hours or until desired tenderness.

Yield: serves 6 to 8

Ken Gill
Binghamton, NY

CHAPTER 6
VENISON RECIPES

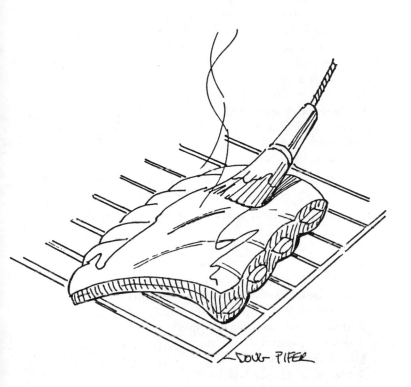

DOUG PIFER

Barbecue

Steve's Venison Barbecue

Barbecue Sauce:

  3 sticks margarine
½ teaspoon worcestershire sauce
  8 ounces tomato sauce
    dash of Liquid Smoke
  1 teaspoon black pepper
½ cup chopped onion
½ cup lemon juice
½ cup ketchup
½ teaspoon oregano
½ teaspoon garlic salt
½ teaspoon dry mustard
½ teaspoon rosemary
½ teaspoon thyme
½ teaspoon salt

Heat three sticks margarine in a one quart saucepan. Add remaining ingredients and simmer 10 minutes.

1½–2 pounds venison roast or steak (beef optional)
½ large onion, sliced
  1 green pepper, sliced
  1 (4 ounce) can mushrooms
    barbecue sauce (see above)
½ cup Gold Medal flour (minimum)
½ teaspoon red pepper (optional)
  2 stalks fresh celery, chopped
  1 pound sweet Italian sausage (bulk)
½ cup red wine
  1 teaspoon season salt
  1 teaspoon black pepper

Fry bulk sausage in a dutch oven and remove to a bowl, leaving drippings in pan. Cube roast or steak, dredge in flour seasoned with seasoned salt and black pepper. Fry pieces of cubed meat in dutch oven until brown. Simmer for 30 minutes. Return sausage to pan and add wine, green pepper, mushrooms, barbecue sauce, celery, red pepper (optional) and any leftover flour. Simmer 30 minutes or until tender. Serve over your favorite rice with hot bread.

Yield: serves six

Steve Loder
Lansdale, PA

Barbecued Deer Ribs

Method 1: Place five pounds deer ribs in a large heavy pan. Cover with water and simmer for one hour. Drain.

Method 2: Wrap ribs in heavy duty foil and bake in 350 degree oven for one and a half hours. Unwrap and drain drippings.
   Combine the following:

    1 cup firmly packed brown sugar
 ¼ cup worcestershire sauce
 ⅓ cup soy sauce
 ¼ cup cider vinegar
 ¼ cup chili sauce
 ½ cup catsup
2 ½ teaspoons yellow mustard
    2 crushed garlic cloves
 ⅛ teaspoon pepper

Pour over ribs. Marinate one to three hours at room temperature. When ready to cook, remove ribs from sauce and arrange on grill about four to five inches over moderately hot coals, basting frequently with sauce and turning often until sauce is used and ribs are crisp and brown (about 20 minutes).
   Depending on how meaty ribs are, allow three quarters to one pound per person.

Danny B. Ball
Pearisburg, VA

E-Z Indoor B-B-Q

4–6 venison chops or steaks
 1 (10 ounce) jar barbecue sauce
 1 onion, diced
 2 (16 ounce) cans baked beans

Place venison in 6x9 inch pan, lightly coat with barbecue sauce (save the rest for later). Top with diced onion. Pour beans over the top of the onion until completely covered. Pour remaining barbecue sauce over beans, mixing well. Bake in 350 degree oven for 45 minutes to one hour.

Stephen Hartin
Baltimore, Maryland

Barbecue Venison Speedies Appetizer

3 pounds venison
¼ cup pure virgin olive oil
2 cups zesty Italian salad dressing
1 tablespoon steak sauce
1 tablespoon soy sauce
1 splash hot sauce (optional)
½ teaspoon dried basil
½ teaspoon crushed thyme
½ teaspoon dried parsley

Mix all ingredients except venison in a large mixing bowl, blend well with a hand wisp and then set aside.

Cut venison into three inch strips, about a half an inch thick. Place venison strips into marinade and refrigerate, covered, for one hour. After one hour, remove directly from marinade onto hot barbecue grill, turning pieces frequently. Remove speedies when they are medium rare. This is essential or meat will become tough.

Serve with your favorite dipping sauce.

John Campanella
Syracuse, NY

Venison B-B-Q

1 venison roast (2½ to 3 pounds)
4 beef bouillon cubes
½ cup water
1 teaspoon chili powder
½ cup barbecue sauce
¼ cup ketchup
1 large onion, quartered

Cut venison, place in crock pot with water and beef bouillon cubes. Add chili powder, barbecue sauce and ketchup. Add quartered onion, salt and pepper. Cook overnight on low heat.

Peggy Ivy
Paducah, KY

Barbecued Venison

3-4 pounds venison
  2 bottles Hunt's country or southern style barbecue
     sauce
  1 cup ketchup (approximately)
  1 cup spaghetti sauce (approximately), homemade or
     store-bought

Pot roast venison until tender and remove from heat until cool
enough to handle. Shred meat. Combine other ingredients to
taste. Add meat to sauce. You should have a lot of sauce. If not,
add more sauce ingredients so that it is very moist. Heat and
serve on good, crusty rolls. This is very easy, very tasty, and goes
in a crock pot well. I've served this as barbecued beef to many
people who love it and did not know it was venison.

Margie Dehnhard
Clarksboro, NJ

Chili

Big Game Hunter's Chili

Best to make 24 hours ahead, chill and de-grease, then re-heat slowly.

6 tablespoons oil (better if corn oil or bacon fat)
3 pounds chili-ground chuck (better if chili-ground venison)
1 pound chili-ground pork (better if chili-ground wild boar)
10 stalks celery, coarsely chopped
8 tablespoons chili powder (prefer Gebhardt's) added throughout cooking
2 teaspoons brown sugar
4 bay leaves (remove before serving)
2 tablespoons fresh French thyme or 1 tablespoon dried thyme
½ teaspoon basil
1 tablespoon ground cumin or 3 tablespoons dried oregano
4 teaspoons salt
8 cloves garlic, very finely minced
½ cup chopped fresh cilantro
2 large yellow onions, minced
2 pounds (12 ounce can) tomatoes (stewed or whole, peeled), drained. If whole, mash or cut in half.
2 cups dry red wine
2 green peppers, seeded and chopped
4 minced jalapeño peppers and 4 minced serrano or Japanese peppers or 8 crushed small dried red peppers to taste (4 is often enough) or 2 to 4 ounce can chopped green hot chilies
4 cups beef broth
2 tablespoons red wine vinegar
2 tablespoons tequila
½ cup Mexican beer

In a skillet, sauté onions, green peppers and garlic in oil. Remove from pan and brown meat in the same skillet. Pour off grease from meat. Put meat, tomatoes, onions, peppers, garlic, and seasonings (one half the chili powder) in a large dutch oven and simmer covered for one hour.

Add red wine, tequila, beer, the rest of the chili powder, and enough water to cover (four to eight cups) and cook another 30 minutes without the cover until thickened. Add one cup boiling water to thin if necessary.

Adjust seasoning with salt and chili powder.

To increase quantity, add the following to each additional two pounds meat: four teaspoons chili powder, one teaspoon cumin, and garlic to taste.

Serve with: slabs cheddar or jack cheese, corn bread sticks, warm tortillas or French bread, beer or tequila.

Yield: two gallons serves 16

Fred W. Williams
Brownsburg, IN

Fred's Famous Venison Chili

1-1½ pounds venison burger, browned and drained
  ½ pounds fresh mushrooms, coarsely chopped
  1 green pepper, coarsley chopped
  1 (14½ ounce) can sliced stewed tomatoes, undrained
  1 (6 ounce) can tomato paste
  3 (14½ ounce) cans dark red kidney beans, undrained
  2 tablespoons chili powder
  1 teaspoon cumin powder
  ¼ teaspoon Tabasco sauce
  ½ teaspoon cayenne pepper
3-4 dashes crushed red pepper
1-2 dashes celery salt
    grinding of black pepper
  2 cloves garlic, crushed

Combine all above ingredients in a four quart slow cooker (crock pot) and preferably refrigerate overnight. Cook on low heat setting for eight to ten hours. Top each serving with freshly chopped onion and shredded cheddar cheese.

Note: this is a very good, mildly hot chili that is complimented by a freshly baked loaf of bread.

Yield: six to eight servings

Fred W. Williams
Brownsburg, IN

Chimichangas

1 pound ground venison
1 medium onion, chopped
⅓ cup Pace picante sauce
   salt and pepper to taste
⅔ cup cheddar cheese, shredded
1 package egg roll wraps
   oil

Brown venison with onion, making sure you crumble till fine texture. Drain. Add picante sauce, salt and pepper and simmer till juice is gone. Add cheese and stir until mixed well. Roll into egg roll wraps and fry until golden brown. Serve on a bed shredded lettuce, top with either more cheese, sour cream or a spoonful of guacamole.

Yield: 16 servings

Mrs. Ken Stormont
Scott City, KS

Venison Chili (Without Tomatoes)

1 pound ground venison
1 cup dried navy beans
2 medium onions, chopped
1 cup sliced fresh mushrooms
¼ teaspoon chili powder (or more according to your
    fondness for chili flavor)
1 pinch cayenne pepper
¼ teaspoon cumin
¼ teaspoon summer savory
¼ teaspoon chervil
2 beef bouillon cubes
4 strips bacon
1 tablespoon bacon fat
1½ teaspoons butter, margarine, or cooking oil
1 bay leaf

Preheat oven 325 degrees.

Soak beans for a long time, preferably overnight.

Place beans in kettle with approximately two quarts water
(depending on your tastes, you might want to also add to the
cooking water a half cup or so sherry, red wine or apple cider),
bouillon cubes, spices, whole onion, lard and bay leaf. Cook until
beans are just shy of tender.

Cut bacon strips into quarters, begin to cook. When bacon
is almost done, add venison. Cook until venison is brown but
not well-done. Drain meat and reserve.

Melt butter in a small fry pan. Sauté onions and mushrooms
together until cooked but still firm.

Place venison/bacon and onions/mushrooms into a covered
casserole and, with a slotted spoon, add beans. Discard bay leaf
and whole onion. Pour one inch bean liquor into casserole and
stir. Place in 325 degree oven for one half hour (or in microwave
for five to seven minutes on high setting).

Yield: four hearty servings

James B. Heath
Norfolk, CT

PJ's Venison Chili

3 pounds venison, cut into ½ inch cubes
1 pound ground venison (with pork added)
1 pound hot Italian sausage, chopped
5 tablespoons vegetable oil
2 large onions, chopped
8 cloves garlic, chopped
2 stalks celery, chopped
4 tablespoons chili powder
1 teaspoon oregano
1 teaspoon ground cumin
1 teaspoon salt
1 teaspoon red pepper flakes
1 (6 ounce) can tomato paste
4 cups beef stock or beef gravy
2 cans red kidney beans
2 cans great northern beans
1½ pounds monterey jack cheese, grated or cubed (¼ inch cubes)

Pat meat dry with paper towel. Heat oil in skillet and brown meat for two or three minutes. Put browned meat into large cast iron dutch oven or slow cooker (if slow cooker, cook for six hours). Sauté garlic, onions and celery for four to five minutes, stirring often.

Add garlic, onions and celery to meat and stir well over medium heat for two minutes. Turn heat to high and add rest of ingredients except beans and cheese. Bring this mixture to a boil and simmer for one and a half hours. Add beans and simmer an additional 20 minutes, turn off heat and add cheese. Cover pot while simmering and stir every 15 minutes. Serve with Italian bread and butter or home made biscuits.

Yield: eight to ten servings

Paul J. Howshall
Effort, PA

Brimm's Alaskan Bowhunters Chili

1 pound venison, de-fatted and ground with ¼ pound
    beef fat
2 large green bell peppers
1 hot jalapeño pepper
2 (15 ounce) cans jalapeño pinto beans or red kidney
    beans
2 (14½ ounce) cans peeled tomatoes
2 cups hot water
2 teaspoons chili powder
2 teaspoons ground cumin seeds
1½ teaspoons salt
1 tablespoon vegetable oil
1 teaspoon garlic powder (coarse grind with parsley)
1 teaspoon oregano
½ teaspoon cayenne pepper (red)
½ teaspoon chili peppers (dried)

Preparation/cooking time: two and one half hours (not including venison preparations).

Using a pot that will hold at least three quarts, stir fry diced onion, hot peppers, and bell peppers (chopped into one half inch pieces and hot pepper finely cut to one eight inch pieces) in vegetable oil over medium heat until slightly brown. At the same time, brown venison in a fry pan (do not overcook), add salt. Dump venison into cooking pot and stir until mixed. Lower heat to minimum, add chili powder to one cup hot water and pour into pot. Mix in tomatoes and add to pot without canning juice. Add jalapeño beans. Grind one half teaspoon chili peppers over mixture. Stir in one cup water until thoroughly mixed. Cover and cook at a simmer over low heat for two hours, stirring occasionally (approximately 15 minutes).

Serve hot with saltine crackers. Leftovers can be frozen in plastic containers and reheated as needed.

Gary W. Brimm
Garland, TX

Ground Venison

Tag-A-Long Venison Pies

This recipe is wonderful for taking on outings. It takes a little time but is worth the effort.

    2 pounds ground lean venison
    4 tablespoons corn oil
    3 medium onions, ground, with juice
    2 tablespoons fresh parsley, finely chopped
    2 tablespoons flour
    ¼ teaspoon each paprika, red pepper and black pepper
      salt to taste
    ½ pound ground pork (mild)
    5 green onions, finely chopped
    2 bell peppers, finely chopped
    1 pod garlic, minced
    2 tablespoons water (if needed)
      pie crust (see below)

In heavy skillet cook meat in corn oil over medium heat, stirring often, until it is mealy in appearance and crumbles. Add onions, bell peppers, parsley, garlic and seasonings. Cook ten minutes more. Remove from heat and stir in flour and water; blend ingredients together. Cool and place in freezer for 30 minutes.

Remove filling from freezer and place on one side of pie crust round (or square). Fold over and crimp crust edges together with fork tine. Place on cookie sheet approximately one inch apart. Bake in 350 degree oven until lightly browned. Freezes well. Also delicious served as a hot entree with sour cream.

Pie Crust:

    4 cups unsifted all-purpose flour (lightly spooned into
      measuring cup)
    1 tablespoon sugar
 1 ¾ cups Crisco
    1 large egg
    2 teaspoons salt
    1 tablespoon white vinegar

Put flour, sugar and salt into large bowl, mix well with fork. Add shortening and mix with fork until ingredients are crumbly. Beat together (in small bowl) one half cup water, vinegar and egg.

Combine the two mixtures, stirring with fork until all ingredients are moistened. Divide dough into five portions and with hands, shape each portion in a flat round patty ready for rolling, or divide dough into 24 small rounds for meat pies (recipe on page 168). Wrap each patty in waxed paper and chill at least one half hour. When ready to roll, slightly flour both sides of dough patty, put on lightly floured board or pastry cloth. Cover rolling pin with stock net and run in a small amount of flour. To keep pastry round, roll from center to about one eighth inch thickness. Tag-a-long rounds should be about 4x4 inches. Press with fingers to remove air pockets and punch with fork to keep flat. Fill with meat mixture or favorite pie filling.

Sugar Ferris
Arlington, TX

Mushroom Glob

1 pound ground venison
salt and pepper
Pennsylvania Dutch style noodles
1 can Campbell's mushroom soup
1 onion, chopped

Salt and pepper venison and brown with onion. Add mushroom soup and heat to boil stirring occasionally. Serve over hot noodles.

Don Shaneberger
Port Murray, NJ

—DOUG PIFER—

Bennett's World Famous Cowboy Beans and Venison

2 ½ pounds ground venison
1 pound link type venison sausage
2 cans barbecue beans
2 cans dark red kidney beans
2 cans spicy Mexican beans
1 can brown sugar beans
1 can stewed tomatoes
½ cup barbecue sauce
3 large onions, diced
12 ounces hot Mexican Velveeta cheese
1 large bell pepper, diced
2 cups rice
1 tablespoon butter
½ cup catsup
1 tablespoon mustard
2 tablespoons sweet pickle juice
¼ cup Tabasco sauce
¼ teaspoon salt
¼ teaspoon pepper
½ teaspoon onion powder
¼ teaspoon garlic powder
1 cup dark brown sugar

Bring two cups water to a boil in a large pan, place diced onion and bell pepper and boil six minutes. Drain. Return to heat and add ground venison. Brown and drain.

Reduce heat to medium and add all ingredients except butter, hot cheese and link venison sausage. Cook mixture for 20 minutes, stirring regularly.

In a separate pan, bring four cups water to a boil, add rice and one tablespoon butter, simmer 20 minutes or until done. When done, serve rice covered with cowboy beans and steamed sausage. Cut chunks of hot cheese and melt over rice, beans and sausage.

Yield: serves eight to ten hungry cowboys or cowgirls

Phil Bennett
Tallahassee, FL

Venison Calzone

1 pound ground venison
1 tablespoon fennel seed
1 teaspoon salt
1 large soft tomato, chopped
   sesame seeds
¼ teaspoon pepper
1 egg, beaten
1 pound frozen white bread dough
1 medium green pepper, chopped

Follow directions on frozen dough. After dough rises double in size, roll out on floured board as for a pie.

Sauté venison, adding fennel seed, salt and pepper. After mixture has cooled, spread on rolled dough. Add chopped green pepper and tomato and spread evenly over venison. Roll jelly-roll fashion. Seal ends and place on cookie sheet that has been sprayed with Pam. Brush top with beaten egg and sprinkle with sesame seeds. Bake at 350 degrees for 40 to 45 minutes. Let cool about ten minutes. Slice in diagonal slices.

Marie Rizzio
Traverse City, MI

Venison Roll-Ups

2 pounds ground venison burger
2 eggs, slightly beaten
¾ cup bread crumbs
½ cup catsup
3 tablespoons chopped parsley
½ teaspoon basil, crumbled
¼ teaspoon oregano, crumbled
¼ cup minced onion
¼ teaspoon sage
¼ teaspoon pepper
½ teaspoon garlic powder
   cracker crumbs
2 (2½ ounce) packages boiled ham slices
2 cups (½ pound) shredded Swiss cheese

Combine eggs, bread crumbs, catsup, parsley, basil, oregano, onion, sage, pepper, garlic powder, and venison burger in large

171

bowl. Mix until well blended. Divide into two equal parts. Sprinkle two 12x12 inch pieces aluminum foil with cracker crumbs. Pat out each half of meat mixture on foil to make a 9x12 inch rectangle that is about three quarters inch thick. Arrange ham slices on top of each meat rectangle. Sprinkle with shredded cheese. Roll up each rectangle of meat like a jelly-roll using foil as an aid. Pinch edges together and seal ends. Place onto lightly greased 13x9 inch baking pan, carefully removing foil as it is placed in pan. Bake at 350 degree oven for 45 to 50 minutes, until meat is done. Slice into 1 inch thick pieces. Serve warm or cool to room temperature and serve.

Yield: two rolls

Mrs. Jeanne Brown
Eureka, MT

Spaghetti and Venison Meatballs

1½ pounds ground venison
½ pound pork
2 eggs
4 slices white bread
2 tablespoons dried parsley
1 teaspoon garlic salt
½ teaspoon coarse ground pepper
3 tablespoons parmesan cheese

Remove crust from bread. Soak bread in water, then lightly squeeze. Break bread into small pieces. Add all ingredients together and mix lightly. Make into balls about two inches in diameter. Brown in skillet in small amount of olive oil. Remove meatballs and place in baking dish. Cover meatballs with sauce made of:

1 large onion, chopped
½ cup cooking sherry
2 cups water
1 (12 ounce) can tomato paste
1 teaspoon oregano

Mix together and pour over meatballs. Cover and bake at 375 degrees for 45 minutes. Serve over spaghetti.

Berneta Austenfeld
Emporia, KS

Venison Spaghetti Pie

1 pound ground venison
6 ounces spaghetti
2 tablespoon butter or oleo
⅓ cup grated parmesan cheese
2 well beaten eggs
½ cup chopped onions
1 cup cottage cheese, drained
½ cup shredded mozzarella cheese
¼ cup chopped green pepper
1 (8 ounce) can tomatoes
1 (6 ounce) can tomato paste
1 teaspoon each salt, oregano, sugar and garlic powder

Cook spaghetti and drain. Stir in butter, parmesan cheese and eggs. Form mixture into a crust in a buttered 10 inch pie plate.

In skillet, cook venison, onion and green pepper until vegetables are tender and meat is browned. Drain off excess fat. Stir in tomatoes, tomato paste, sugar, oregano, salt and garlic powder. Simmer 30 minutes.

Spread cottage cheese over bottom of spaghetti "crust." Fill pie with tomato mixture. Cover with foil. Chill two hours.

Bake, covered, in 350 degree oven for 60 minutes. Uncover, sprinkle with shredded mozzarella cheese and bake five more minutes.

Yield: six to eight servings

Richard Rizzio
Traverse City, MI

Wild Game Log

5 pounds venison, ground (moose or elk may be used)
1 teaspoon peppercorns
3 teaspoons garlic salt
3 teaspoons mustard seed
1½ teaspoons hickory smoke
5 teaspoons onion salt

Mix well. Refrigerate for 24 hours. Roll into logs and bake four and one half hours at 175 degrees on a broiler pan. Let stand one hour. Refrigerate or freeze.

David C. Brown
Clarksville, TN

Venison Gringo

1 pound ground venison
2 tablespoons olive oil
1 medium yellow onion, chopped
1 tablespoon chili powder
½ teaspoon coarse ground pepper
½ cup water
½ cup rice
1 bay leaf
1 (14½ ounce) can Mexican stewed tomatoes
1 large green pepper, chopped

Crumble meat and brown in olive oil. Add onion and cook for five minutes. Add remaining ingredients, cover and cook over medium heat for 35 minutes, stirring occasionally.

Berneta Austenfeld
Emporia, KS

Special Meatball Appetizer

Sauce:

½ cup catsup
¼ cup grape jelly or jam
1 small onion, chopped
1 teaspoon butter
dash of lemon juice

Meatballs:

1 pound ground venison
1 cup bread crumbs (made from fresh piece of bread)
1 tablespoon diced onion
1 egg (optional)
salt to taste

In saucepan combine catsup, grape jelly, onion browned in butter and lemon juice. Cook until jelly dissolves. Combine ground venison, bread crumbs, onion (egg and salt). Shape into meatballs and fry in skillet until done. Add sauce to meatballs and heat through.

Meta Mazur
Chicago, IL

— DOUG PIFER

Venison Fried Rice

½ -1 pound ground venison
1 cup chopped broccoli
½ cup chopped green pepper
½ cup sliced mushrooms
½ cup chopped onion
¾ cup bean sprouts
3 tablespoons peanut butter
2 tablespoons cooking oil
3 cups cooled cooked rice (If you want to cool rice
    quickly you can rinse it with cold water and drain.)
4 tablespoons soy sauce
¼ teaspoon powdered ginger
½ teaspoon garlic powder
  dash of salt
1 egg, beaten

Sauté vegetables in cooking oil in a large skillet until cooked but
still a little bit crunchy. Add soy sauce, ginger, garlic powder and
pepper. Clear a space in the middle of the pan and add egg. Stir
until egg is cooked and then combine with vegetables. Add peanut
butter. Add ground venison. Stir until cooked through. Add
cooked rice.
   Stir until heated through.

Meta Mazur
Chicago, IL

Venison Salami

2 pounds ground venison
½ teaspoon black pepper
½ teaspoon garlic powder
1 tablespoon mustard seed
1 tablespoon Liquid Smoke
2 tablespoons Morton's Tender Quick salt
¾ cup water
1 tablespoon whole peppercorns (optional)

Mix all together and refrigerate 24 hours, stirring once or twice. Mixture will turn a funny color. Shape in two inch thick rolls. Bake on broiler rack for three hours at 250 degrees. Don't brown. It changes colors as it bakes. Remove from rack. Cool. Wrap in foil. Refrigerate for two days or you may slice sooner. It will also freeze well and keep in refrigerator for a long time.

Dr. James N. Little
Walnut Ridge, AR

Venison Meatballs

4 pounds ground venison
1 tablespoon Lawrey's seasoned salt
1½ teaspoons garlic
2 teaspoons oregano leaves
2 teaspoons basil
1½ teaspoons beef bouillon
½ teaspoon dill powder
½ teaspoon sage
1 sleeve Saltines
2 eggs
½ cup chopped onion
1½ teaspoons black pepper

Combine all ingredients and form into small balls.

In a large pan bring the following to a boil:

½ pan water (about 2 cups)
2 tablespoons beef bouillon
1 teaspoon garlic
½ cup wine vinegar

Simmer meatballs in a single layer for about five minutes. Remove meatballs and drain well.

Sauce:
   2 cans jellied cranberry sauce
   2 jars Heinz chili sauce

Melt cranberry sauce and mix in chili sauce. Pour over hot balls.
   Serve hot, but they are delicious cold.

James P. Martin
Rochester Hills, MI

177

Deer Logs

  5 pounds deer burger
2 ½ tablespoons ground mustard
2 ½ tablespoons coarse pepper
2 ½ teaspoons Liquid Smoke
  5 tablespoons Morton's Tender Quick salt
2 ½ teaspoons garlic salt

Mix all ingredients in bowl, cover and refrigerate overnight. Remove once a day for three days to knead well each time for five minutes. One the fourth day, divide into six or seven logs (about the size of a regular drinking glass).

Lay on broiler pan and bake for nine hours at 160 degrees or eight hours at 200 degrees. Turn half-way during baking time.

Remove and roll in paper towels to remove excess grease. Roll in handi-wrap to refrigerate or freeze. Will keep three weeks in refrigerator.

Mr. Kevin Echterling
Lagrange, IN

Venison "Beef" Stick

  5 pounds ground venison (I prefer a 25 percent pork mixture for taste and moisture)
  4 teaspoons Morton's Tender Quick salt
  2 teaspoons table salt
  3 teaspoons garlic powder
  3 teaspoons mustard seed
  3 teaspoons ground black pepper
  2 teaspoons sugar (optional)
  1 teaspoon ground red pepper
1 ½ teaspoons Liquid Smoke

Mix all ingredients well, cover and set in refrigerator for 24 hours. Remove and shape meat into rolls or very small loaves, cover loosely and return to refrigerator for another 24 hours.

Put loaves on baking sheet/pan and bake at 150 degrees for four hours, turn and bake for approximately another four hours. Be sure to check to make sure they do not become overdone.

Remove loaves and set on paper towels to drain. When cool, they can be wrapped in heavy foil and frozen.

These little fellas make wonderful sandwiches or taken wrapped and whole, a great snack to take fishing or hunting. Enjoy!

Tom Fisher
Homerville, OH

Italian Dishes

Venison Brazziole

1 steak, pounded with meat mallet to flatten
1 teaspoon minced garlic
⅛ teaspoon ground pepper
⅛ teaspoon oregano
⅛ teaspoon basil
⅛ teaspoon marjoram or ½ teaspoon Italian seasoning

Mix above. Spread evenly over steak. Use more or less according to taste. Roll in jelly roll fashion and secure with toothpicks or string.

Tomato Sauce:

2 (14–16 ounce) cans whole peeled tomatoes (fresh
  tomatoes in season can be used)
2 tablespoons onions, minced
1-2 cloves garlic, minced
¼ teaspoon fresh ground pepper
¼ teaspoon each: oregano, basil and marjoram or
  ¾ teaspoon Italian seasoning

Coarsely chop tomatoes with juice in processor. Mix in other ingredients. Microwave until hot, four or five minutes. Place sauce in oven proof covered casserole. Add meat. Cook in microwave for 10 minutes, turn meat and cook another 10 minutes or until meat is fork tender. May also be cooked in regular oven 325 to 350 degrees for 45 minutes or until fork tender.

Suzy Stefani
Rillton, PA

Venison Lasagna

2 pounds ground venison
1 medium onion
1 garlic clove
2 tablespoons olive oil
1 (4 ounce) can sliced mushrooms, undrained
2 (8 ounce) cans tomato sauce
1 (6 ounce) can tomato paste
1 can tomato soup
2 teaspoons salt
1 egg
1 (8 ounce) package wide lasagna noodles
1 package frozen chopped spinach, thawed and drained
1 cup ricotta or cottage cheese
⅓ cup parmesan cheese
1 (8 ounce) package grated mozzarella cheese
1 teaspoon oregano
½ teaspoon basil

Finely chop onion and garlic, then lightly brown both in one tablespoon olive oil. Add venison and cook until brown. Stir in mushrooms, tomato sauce, tomato paste, tomato soup, oregano, basil, and one teaspoon salt. Let simmer gently for two hours. During the last hour, cook lasagna noodles until tender and drain. Beat egg slightly and add to thawed spinach: add one tablespoon olive oil, ricotta (or cottage cheese), parmesan cheese, and one teaspoon salt and mix together well. Ladle half the meat sauce into a three quart oblong baking dish. Layer half the noodles over meat sauce; spread spinach/Ricotta mixture evenly over noodles. Place remainder of noodles on top of spinach mixture; top with remaining meat sauce, cover with foil and bake at 350 degrees for 45 minutes. Remove foil and sprinkle grated mozzarella cheese on top and bake another 5 minutes until cheese is lightly browned. Serve with tossed salad and garlic bread.

Robert A. Bianchi
Victoria, TX

Venison Scallopini

3 pounds tender venison
  butter and olive oil
1 bunch green onions
1 clove garlic
2 sprigs fresh rosemary
1 pinch dry marjoram
2 small cans tomato sauce
1 large can B&B sliced mushrooms
1 bunch parsley
1 pint dry sauterne or sherry

About 45 minutes before preparing venison, start the sauce. Heat a small skillet, add half butter and half olive oil, enough to sauté. After chopping very fine (the good old way) or using modern day blender, add the following mixture and cook on medium heat for about 20 minutes: green onions (tops and all), garlic, parsley (not the stems), rosemary (not the stems) and marjoram. After 20 minutes add tomato sauce and mushrooms (mushrooms only, save juice for later). Stir well and cook for additional 10 minutes and then let simmer on low heat while cooking venison.

Cut venison into three inch squares and trim off all fat. Pound well and shake in seasoned flour (salt and pepper). This can be done while cooking sauce. Brown venison in hot skillet in half butter and half olive oil (about a minute or so on both sides). Add sauce and mix thoroughly. Let simmer for additional 15 minutes. During last four minutes add one full cup sauterne or sherry. During last two minutes add juice of mushrooms (saved when mushrooms were added to sauce).

Serve while hot! Great when served with rice or polenta, also buttered noodles. Accompany this with your favorite white or red wine

Yield: serves eight

Harold E. Doughty
Middletown, CA

Venison Saltimbocca Rolls

      2 pounds venison, boned and sliced thin
      1 teaspoon sage
      ¼ pound ham, sliced thin
      3 tablespoons butter
        salt and pepper
      2 tablespoons water

Cut venison into pieces about five inches square and sprinkle on both sides with a little sage. Melt two tablespoons butter in a heavy skillet and cook venison over high heat until well browned on both sides. Let cool, then place a slice of ham on each piece of venison, roll up and keep rolled by inserting toothpicks though meat. Place in a 300 degree oven, uncovered, for a few minutes until heated. While meat is heating add water to skillet and scrape bottom well. Add the other tablespoon butter and mix well over low heat. Place heated, rolled meat on a serving dish, pour gravy over and serve.

Jerry Ponder
Fairdealing, PA

Deer Chops — Italian Style

    4-6 deer chops
      1 bay leaf
      1 cup chianti wine
      2 cloves garlic
      1 tablespoon oregano
      1 tablespoon cooking oil
        water

Trim all fat from chops. Brown chops in hot fat along with garlic (garlic may be sliced or left whole). In same pan add bay leaf, oregano and wine. Add enough water to cover chops. Simmer covered until tender one and half to two hours.

Deer steak may be substituted for chops.

Mrs. Barbara Carter
Philadelphia, PA

Venison Scallopini

1 ½ pounds venison round steak
     flour seasoned with salt and pepper
  4 teaspoons olive oil
  2 tablespoons butter
  1 clove garlic, minced
     a sprinkle each, sage and thyme
  ½ cup dry sherry
  ½ cup water
     salt and pepper to taste

Slice venison into ½x4 inch servings. Pound well, coat pieces well (dredge) with flour mixture. In a heavy frying pan with lid, heat oil and butter. Add venison and brown on both sides. Add garlic, salt and pepper to taste. Sprinkle with sage and thyme. Mix sherry and water and pour over meat. Cover and bake at 350 degrees for 45 minutes to one hour till tender.

Serve over linguine pasta or mashed potatoes and please . . . with a hearty burgundy.

William C. Wallace
Dixie, ID

—DOUG PIPER

183

Jerky

Venison Jerky

    4 pounds venison
2 ½ cups apple juice
    ½ cup brown sugar
    1 teaspoon onion powder
    2 teaspoons Liquid Smoke
    2 cups soy sauce
    ¼ cup salt
    2 teaspoons black pepper
    1 teaspoon garlic powder
    1 tablespoon ground ginger

For a mild Venison Jerky:

5-6 pounds venison
    1 (20 ounce) bottle teriyaki sauce
    2 cups apple juice
    2 tablespoons Liquid Smoke

Slice venison into one eighth or one fourth inch thick strips and marinate for 24 hours, turning occasionally.

Line the bottom of oven with aluminum foil and place oven rack as high as possible. Set oven temperature as low as possible.

Pierce strips of venison with a toothpick about one fourth inch from top and hang from oven rack. Let dry for about six hours for one eighth inch strips and seven and a half to eight hours for one fourth inch strips.

Bob Taylor
Meriden, CT

Andy's Venison Jerky

60% worcestershire sauce
40% soy sauce

Per each cup of sauce used, add the following:

    2 teaspoons Accent
    1 teaspoon onion powder
    1 teaspoon garlic powder
    ½ teaspoon black pepper
    Tabasco or Frank's Louisiana hot sauce to taste

Any cut of venison will do. I peel meat off the deer's ribs, and I use all scrap meats such as the front legs and shoulders as well as any trimmings I have left from cutting steaks and roasts. Cut venison into strips about three eighths by three eighths by three inches. Use enough worcestershire sauce and soy sauce to cover meat in whatever container you are going to use for marinating.

Marinate at room temperature a minimum of 24 hours, no more than 72 hours. Lay strips on cookie sheets. Dry strips in oven at 150 degrees for six to eight hours until strips are dried through. Do not allow strips to become crunchy. Store in air tight container.

Andrew F. Sweeton
Skillman, NJ

Deer Jerky

Marinade:

        2 pounds venison
   ¼ cup red wine
   ¼ cup soy sauce
   ¼ cup worcestershire sauce
   ½ teaspoon Liquid Smoke
1-1½ teaspoons seasoned salt
   ½ teaspoon garlic powder
   ¼ teaspoon curry powder
   ¼ teaspoon pepper
      1 teaspoon MSG (Accent)
⅛ - ¼ teaspoon cayenne pepper

Trim any fat from meat. Cut into strips with the grain approximately one fourth inch by one half inch wide. Put meat and marinade into strong plastic bag or marinating container. Marinate about 24 hours, turning several times.

Oven Method: Lay foil in bottom of oven to catch drippings. Lay meat strips over oven racks. Cook at 140–160 degrees for six to eight minutes. Leave oven door open a crack for air circulation.

Smoker Method: You may want to delete Liquid Smoke from marinade. Lay meat on smoker racks, process according to smoker directions or at approximately 100 degrees for about two days.

When jerky is done it will break when bent. Will keep for several months without refrigeration.

Berry Meyers
Chiloquin, OR

Venison Jerky

⅓ cup sugar
1 cup worcestershire sauce
1 cup red wine
½ teaspoon pepper
½ teaspoon Tabasco
¼ cup salt
2 cups water
½ teaspoon onion powder
½ teaspoon garlic powder

Mix these ingredients together and set aside. Prepare about 5 pounds venison by trimming all fat and waste away. Slice the meat with the grain in slices one fourth thick and one inch wide at most. (If meat is semi-frozen, it will be easier to work with). Layer meat in a large, flat, glass dish, covering each layer with marinade before starting the next. Cover with plastic wrap and put in the refrigerator overnight.

In the morning, remove strips from marinade and dry on paper towels for about one hour. If you have an electric smoker, put meat in and smoke it for 12 to 18 hours, depending on how dry you like it and how large the pieces are. If you don't have a smoker, set oven on a low heat 150–175 degrees and cook. Store your jerky in a plastic bag or glass jar in the refrigerator. Its shelf life depends on how dry you let it get and how many people you tell about it. Mine lasts a week if I'm careful.

I hope you like this one as much as we do.

Charles Hofmeister, III
Spencer, OH

Jerky

2-4 pounds lean roast or steak meat
 small bottle each: worcestershire sauce, soy sauce
  and A-1 sauce
 garlic salt to taste
12-16 ounces Lambrusco red wine
 large bottle Liquid Smoke
 lemon pepper
 tooth picks

Cut meat into three eighths to one half inch thick strips and one to one and one half inches wide. Remember to cut with grain of meat. Wash meat in cool water and allow to drain.

Meanwhile, mix together worcestershire, soy and A-1 sauces. Add garlic salt to taste. Combine above with Lambrusco wine. Mix well.

Place meat in above ingredients and soak 10 to 12 hours in refrigerator (Large Ziploc bags are best for this). Make sure meat gets coated well. Mix once or twice during soak time.

After soaking, remove meat, wash lightly. Drain. Roll meat in Liquid Smoke, dust with lemon pepper. Stick toothpick through one end of strips and hang in oven. Hang 16 to 18 hours in 105 to 115 degree temperature. Prop door open to allow moisture to escape. Jerky is done when meat is dry, not brittle! It is best to use aluminum foil in bottom of oven to catch drippings. I have also used a 100 watt bulb to maintain oven temperature, when the oven setting is too high.

If you have a regular smoker, delete Liquid Smoke and use whatever flavor wood chips you desire.

Happy hunting and good eating.

R. Sycks
Ashland, KY

Easy Jerky

2 pounds elk or deer meat, round steak works well
¼ cup soy sauce
1 tablespoon Liquid Smoke
1 tablespoon worcestershire sauce
½ cup water
½ teaspoon seasoned salt

Combine all ingredients except meat in a large covered bowl and set aside. Trim meat to remove fat and slice into strips one eighth inch thick. Mix meat with marinade, cover and refrigerate overnight.

Remove racks from oven and pre-heat to lowest possible setting, 150 to 175 degrees. Spray oven racks with cooking spray and lay meat strips directly on racks. Foil in the bottom of oven may be helpful to catch drips. Place racks with meat in oven and leave oven door cracked open to provide air flow over meat. Allow meat to dry in oven four to six hours.

Bob and Carol Greuter
Los Alamos, NM

Hunter Jerky

When you select your piece of meat, place it in freezer for three or four hours until it begins to set. This will make slicing easier.

3-4 pounds red lean beef, venison or other game.

Slice across the grain one fourth to three eighths inch thick.

Marinade:

6-8 cups water
4-8 cloves minced garlic (to taste)
  2 tablespoons salt
  1 tablespoon pepper
  1 stalk celery
  10 tablespoons soy sauce
  5 large strong onions
1-2 tablespoons oregano
1-2 tablespoons hot sauce (to taste)

Place all marinade ingredients into boiling water. Boil three to four minutes, cover and simmer five to six more minutes. Let cool under cover for 30 minutes. Strain through a large strainer using a large spoon to push some pulp through strainer. Place sliced meat in bread pans, cover with marinade. Place in refrigerator for two days. Remove and stir occasionally.

Dry in a dehydrator or on racks in your oven at 115 to 125 degrees.

When done pack in Ziploc bags and freeze for long-term storage.

Edd Higgs
Columbia, MD

Deer Jerky

1 ½ pounds deer round steak (trimmed)
½ teaspoon seasoned salt
¼ teaspoon each: pepper, oregano, marjoram, basil,
       thyme and garlic powder
 1 teaspoon onion powder
¼ cup soy sauce
 2 tablespoons Liquid Smoke
¼ cup worcestershire sauce

Slice steak into one fourth inch thick slices along the grain. Place
in a shallow dish.

In a small bowl, combine remaining ingredients. Pour over
steak strips. Cover and refrigerate overnight.

Preheat oven to 150 degrees.

Line bottom of baking pan with aluminum foil, lay steak strips
on foil and place in oven. Prop oven door open with a pencil.
Bake eight to 12 hours or until meat is dry and chewy.

Yield: six servings

Mr. Kevin Echterling
Lagrange, IN

Moose Jerky

3-5 pounds moose or venison
 10 ounce bottle worcestershire sauce
 10 ounce bottle soy sauce
 10 ounces hot water
  5 teaspoons each: seasoning salt, Accent and onion salt
1 ½ teaspoons black pepper
1 ½ teaspoons garlic powder

Slice meat one eighth to one fourth inch thick and trim off any
fat. Dissolve spices in hot water. Add soy and worcestershire sauce.
Marinate meat overnight (eight or ten hours). Air dry slices on
oven or smoker racks for about one hour. Dry in smoker eight
to ten hours or in oven at lowest possible setting with door open
three to five inches, for three to five hours.

Marinate may be kept refrigerated and used for two or three
batches.

Anthony J. Pohl
Maple Grove, MN

189

Marinades and Sauces

Marinade for Venison

Cover venison with 1 cup each water and dry red wine and add the following:

     8-10 black peppercorns
        2 bay leaves
     1-10 whole cloves
        2 slices medium onion
        1 small sprig rosemary

Marinate meat for three days, covered, in the refrigerator. Turn from time to time. It is better if venison is left in marinade for a longer period, five days or so. Above marinade may be used for venison stew, goulash, steak, or venison roast.

D. F. Donnell
Newbern, NC

Buffalo Tro Marinade

     ⅔ cup ketchup
     ½ cup lemon juice
     1 teaspoon each: allspice, basil, coarse black pepper
    2-3 bay leaves
        dash of Tabasco sauce
     ½ cup beer
     2 tablespoons worcestershire

Mix ingredients, simmer for 10 minutes, cool marinade. This marinade is for one pound steak.

Mr. John Rockaway
Rolla, MO

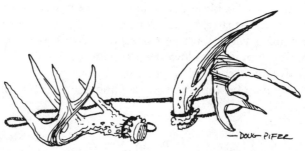

— DOUG PIFER

Marinated Venison

1 venison top round (London broil), about 1½ to 2
   pounds
2 tablespoons prepared Dijon mustard
3 tablespoons each: dry red wine, lemon juice, soy
   sauce, worcestershire sauce

Score steak on both sides in diamond patterns. Brush mustard
on both sides of steak and place it in a large, shallow dish. Combine wine, soy sauce, lemon juice and worcestershire sauce and
pour over venison. Cover dish and marinate in refrigerator for
five to six hours.

Remove venison from marinade and place it in a broiling pan.
Broil venison five inches from heat for five minutes on each side
for medium rare, or broil it to desired doneness, basting with
remaining marinade. This can also be done on the barbecue.
To serve, thinly slice steak diagonally across the grain.

Gary C. Garran
Demarest, NJ

Richard's Grilled Venison

Rinse and trim all sinew, bone and other tissue from venison
steaks or chops and soak in salt water for one hour. Remove and
rinse venison. Add the following ingredients in a medium
saucepan:

1 tablespoon butter
1 tablespoon soy sauce
½ teaspoon onion salt
¼ teaspoon each: garlic powder, black pepper, and
   ground basil
¼ cup Italian dressing
¼ cup Russian dressing

Heat ingredients in saucepan over low heat and stir until butter
is melted and all ingredients are blended. Pour immediately over
venison on both sides and let meat marinade in the refrigerator
for at least six hours (can be left overnight). When ready to grill,
remove venison from marinade and grill over medium heat until meat is pink in the middle. Be sure and save remaining
marinade to use as a basting sauce for your ground deer burgers.

Richard A. Foote
Jackson, TN

191

Meatloaf

Venison Mini-Meatloaf

1 ½ pounds venison, chopped
  1 medium onion, chopped
  3 green onions, chopped
  2 celery ribs, chopped
  1 carrot, chopped
  2 cloves garlic, chopped
  3 dashes of worcestershire sauce
  1 teaspoon garlic powder
    salt and pepper to taste
1 ½ cups bread crumbs
  2 eggs
  2 green peppers, cut into strips*
  1 (29 ounce) can tomato sauce*
    vegetable oil

Combine all ingredients with meat except green pepper slices and tomato sauce. Shape into small loaves. Brown on both sides in fry pan coated with vegetable oil. Add green pepper strips and tomato sauce, simmer covered one half hour or until peppers are tender. Serve on a bed of white rice.

*Variety: Eliminate green pepper and tomato sauce, add instead one to two cups beef broth and thicken with flour or cornstarch. Or, eliminate green pepper and tomato sauce, make one large meatloaf and bake in oven 350 degrees for one hour. Serve with buttered noodles and vegetables or mashed potatoes.

Mary E. Carvalho
Cranford, NJ

Venison Meatloaf

1-1 ½ pounds ground venison (can mix with ground pork)
  3-4 slices bread
    2 cans condensed tomato soup
  1-2 eggs
  1 large onion
    ½ teaspoon salt
    ½ teaspoon pepper
    1 teaspoon Bell's poultry seasoning
    1 can cream of mushroom soup
    Gravy Master

Cut bread into small cubes. Mix one can tomato soup with bread. Dice onion. Add diced onion, eggs, salt, pepper and Bell's seasoning to bread mix. Add ground venison and mix well. Form into a loaf and bake in a loaf pan at 350 degrees for one and a half hours. After one hour of baking, pour second can tomato soup over loaf and bake 30 more minutes.

To make gravy, add one can cream of mushroom soup, milk as needed, and Gravy Master for color to pan drippings. Cook over top burner until gravy is mixed thoroughly.

Brian T. Neylon
East Lyme, CT

Mexican Dishes

Venison Fajitas

    1 pound venison, sliced in thin two-inch strips
    1 large red or yellow onion, sliced
    1 green pepper, sliced
    1 tomato, cut in wedges
    ¾ cup Italian dressing (I like Good Seasons)
    2 tablespoons worcestershire sauce
    2-3 tablespoons Liquid Smoke
       tortillas
       salsa

Mix all ingredients except tortillas in shallow bowl, marinate for 30 minutes. Drain off marinade. In hot skillet (cast iron works best), quickly fry one third of meat and vegetable mixture just until meat is cooked through. Cook remaining mixture in two separate batches, re-heating skillet in between. To serve, wrap meat and vegetables in tortillas, add salsa if desired. Preparation time: 40 minutes.

   Yield: four servings

Leslie York
Windsor, VA

193

Venison Carne Guesada

1 ½ pounds small venison steaks
  1 can rotel tomatoes
1 ½ teaspoons ground cumin
  2 tablespoons chili powder
  ¼ cup corn oil
  2 cloves minced garlic
2 ½ –3 cups water
  2 tablespoons flour
  salt and pepper to taste

Salt and pepper venison and lightly flour. Brown slowly in large skillet containing oil. Add cumin, chili powder and flour, cook a few minutes and then add water, as you would for making gravy. Pour over meat and add garlic, stirring constantly. Add tomatoes. Bring to a boil, then simmer for two hours. Eat as is or put it in a flour tortilla for an excellent taco.

Mike Sauncers
Cotulla, TX

Venison Surprise with Honey and Jalapeños

1 pound venison backstrap
3 jalapeño peppers (pickled)
6 strips bacon
  honey

Cut backstrap into six and a half inch thick steaks. Pound to tenderize and flatten. Slice jalapeño peppers lengthwise and remove seeds. Place strips of jalapeño pepper on each steak and cover with honey. Roll up steak with jalapeño and honey inside. Wrap each steak with strip of bacon and secure with toothpicks. Place on charcoal grill. Baste with honey, turning frequently until cooked through. Do not overcook. Serve with long grain and wild rice.

Yield: serves six

Dan Breeden
Brownsville, TX

Tenderloin Tacos

1½ pounds venison tenderloin, sliced into thin strips
1 envelope brown gravy mix
1 envelope Ortega taco seasoning
⅛ teaspoon black pepper
    dash of garlic powder
1 teaspoon butter or margarine
1 large white onion, chopped
1 large tomato, chopped
¼ head of lettuce, shredded
1 cup shredded mild cheddar cheese
1 medium green bell pepper, chopped
1 package soft white flour taco shells
1 cup water

Melt butter in a large skillet over medium heat. Add sliced tenderloin and onion. Stir fry until meat is browned. Add water, black pepper, garlic, taco seasoning, and brown gravy mix. Mix together and simmer for 15 minutes. Add green pepper and simmer 10 more minutes. Salt to taste.

Warm taco shells one at a time in a greaseless pan over medium/high heat (about 15 seconds). To serve, spoon meat mixture onto shell, add cheese, lettuce and tomato. Roll into taco or serve open face.

Yield: serves four

Debby Erwin
Lawrenceville, GA

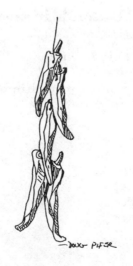

195

Venison Taco

1 ½ pounds venison backstrap
  2 eggs
  1 can evaporated milk
    saltine crackers
    flour
    seasoned salt
    onion powder
    salt and pepper

Slice venison in one fourth inch slices. Place in glass baking dish in two layers. Season to taste with seasoned salt, onion powder, salt and pepper. Pour in evaporated milk and one can water. Marinate over night.

Pour out marinade and rinse meat. Place each slice of meat in beaten egg and then roll in crushed crackers mixed with flour. Fry in one fourth inch vegetable oil until done. Make sure you wipe out pan after each batch to prevent burning. Serve sliced in warm flour tortillas. Picante sauce optional. Delicious!

Yield: serves six

Pam Ramirez
Brownsville, TX

Mincemeats

Venison Mincemeat

1 cup water
1 heaping cup ground venison
3 cups diced apples
½ can chopped, drained mandarin oranges
1 cup brown sugar
1 cup raisins
½ cup vinegar
1 teaspoon cinnamon
½ teaspoon cloves
½ teaspoon nutmeg
½ teaspoon allspice
1 tablespoon butter

Simmer meat and water until meat loses its color. Add remaining ingredients. Simmer 45 minutes or until thick. Makes two pies. Can be put in freezer for future use.

Faye Berry
Lewistown, IL

Venison Mincemeat

4 pounds lean venison, ground
2 pounds beef suet, ground
8 quarts peeled sliced apples
3 pounds sugar
2 quarts cider
4 pounds raisins
3 pounds currants
1½ pounds chopped citron
1 gallon sour cherries with juice
½ pound dried orange peel
½ pound dried lemon peel
  juice and rind of one lemon
1 tablespoon mace
1 tablespoon cloves
1 teaspoon salt
1 teaspoon pepper
2 whole grated nutmeg
2 pounds chopped walnuts

Cook all ingredients over low heat for two hours. Stir frequently. Seal in jars; can also be frozen.

To make pie, add two tablespoons brandy and one fourth teaspoon ground tapioca to one quart mincemeat. Pour into pie shell and bake at 450 degrees for 30 minutes.

This mincemeat filling can be used as a filling for sugar cookies or coffee cake. Just use your imagination and surprise everyone.

Oneta Keister
Rupert, ID

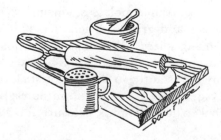

Mincemeat for Pies

    1 hog jowl
    3 pounds lean pork
 1 ½ pounds beef suet
 2 ½ pounds lean beef (4 ½ pounds beef, elk or other lean
        meat if deer meat is not used)
    2 pounds deer meat
    2 gallons apples
    2 quarts sour cherries
    1 box raisins
    2 boxes currants
    1 (12 ounce) bottle Bre'r Rabbit molasses
 1 ½ cups cider vinegar
    2 pounds brown sugar
    2 whole lemons
    ½ gallon apple cider
    1 pound citron
    2 teaspoons each, cinnamon, cloves and allspice

Cook meat and fat from one hog jowl, approximately three pounds, save broth to use later. Cook until fat can easily be cut with dull knife (two hours). This is one ingredient that should not be left out. Mincemeat is worthless without hog jowls (tame or wild hog).

Cook together three pounds lean pork (save broth), one and a half pounds beef suet, two and a half pounds lean beef and two pounds deer meat. Again, use four and one half pounds beef, elk or other lean meat if deer meat is not used. All meat should be cooked in enough water to cover it till done (easily cut apart). After meat and suet are cooked, save broth and grind meat and suet in a grinder. These things can be done during a couple of days and kept refrigerated.

Peel, core and quarter apples and grind in a grinder. Remove seeds from cherries and grind. In a large kettle (stainless steel is best), add raisins, currants, molasses, vinegar (to taste), brown sugar, remove seeds and grind two lemons, skin and all. Add apple cider, citron and spices. Mix well, add one quart beef broth and one half quart pork broth. Bring to a boil and cook for one half hour, stirring constantly so it will not stick or burn.

Can in open water bath in jars for 30 minutes, or can in jars in a pressure cooker at 10 pounds pressure for 30 minutes.

Great for Christmas and Thanksgiving pies with old-time flavor!
Yield: 16 to 18 quarts

Thomas E. Cave
Winchester, VA

Old Fashion Venison Mincemeat

4 pounds lean boiled venison
8 pounds tart green apples, chopped
1 pound chopped suet
3 pounds raisins
2 pounds currants
1 pound brown sugar
1 quart cooking molasses
2 quarts sweet cider
1 pint boiled cider
1 tablespoon salt
1 tablespoon pepper
1 tablespoon allspice
1 tablespoon mace
4 tablespoons cinnamon
2 grated nutmeg
½ pound citron

Mix all ingredients thoroughly and warm in large pan on stove until heated through. Remove from stove and when nearly cool, stir in a pint of very good brandy and a pint of Madeira wine. Put mixture in a crock, cover it tightly and set it in a cool palace where it will not freeze, but keep perfectly cold. This will keep all winter. You may also can it if you like.

Sharren Skanes
Crobitt, OR

Miscellaneous Venison Dishes

Venison and Rice

½ pound venison, cubed
   salt, pepper and garlic powder
2 tablespoons olive oil
1 large onion, diced
6 cloves garlic, minced
4 sprigs parsley, chopped
1½ cups rice
3½ cups water
1½ teaspoons salt (optional)
1 cup frozen peas

Sprinkle meat with salt, pepper and garlic powder. Heat pan, add olive oil, add meat and sauté garlic and parsley, sauté 5 minutes more. Add rice, stir to coat, add water, salt, tomato sauce and peas, bring to boil, cover and simmer 20 minutes. Let stand a few minutes before serving.

Serve with a crisp green salad.

Mary E. Carvalho
Cranford, NJ

Barbecue Bean Stew

1 pound leftover barbecued venison
½ –1 cup barbecue drippings, sauce and onions
1 (12 ounce) can black beans (or about ½ pound dried, cooked)
1 (14 ounce) can stewed whole tomatoes

Chop venison into bite-sized chunks. In a large pot, combine all ingredients and simmer for one hour. More water can be added for desired consistency.

Cindy Walker
San Antonio, TX

Dirty Rice
Grandma Hetherwick's Venison

2 or 3 stalks celery, cut fine
    ½ cup (more or less) chopped parsley
    2 slivers green pepper (finger size)
    1 pound ground chuck (or any meat or fowl you
        have in the refrigerator), brown in skillet before
        combining with the rest of the ingredients
2 or 3 cloves garlic
    3 green onions with tops
    1 large onion
    6 cooked chicken gizzards (ground)
    1 piece smoked pork sausage (about the length of
        your finger)
    1 serving smoked ham

Grind all the above together, mix well, then add:

    1 tablespoon worcestershire sauce
    1 teaspoon mustard (I use Kraft)
    2 shots Tabasco (be careful, it's hot!)
    3 cups chicken, duck or beef broth (not water)
    1 cup raw rice

Put all this into a deep, heavy pot, and of course, salt to taste.
Bring to a boil, lower flame and cook one hour (or less) with
lid on. Stir once or twice before boiling point, but not after it
has started to cook. Rice should come out in whole grains, not
mashed.
    That's it. Hope it all works out.

Ken Hetherwick (Grandson)
Shreveport, LA

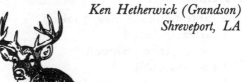

Venison Paprika with Hazelnut Rice

4 pounds venison, chunked 2x2 inches
2 pounds onions, diced
3 stalks celery, chopped fine
1 bell pepper, chopped fine
4 cloves garlic, minced
5 large carrots, peeled and sliced one inch thick
1 cup sliced mushrooms
1 (#2) can tomatoes, juice and all
1 can tomato sauce
3 cups red table wine
4 tablespoons paprika
2 teaspoons celery seed
1 teaspoon garlic powder
½ teaspoon cumin
3 tablespoons Louisiana hot sauce
2 tablespoons worcestershire sauce
1½ cups flour
½ - ¼ cup oil
water
salt

Heat oil in large dutch oven, mix flour, garlic powder, paprika, cumin and pepper. Dredge meat well. Brown meat in hot oil. Add celery, onion, bell pepper and minced garlic. Continue to cook until onion is soft. Add carrots, mushrooms, tomatoes, tomato sauce, wine, celery seed, Louisiana hot sauce and worcestershire sauce, add water if needed to build sauce. Simmer until meat is tender and sauce is reduced and thick. Salt to taste. Serve over hazelnut rice.

Hazelnut Rice:

3 tablespoons butter, melted
1 onion, minced
1 clove garlic, minced
1 teaspoon salt
1 teaspoon celery seed
½ cup wild rice
2½ cups white rice
6 cups water
2 tablespoons lemon juice
¾ cup hazelnuts, chopped
4 green onions, chopped

Sauté onion, garlic and wild rice in butter until onion is clear. Add white rice, spices, water and lemon juice. Cover and reduce heat. When rice is cooked, stir in nuts and top with green onions.
  Yield: serves eight

L. C. Vernon
Cheyenne, WY

Venison Burgundy

2 pounds venison, cubed in bite size pieces
1 pound mushrooms, sliced
1 large onion, finely diced
1 cup burgundy
1 cup beef stock
1 bay leaf
1 tablespoon rosemary
1 teaspoon thyme
  salt and pepper to taste

In a large covered casserole, mix together venison, mushrooms, onions, rosemary, thyme, pepper and salt. Pour over burgundy and beef stock. Cover and bake in 325 degree oven for three to three and a half hours (depending on cut of venison). Serve over rice.
  Recipe works equally well with beef.
  Yield: four servings

Charles W. Long, Jr.
Morrisville, PA

Venison with Cheese and Tomato Sauce

1 pound venison, swissed or pounded thinly
½ cup bread crumbs
½ cup corn meal
⅓ cup grated parmesan cheese
½ teaspoon salt
½ teaspoon pepper
2 eggs, beaten
2 tablespoons butter
2 tablespoons oil
4 slices muenster cheese
8 ounces Velveeta, diced
   tomato sauce (recipe below)

Combine bread crumbs, corn meal, parmesan cheese, salt and pepper. Heat frying pan to medium high temperature and add olive oil and butter. Dip serving size pieces of venison into beaten eggs and thoroughly coat with crumb mixture. Brown meat lightly on both sides and transfer to a lightly oiled baking dish. Cover well with tomato sauce and top with Velveeta, then muenster cheese. Bake for 10 to 15 minutes at 400 degrees until heated through and cheese has melted.

Tomato Sauce:

½ cup olive oil
½ cup yellow onion, sliced
2 green onions, diced
2 garlic cloves, chopped
½ cup dried parsley flakes
½ teaspoon crushed red pepper seeds
1 (8 ounce) can chopped mushrooms, drained
1 (29 ounce) can chopped tomatoes, drained
¼ cup burgundy
1 teaspoon oregano
¼ teaspoon each: thyme, rosemary, marjoram, basil and
   sage
2 tablespoons chicken flavoring
2 tablespoons pimento stuffed olives, chopped

Heat oil in a saucepan. Add garlic, pepper seeds and yellow onion. Cook until onions are slightly browned. Add mushrooms, green onions, tomatoes, wine, olives, chicken flavoring and spices. Stir to mix, add salt and pepper to taste, simmer for ½ hour.

William B. Warton, D.V.M.
Chesterton, IN

Venison with Sauerkraut and German Potato Salad

   1 pound deer meat
   1 (15 ½ ounce) can sauerkraut
   1 (15 ½ ounce) can German potato salad
   salt and pepper to taste

Cut meat into strips ¾ inch by 1½ inches long. Brown meat in skillet with a little oil. When brown add sauerkraut and potato salad and heat throughly.

G. Marione
Annandale, VA

Bavarian Venison

1 ½ pounds venison loin or steak
   2 tablespoons olive oil
¼ cup flour
   salt and pepper to taste
   1 can consommé
¾ cup red cooking wine
   1 medium onion, sliced
   1 slice bread, cut in ½ inch cubes

Cut meat into 2 inch pieces. Coat meat well with flour and brown in oil in large skillet. Add remaining ingredients. Cover and cook over low heat for one hour, stirring occasionally. Serve over mashed potatoes.

Berneta Austenfeld
Emporia, KA

Cuban Venison

A traditional Cuban/South American way of preparing pork which lends itself to venison.

    1 venison shoulder roast or ham
    1 medium onion
    1 large whole garlic
      salt/pepper
      oregano
    6 sour oranges (can substitute 4 oranges mixed with 4
        lemons or limes
      sage

Begin by juicing oranges into mixing bowl. Flavor is enhanced if orange pulp is also included. Peel and mince garlic. Prepare venison by removing all traces fat and exposed gristle. With pork hams fat and skin are left intact. Venison fat imparts a strong gamey flavor. Place meat in covered roasting pan. The venison is now pierced by a long thin knife about every three inches. Using your index finger enlarge all the slits. Salt is liberally sprinkled over meat and worked into slits with finger. Pieces of finely chopped garlic are then forced into slits. The process is repeated on the opposite side. The remainder of the chopped garlic is now added to juice, along with one teaspoon salt, one half teaspoon freshly ground pepper, dash of sage, and one teaspoon oregano. These ingredients are mixed so the herbs are moistened. The juice mixture is then poured over meat, making sure liquid enters all slits and covers all surfaces. The onion is cut into chunks and added to marinade. Cover dish and place in refrigerator for 24 hours. After 12 hours meat is turned. Pre-heat oven to 360 degrees and cook venison in covered pan approximately one half hour per pound.

Serve with beans and rice.

Morris Gallo
Ft. Meyers, FL

Venison Scrapple

Scrapple is a favorite breakfast dish in the Southwest, but my family wouldn't eat it after watching me boil unappealing pork scraps left over from butchering. Now I make it outside in my harvest kitchen, put it up in cupcake tins, and thinly slice and fry for a Sunday breakfast special called "holiday bacon." Everyone enjoys it and asks no questions. Two years ago I tried substituting the trimmings from venison and I think it actually tastes better than pork scrapple. Here is my formula for venison scrapple:

    16 cups cooked and chopped venison
     8 cups venison broth
     1 cup lard
     4 cups corn flour or corn meal
     1 cup buckwheat or rye flour
     1 cup rolled oats
     1 teaspoon salt
     1 teaspoon black pepper
     1 teaspoon jalapeño juice (to taste)
     1 dash Wrights Liquid Smoke
     1 sprinkle Morton's sausage and meat loaf seasoning

All quantities are in proportion so it can be multiplied or divided, depending upon the amount of available meat.

Trim fat from venison trimmings, place them in a pot, cover with water and cook until meat separates from the bones (about 30 minutes in a pressure cooker). Save broth. Separate meat from bones and chop in a food processor. Meanwhile, to two cups broth, add corn meal, rolled oats and buckwheat flour. Mix thoroughly so there are no lumps. Bring meat in remaining broth to a boil. Add lard, cereal and broth mixture and cook until it has the consistency of thick mush. Stir in salt, pepper and spices (jalapeño juice is brine from preserved jalapeño peppers and a little goes a long way). Remove from heat and pour into muffin tins using cupcake liners. The finished product can be stored frozen for six months or so. Properly made, venison scrapple can be thawed and sliced easily for frying with little crumbling.

H. E. Cottrell
Las Cruces, NM

Portuguese Venison

Place "fist size" pieces with bone (legs/spinal area) in a clay pot.

- **3 cloves sliced garlic**
- **1 teaspoon black ground pepper**
- **2 bay leaves**
- **1 teaspoon black peppercorns**
- **1 tablespoon salt**
  minced parsley
- **1 teaspoon paprika**
  equal parts red and white wine
- **8 slices bacon**
- **2 medium onions**
- **3 small cans tomatoes**

Add garlic, ground black pepper, bay leaves, black peppercorns, salt, parsley, paprika and wines until meat is almost covered. Marinate six hours, mininum.

Fry bacon and onions, place into pot along with tomatoes. Bring to a boil. Bake 350 degrees for two and a half to three hours, turning meat over every 30 minutes so it will not dry out.

Serve with potatoes and vegetables.

Mario Alberto
Greenwich, CT

Venison Fondue

- **2 pounds vension loin (fat and bone removed)**
- **1 teaspoon salt**
- **1 teaspoon tenderizer**
- **¼ teaspoon each, fresh ground black pepper, garlic powder and seasoning salt**
- **2 cups extra virgin olive oil**
- **1 cup peanut oil**

Cut venison into ¾ inch cubes. Mix seasonings together. Place a layer of meat cubes in a two quart casserole dish, sprinkle with some of the seasoning, repeat layers with rest of meat and seasoning. Stir well. Cover and refrigerate for about six hours. Heat oils in electric fondue pot according to manufacturers directions. Oil is hot when a one inch cube of soft bread browns in 45 seconds.

Each guest spears a piece of venison and cooks it from 15 (rare) to 60 seconds (well done).

Can be served with a dipping sauce, such as bearnaise, or a horseradish sauce. If watching calories or cholesterol, cook in three cups beef bouillon, still very tasty.

Yield: serves four to six people

Mrs. Charles (Jean) Campbell
Petoskey, Michigan

V-8enison Soup

4 cups cubed venison
1 package Lipton beefy onion soup mix
3 cups water
1 package Lipton onion mushroom soup mix
4 cups V-8 juice
1 cup carrot slices
2 cups cubed potatoes

Place venison in roasting pan. Mix soups with water and pour over meat. Cover with aluminum foil and roast in 325 degree oven for two and a half hours. When cooked, put meat and juices into pot. Pour four cups V-8 juice and two cups carrot slices into pot with meat and juices. Simmer on top of stove until carrot slices are soft. In a separate pot of water, cook cubed potatoes. Put cooked potatoes into venison soup before serving. Cooking potatoes separately will eliminate the potato taste in the soup.

Gerri Bryant
Andover, NJ

Venison Supreme Casserole

4 pounds venison cut into 2 inch cubes (caribou, elk or moose may also be used)
1 can cream of mushroom soup
1 can cream of celery soup
1 can cream of chicken soup
2 packets Lipton onion soup mix
½ - ¾ cup burgundy wine

Put all ingerdients in covered casserole and bake in 325 degree oven for at least three hours. Stir once or twice while baking.

When browning the meat additional seasonings are not needed. Serve over noodles, potatoes or toast points.

If more meat is needed, just add one or more cans of any of the soups.

R. Earl Ash
Norwich, NY

Venison Supreme

- 6 venison chops
- 6 strips bacon
- 2 medium onions, sliced
- 1 apple, peeled and sliced
- 1 (8 ounce) can mushrooms
- 1 (16 ounce) can sauerkraut
- 1 large clove garlic, chopped
- 2 beef bouillon cubes
- ¼ cup burgundy wine
- ⅛ teaspoon black pepper

Take venison chops and with a small sharp knife remove loin from the bone. If your chops are more than three fourths inches thick, split in half. This will be easier when chops are still slightly frozen. In anticipation of this recipe I remove the bone from the loin when preparing my meat for the freezer. Leave meat in one piece and slice it when you are ready to use in any recipe. In small saucepan combine sliced apple and sauerkraut. Season with black pepper, cover and bring to a boil. Turn down heat and simmer for one hour or more before starting recipe.

In large fry pan lay strips of bacon flat in pan. Fry until half done, remove, drain on paper towel, reserve about two tablespoons fat, discard the rest. Fry chops in reserved fat, turning until they are brown. Add sliced onions and chopped garlic and sauté until onions are limp. Add bouillon cubes that have been dissolved in a slight amount of hot water. Stir, add mushrooms that have been drained. Heat through and put in your favoite baking dish. Add wine to fry pan and simmer, scraping any paricles of gook that stuck to the pan. Pour over meat and sauerkraut mixture. Add strips of bacon to top of mixture and place uncovered in 350 degree oven for one hour.

Serve with whipped potatoes, garlic bread and your favorite vegetable, this is "a feast fit for a king."

Jim Austin
Honesdale, PA

Super Venison Chops

2 venison chops
2 pork chops
4 onions, sliced
4 lemons, sliced
8 tablespoons tomato catsup
8 tablespoons brown sugar

Pre-heat oven to 350 degrees. Rinse chops and place flat on baking dish that is approximately one and one half to two inches deep. Place a slice of onion and a slice of lemon on each chop. Spread two tablespoons brown sugar on each chop and pour approximately 2 tablespoons catsup on each chop.

Cover with foil and bake 45 to 60 minutes depending on thickness of chops (one inch about one hour; three fourths inch about 45 minutes). Uncover and baste every 10 minutes for another 30 minutes. Makes two servings.

Variations include using all venison chops and adding several strips pork fatback or standing chops on the "bone" edge in a dutch oven like a crown roast with onion and lemon slices between chops with brown sugar and catsup liberally spread over all. Cooking time is about the same.

James A. Rowdon
Chester Heights, PA

Braised Venison Heart

1 deer heart (1 pound), 1 antelope heart or ½ elk
    heart
⅛ pound bacon
1½ tablespoons butter
1 onion
4 peeled tomatoes, diced
3 tablespoon white wine
½ cup sour cream
1 egg yolk
1 teaspoon lemon juice
    dash of basil leaves
    salt and pepper to taste

Wash, trim veins and fat from one venison heart. Dice into large cubes (1x2 inches). Dice bacon and sauté in butter. Add cubes of heart, brown slightly, then add one half cup water. Add peeled and diced tomatoes together with white wine. Braise slowly for an hour and a half, or until heart cubes are tender, then remove cover and simmer slowly 30 minutes. Remove from heat and stir in sour cream and egg yolk, which have been mixed thoroughly together. Season with basil, salt and pepper, and serve with rice or mashed potatoes.

A marvelous way to do heart, which I purloined from the kitchen of a hunting collegue in Germany's Fichtel Mountains. His wife's mother claimed that this was the way they had always done the deer and elk hearts, and even used it for wild boar hearts.

Gary Lease
Santa Cruz, CA

Cynthia's Venison Soup

    5 pounds venison
    2 large chopped onions
    2 large chopped bell peppers
    3 tablespoons worcestershire sauce
    ½ teaspoon Tabasco
    1 chopped garlic clove
    1 cup chopped shallots
    3 (16 ounce) cans cut green beans
    3 (16 ounce) cans whole kernel corn
    2 (16 ounce) cans lima beans
    2 (16 ounce) cans mixed vegetables
    1 (16 ounce) can diced carrots
    4 (8 ounce) cans tomato sauce
    1 cup chopped cabbage
    8 large cubed red potatoes
    1 (8 ounce) package elbow macaroni
    ½ teaspoon salt
    ½ teaspoon cayenne pepper
    7 gallons water

In four and one half gallon soup pot, add venison, two tablespoons worcestershire sauce and three and one half gallons water. Boil venison for two hours. Remove vension and cube. Discard water. Add venison, onions, bell peppers, shallots, green beans, whole kernel corn, lima beans, mixed vegetables, tomato sauce, one tablespoon worcestershie sauce, three and one half gallons hot water, salt, and cayenne pepper to soup pot. Cover loosely and bring to a boil. Reduce heat to medium and cook for two hours. Then add potatoes, carrots, macaroni and cabbage. Simmer another hour.

Yield: servings for 10 to 12 people

Cynthia Babineaux Lopez
New Iberia, Louisiana

Biscuits and Gravy

Gravy:

   1 pound cubed venison
1 ¼ cups flour (seasoned flour works better)
   ¼ teaspoon garlic salt
   ¼ teaspoon onion salt
      dash of table salt
   ½ teaspoon black pepper
   ½ cup light oil (canola works well), may be reduced

Dredge meat in flour, brown in oil using a large cast iron skillet. Add the rest of flour and brown with meat. You may need more oil to keep mixture moist.

Add two cups milk (1% milkfat) and 1 cup water. Bring to boil, stirring constantly. You may add more water to desired thickness; it is best when creamy.

Yield: serves four people

Biscuits:

   4 cups flour
   5 teaspoons baking powder
   ¼ cup light oil

Blend together until cornmeal like mixture. Add 1½ cups milk (1% milkfat). Do not over-thin.

Shape biscuits by hand or with cutter. Bake 12 to 15 minutes at 475 degrees. Serve hot and enjoy.

Yield: 16 to 18 average size biscuits

Deloy Spencer
Pleasantview, Utah

Blue Dog Butterflies

   2 pounds butterfly chops, deer or antelope
 ½ teaspoon paprika
 ½ teaspoon white pepper
   1 cup flour, mix with white pepper and paprika
 ¾ cup white wine
 ¾ cup chicken stock
   2 tablespoons butter
   2 egg yolks
     juice of 2 lemons
   1 cup heavy cream
     lemon slices
     butter for sautéing

Pound butterfly chops between two pieces of waxed paper until one fourth inch thick. Dredge in flour mixture. Melt a walnut-sized piece of butter in a good frying pan, moderate heat, and sauté each chop just until brown or each side, turn only once and do not overcook. Don't crowd the frying pan. Add more butter if necessary. As each chop is done, remove onto a warm serving platter.

After all chops are done, add chicken stock, wine, and two tablespoons butter to pan. When butter is melted add lemon juice. Cook until reduced to about three fourths cup. Mix together cream and egg yolks. Add to pan, stirring constantly with a whisk to desired thickness. Serve over chops with lemon juice. Garnish. Best with rice.

Jane Peirce
Orange, MI

One Pan Dinner

   5 venison or antelope chops, ½ inch thick
 2-3 medium potatoes, quartered
   4 carrots, sliced
   4 small onions
 4-5 stalks celery, sliced
   1 tablespoon parsley
     salt and pepper

Brown meat in small amount of butter. Add vegeatables, sprinkle with salt, pepper and parsley. Add enough water to almost cover.

Cover and simmer about 40 minutes, checking occasionally, so it does not cook dry.

Yield: two servings.

Mrs. Thomas Sanders
Hanover, PA

Best Chicken Fried Steak

This recipe works well with deer, antelope and elk.

1½ –2 pounds steaks
    Lawry's seasoning salt
    worcestershire sauce
    Crisco cooking oil
2 eggs
    milk
1 cup all purpose flour

Soak steak in salt water for six to eight hours. Trim all fat and membrane away and rinse. Chop steaks with a serrated knife blade until it is about one half inch thick. Sprinkle with a seasoning salt and about three drops worcestershire and pound in with knife. Let steaks stand for 15 to 20 minutes.

Make a batter using eggs and add a dash of milk and one half teaspoon seasoning salt. Dip steaks in batter and then cover both sides with flour. Cover the bottom of fry pan with crisco and heat to 375–400 degrees. Brown on one side and then turn and reduce heat to simmer. Cover and cook 10 to 15 minutes, depending on steak thickness. Remove cover for last five mintues cooking time. Enjoy!

Gene Galitz
Lander, WY

Toothsome Tenders

2½ pounds lean venison (deer, elk, moose, sheep or
     pronghorn), trimmed of any fat or sinew strings
   3 cups cooking oil or shortening
   3 cups white flour
   2 eggs
1½ cups whole or powdered milk
   1 cup Italian salad oil
   2 tablespoons worcestershire sauce
   1 teaspoon Tabasco or hot sauce
     salt and pepper

Slice meat across grain, into three fourths inch thick cutlets of
about fruitjar lid size. With a clean hatchet or hammer pean,
lightly pound and tenderize tenders into half inch thickness or
less. Salt and pepper tenders to taste and marinate them for one
half hour in a shallow pan or cupped foil, using a marinade of
Italian dressing, worcestershire sauce and Tabasco. Remove, when
tender, pat with paper towels.

Whip eggs and milk into a loose batter. Dredge tenders through
flour, batter, and then flour again until well coated. Fry for three
minutes each side in a frying pan or a dutch oven with oil or
shortening bubbling slightly. Do not overcook. Remove tenders
onto paper towels for draining. Eat them while hot or warm. Any
leftovers make fine sandwiches for your lunch afield.

C. P. Wade, Jr.
Galveston, TX

Cutlets Venison, Bear, Beef or Other Meat

2 pounds cutlets, cut in small steaks, cubed and
     pounded

Make a batter of:

   3 eggs, slightly beaten
   ½ cup grated romano cheese
   1 tablespoon parsley
   1 tablespoon crushed basil
2-3 cloves garlic
     grated rind and juice of lemon
     wine
     bread crumbs, ground

Mix well, saturate each piece well and let stand in bowl for three hours. Dip each piece in wine and ground bread crumbs and deep fry, four to five cutlets at a time until browned. Drain on paper towel. Serve with lemon wedges. Good hot or cold.

Mark Hewlett
Hermon, NY

Otter's Venison Sauerbraten

Beg, borrow or steal 7 to 8 pounds venison haunch from hunter friends, or shoot your own.

4 tablespoons all purpose white flour
3 stalks celery, cut small
1 tablespoon cornstarch
20 gingersnaps, crushed fine
½ cup dry madeira wine
1 tablespoon bacon fat or any cooking oil
4 carrots, chopped small
1 cup raisins
1 cup dry mushrooms, soaked in 2 cups water for 20 minutes
1 cup sour cream

Marinade:
4 cups good dry red wine
1 tablespoon salt
1 teaspoon thyme
½ teaspoon sage
1 tablespoon dry mustard
20 whole cloves
3 large cloves garlic, smash 'em
2 cups tarragon vinegar
12 black peppercorns
1 teaspoon mace
½ teaspoon allspice
3 bay leaves
3 large yellow onions, chopped

Combine marinade ingredients and place in plastic bag with venison. Marinate in refrigerator for three to four days (four days is better).

Remove meat from bag, reserving marinade. Dry meat, dredge

it in flour and brown it well in oil or bacon fat. Place meat in enamel or steel kettle (not aluminum). Add chopped celery, carrots and marinade. Simmer slowly, covered, for two hours.

Remove meat — keep warm. Strain remaining liquid and boil to reduce. Add cornstarch if too thin. Add raisins, mushrooms and gingersnaps. Simmer on low heat for 20 mintues. Salt to taste. Add madeira and sour cream.

Serve with rice or buttered noodles.

Yield: serves 8 to 10 good eaters

Albert M. Otter
Walnut Creek, CA

Deer Ribs

1 large bottle French dressing
1 cup Bermuda onion, chopped
5 pounds deer ribs

Marinate ribs with onions and dressing overnight in refrigerator in covered glass Pyrex dish.

Bake as is at 350 degrees for 30 minutes or until done.

Kenneth Kronvoid
Whelling, IL

Venison Sausage Stick Soup

1 pound venison steaks
1 cup onions, chopped
1 cup cubed potatoes
1½ quarts water
1 cup sliced carrots
½ cup diced celery
1 cup shredded cabbage
1 (16 ounce) can great northern beans
¼ cup rice
1 (#2 can) tomatoes
1 small bay leaf
½ teaspoon thyme
¼ teaspoon basil
3 teaspoons salt
⅛ teaspoon pepper
grated parmesan cheese

Cook all ingredients except cheese. Cover and simmer for one hour. Serve sprinkled with cheese.
Yield: six to eight servings

Wanda V. Richardson
Coolville, OH

Oriental Dishes

Thai Waterfall Venison
(Yam Nay Kwang Nam Toke)

1 pound venison steak
1 teaspoon worcestershire sauce
2 teaspoons oyster sauce
Jane's season salt
5 teaspoons fish sauce (Nam Pla can be purchased in any oriental food store or oriental section in many supermarkets)
1 teaspoon sugar
2 teaspoons uncooked brown rice
2 cloves shallots
handful fresh mint (much better than dry)
1 tablespoon chopped green onions
1 small dried red chili pepper

Ahead of time, brown two tablespoons raw rice in oven at 300 degrees. Take out when light brown. When cool, grind in a blender or a coffee grinder, save.

Grind dried chili pepper in a blender and save separately.

Combine worcestershire sauce, oyster sauce and a dash of Jane's season salt.

Marinate venison steak in above mixture for two hours.

Cook venison steak on grill to taste. When done, slice venison steak diagonally across grain into thin strips. Mix venison slices together in a bowl with fish sauce, lemon juice, one half teaspoon ground chili pepper (vary to taste), sugar and two teaspoons ground browned rice. Slice shallot cloves in thin slices. Mix in sliced shallots, green onion and mint leaves.

Serve with raw cabbage or lettuce and green onions. In Thailand, the dish is served as an appetizer with beer and other drinks. Each hunter can pick pieces from a central plate with a fork.

Maurice M. Tanner
Moscow, ID

Szechwan Venison with Cashews

1 pound venison loin or sirloin, trimmed of fat
2 teaspoons flour
   Lawry's seasoned salt to taste
   white pepper to taste
1 tablespoon peanut oil
3 cloves garlic, minced
1 teaspoon fresh ginger, minced
10 (about) dried red chili peppers
1 (8 ounce) can sliced bamboo shoots
10 whole green onions cut in 1 inch length
1 tablespoon sugar
1 tablespoon rice vinegar or white wine vinegar
1 tablespoon dry sherry
2 tablespoons soy sauce
3 tablespoons chicken broth
2 teaspoons corn starch
¾ –1 cup roasted cashews
   cooked white rice

Preferably, venison should be fresh from a fat, young doe. Slice venison across grain on a slant in one eighth inch thick slices (such as with flank steak or for fajitas). Mix flour, salt, pepper, and sherry in a bowl. Add sliced venison and let stand for 20 minutes to marinate.

Mince garlic and ginger and place on saucer with dried chili peppers. Drain bamboo shoots and place in a bowl with sliced green onions. Mix sugar, vinegar, dry sherry, soy sauce, and chicken broth in a bowl. Add corn starch and mix well.

Heat a wok or frying pan over high heat. Add three tablespoons peanut oil. When oil begins to smoke add garlic, ginger and dried chili peppers. Stir continuously. When garlic begins to brown add marinated venison immediately and stir vigorously until pan begins to cool. Continue stirring until meat browns (for three or four minutes.) Remove from pan. Drain any available liquid from venison back into wok.

Add remaining tablespoon peanut oil and heat. Add bamboo shoots and green onion and stir for one minute. Add venison and cashews. Re-stir cooking sauce and add to wok. Stir until sauce thickens. Remove from heat. Serve over fluffy white rice.

Yield: serves four

Larry Lucas
Seguin, TX

Chinese Deer Pot Roast

4–5 pounds roast (elk or moose may also be used)
2 teaspoons salt
½ teaspoon black pepper
2 teaspoons LaChoy brown gravy sauce (or Kitchen Bouquet)
1 tablespoon worcestershire sauce
½ cup soy sauce
2 tablespoons butter
2 cups water
6 small onions

Mix salt and pepper with sauces and rub well into meat. Let marinate a few minutes. Brown meat well in dutch oven (or other heavy pan). Add water, onions and left over marinade sauce. Cover tightly and cook slowly on top of stove three to three and one half hours (until meat is tender). Add more water if necessary. Turn meat once or twice during cooking. When meat is nearly done, potatoes, carrots and more onions may be added if desired. Preparation time is 3 to 4 hours.

Yield: six to eight servings

Joe Hulver, Jr.
Winchester, VA

Kung Fu Deer

1 pound venison roast, sliced very thin

Marinate for at least two hours in:

2 tablespoons soy sauce
2 tablespoons water
2 tablespoons sesame or olive oil
1 level tablespoon sugar
2 tablespoons sesame seed
2–3 cloves garlic, minced
1 large thinly sliced onion
dash of black pepper, to taste
1 tablespoon fresh grated ginger root, or to taste
½ cup drained Vlasic pepper rings, mild or spicy, depending on your taste

Cook in a wok or frying pan, and serve over rice.

The key to this one is fresh ginger. You can use dry, powdered ginger, but then you might as well use dry, powdered venison too.

Tom H. Nagel
Columbus, OH

Sausage and Bologna

Wild Game Bologna/Salami
from Deer, Elk and Moose

This recipe makes a splendid bologna or salami-type roll for excellent eating. Enjoy!

> 2 pounds ground meat
> 1 teaspoon each, onion salt, garlic salt, mustard seed, seasoned pepper
> 2 teaspoons celery seed
> 2 tablespoons Liquid Smoke
> 3 tablespoons Morton's Tender Quick salt
> 1 cup water

Mix all together, make into rolls one foot long by one and one half inches thick. Wrap in foil and refrigerate for 24 hours allowing meat to cure. Punch holes in foil with fork. Put foiled rolls on flat sheet in oven and bake at 350 degrees for one and one half hours. Allow to cool in foil, then enjoy!

Pichaway County Sportsman
Stoutsville, OH

Venison Bologna

> 10 pounds venison
> 1 pound hamburger
> ½ cup Morton's Tender Quick salt
> 2 ½ cups vegetable oil
> 5 teaspoons garlic powder
> 2 teaspoons hickory smoke salt
> 2 teaspoons onion powder
> 4 teaspoons black pepper
> 5 teaspoons Liquid Smoke
> 1 tablespoon hot pepper sauce
> 2 envelopes Lipton beefy onion soup mix

Use casings or shape into logs one and a half inch diameter. Wrap in foil. Bake in 200 degree oven for one hour and 45 minutes.

Ernest Anderson
Titusville, PA

Venison Salami

4 pounds venison, elk or antelope, as fat free as
    possible
1 pound fatty ground pork
¼ cup curing salt*
2 tablespoons Liquid Smoke
1½ teaspoons garlic powder
2 tablespoons worcestershire sauce
2 teaspoons cracked pepper or 1½ teaspoons ground
    pepper

Mix well in glass bowl and chill for 24 hours.

After chilling, divide into quarters, shape and roll into "logs" about eight inches long, place each log on a piece of 12x18 inch nylon netting.** Roll up tightly and tie each one with string. Place logs on rack on top of a cookie sheet (spray rack with "Pam" to make clean-up easier). Bake in a 225 degree oven for about four hours. Remove logs from oven and pat with paper towels to remove excess fat and oil. After 15 minutes remove netting slowly and allow venison salami rolls to cool. Wrap first in plastic wrap and then in foil. Since there are no preservatives in this recipe, the salami will keep for several weeks in the refrigerator or six months or more in the freezer.

Make plenty because once your hunting buddies get a taste of this, they're liable to take your rifle away and hand you an apron.

*The curing salt can be obtained from some butcher shops or from Morton Salt Company, Dept SM, Box 355, Argo, IL 60501

**Nylon netting is sold by the yard at most stores where fabric is sold. Buy the least expensive type of netting with large holes.

Gilbert Yanuck
Chatsworth, CA

Easy Smoked Venison Summer Sausage

3 pounds venison ground with beef tallow
3 tablespoons Morton's Tender Quick salt (cure for
fresh and frozen meat)
1 tablespoon mustard seed
1 cup water
½ teaspoon garlic salt
½ teaspoon onion salt
1½ teaspoons Liquid Smoke

Put ground venison in large bowl. Mix all other ingredients in one cup water. Mix well. Pour liquid mix into bowl with venison and mix well. Separate mixture into four rolls, similar to pepperoni rolls, and wrap tightly in plastic wrap. Refrigerate 24 hours. Unwrap and bake on broiler pan or rack with drainage; bake in 250 degree oven for two and one half hours. Turn once halfway through baking. Let cool completely. Wrap in aluminum foil. Will keep in refrigerator up to four weeks, and can be frozen up to six months.

Marion 'Mame' Martell
Midland, PA

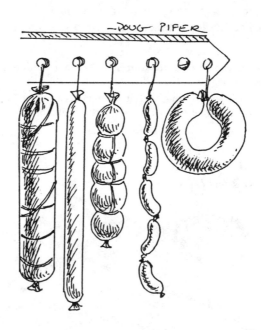

Andouille Smoked Sausage

5 pounds coarsely ground venison
5 pounds coarsely ground pork butt
2 level teaspoons Prague powder curing salt
2 cups ice water
3 tablespoons salt
2 tablespoons cayenne red pepper
2 teaspoons chili powder
1 teaspoon mace
1 teaspoon cloves
1 teaspoon allspice
2 teaspoons garlic powder
1 tablespoon thyme
2 tablespoons parsley
1 tablespoon marjoram
1 teaspoon ground bay leaf
2 large onions, sauteed (optional)

Dissolve curing salt in ice water, stirring thoroughly. Add remaining seasonings to water. Add to meat and mix thoroughly. Stuff into hog casings and tie off into five or six inch links. Place sausage on smoke house sticks and space properly. Place in a preheated 160 to 165 degree smoke house with dampers one fourth open. Apply heavy smoke and keep in smoke house until the internal temperature is 152 degrees, about 12–24 hours. To make smoke, use dampened mesquite or hickory sawdust placed in a pan on smoke house burners. This recipe is my favorite for smoked sausage.

Philip Sauber
Beaumont, TX

225

Salami

Venison Salami:

(Fast, easy and great for outings or served as hors d'oeuvers)

     12 pounds ground venison
      3 pounds pork sausage
     ¾ cups curing salt

Divide meat into three equal portions.

Smoked Salami:

      2 teaspoons Liquid Smoke
  1-½ teaspoons garlic powder
      2 teaspoons cracked pepper

Mix well with one portion of meat mixture and chill 24 hours.

Herbed Salami:

      3 tablespoons red wine
      1 tablespoon crushed basil leaves
      1 teaspoon garlic salt
      1 teaspoon oregano
      1 teaspoon onion powder
      2 teaspoons mustard seed
     ⅔ cup fresh grated parmesan cheese

Mix well with one portion of meat mixture and chill 24 hours.

Spicy Salami:

      3 tablespoons dry white wine
      1 teaspoon garlic powder
      2 teaspoon chili powder
      1 teaspoon (or more if you like it hot) crushed red
         pepper
      1 teaspoon ground cummin

Mix well with one portion of meat mixture and chill 24 hours.
  Divide each mixture into fourths. Shape, roll into compact eight inch logs. Place on cheesecloth square, 12x18 inches. Roll tightly and tie with cotton string at both ends. Place logs on broiler pan rack and bake at 225 degrees for four hours.
  Freezes nicely but must be kept refrigerated until used.

Sugar Ferris
Arlington, TX

Easy Homemade Deer Sausage

2 pounds ground deer meat
¾ pound ground pork
½ teaspoon coarse black pepper
1½ teaspoons mustard seed
½ teaspoon garlic powder
¼ teaspoon onion powder
3 tablespoons Morton's Tender Quick salt
1 tablespoon Liquid Smoke

Combine all ingredients and mix well. Shape into two log rolls and wrap in foil. Refrigerate overnight. Unwrap and bake at 300 degrees for one hour. Remove from oven and cool. Wrap in foil and refrigerate.

Makes delicious party snacks served on club crackers.

Frank Wilson
Sainte Genevieve, MO

Venison Sausage

6 pounds venison, trimmed
6 pounds pork
¼ cup salt
1½ tablespoons sage
1½ tablespoons ground black pepper
1 tablespoon cayenne pepper
1 teaspoon garlic salt
1 teaspoon mustard seed
1 teaspoon coriander seed

Cut meat into chunks, combine with remaining ingredients and grind. Grind with coarse cutter first then with a finer grinder. Can be formed into patties or stuffed into casings.

Bob Rayburg
Girard, PA

Venison Sausage Cacciatore

2 pounds venison trimmings
2 pounds pork butt
1 pound mushrooms, sliced
2 large green peppers, sliced
2 large yellow onions, coarsely chopped
1 cup rosé wine
1 tablespoon ground coriander
2 tablespoons whole fennel seed
2 tablespoons crushed pepper (optional)
6 large cloves garlic
1 (16 ounce) can crushed tomatoes
5 tablespoons olive oil
1 large hank sausage casings

The day before the feast, coarsely grind venison trimmings and pork butt. In large pan, place ground meat, 4 pressed cloves garlic, fennel seed, crushed red pepper, ground coriander and half the rosé. Mix thoroughly and allow to marinate refrigerated from one to three hours. Then stuff casings, tying off every six inches. Refrigerate sausages overnight.

The day of the feast, brown sausage in just enough oil to coat the bottom of pan to prevent sausage from sticking and breaking the casing (moving the sausage around the pan for the first few minutes also keeps it from sticking). Remove sausage from pan when about three quarters cooked (cooked firm enough to cut). In drippings, saute onions and two pressed cloves garlic. When onions are clear, add one can crushed tomatoes and one half cup rosé and simmer for one half hour. Then add sausage cut into one inch pieces, sliced mushrooms and peppers and simmer for 20 to 30 minutes until peppers begin to soften.

Serve over rice, spaghetti or macaroni.

Yield: six to eight servings

Robert E. Paola
Cranston, RI

Spicy Venison Sausage

2 pounds ground venison
1 pound ground pork
¼ cup wine vinegar
1 teaspoon salt
½ teaspoon black pepper
2 teaspoons oregano
1 tablespoon paprika
½ teaspoon cumin
1½ tablespoons chili powder
2 cloves garlic, crushed

Mix well and store in plastic bag for 24 to 48 hours before using. Make into patties and fry or broil.

Winnie Alphonse
Forked River, NJ

Italian Sausage

Ingredients per 10 pounds:

5 pounds coarsely ground pork
5 pounds finely ground venison
½ cup grated romano cheese
1 cup chopped fresh parsley
1 ounce whole fennel seed (or 1 tablespoon ground
    fennel)
½ tablespoon hot pepper (or to taste)
1 quart spring water
2 ounces natural hog casing
1 cup shredded mozzarella
1 cup semi-sweet white wine
1 tablespoon pepper
3 tablespoons salt

Mix stuffing ingredients well and refrigerate overnight. Stuff into casing or press into patties. Separate into desired portions, wrap in freezer paper and freeze.

Joseph D. Poblock
Buffalo, NY

Polish Sausage

Ingredients per 10 pounds:

   5 **pounds finely ground venison**
   5 **pounds coarsely ground pork**
   ½ **cup dried marjoram (or 2 tablespoons ground
       marjoram)**
   2 **tablespoons black pepper**
   3 **tablespoons salt**
   2 **cloves finely chopped garlic**
   ½ **teaspoon ground ginger**
   1 **quart spring water**
   2 **ounces hog casing**

Mix stuffing ingredients well and refrigerate overnight. Stuff into
casings or press into patties. Separate into desired portions, wrap
in freezer paper and freeze.

Joseph D. Poblock
Buffalo, NY

Venison Sausage

   2 **pounds venison (remove all fat possible)**
   1 **pound firm pork fat (rendered)**
   2 **teaspoons salt**
   3 **teaspoons sage**
   ½ **teaspoon ground black pepper**
   ¾ **teaspoon ground thyme**
   ⅔ **teaspoon ground oregano**
   1 **teaspoon ground cayenne pepper**

Coarsely grind venison and pork fat. Add rest of ingredients and
mix with (clean) hands. Regrind with fine blade in meat grinder.
Refrigerate.

   If not to be eaten within a week, make into patties separated
by two sheets waxed paper and store in freezer.

   This is a simple, basic recipe and is delicious just as it is,
however, strength of spices vary, especially sage (I like a lot of
sage), and amounts may be adjusted to suit individual tastes.

Dr. James N. Little
Walnut Ridge, AR

Deer Camp Breakfast Sausage

2 pounds ground venison
1 pound ground pork
1 teaspoon marjoram
1 tablespoon basil
1 tablespoon sage
1 teaspoon dry mustard
1 egg
¼ cup cooking oil
¼ cup bread crumbs
   salt and pepper to taste

Combine meats and seasonings, mixing together, then add egg and bread crumbs to mixture. Stir well, shape into patties and fry in oil until golden brown on each side.

Dan McNamara
Kennedy, NY

How to Make Deer Sausage or Hamburger

Bone one half as much deer as you want to make into sausage and hamburger. Trim as much fat and ligament as possible. Then add same amount of pork as you have deer meat. Pork should be half fat and half lean. Mix with deer meat. Add 3 ounces salt and 1 ounce pepper for every 10 pounds of mixed meat. Grind, then put in casings or pack for pan sausage or hamburger. If you have a way to smoke sausage, smoke for 2 to 3 days for flavor to eat fried or barbecue. If you want hard sausage to eat like jerky, smoke it until it is as hard as you want it. For extra flavor, add garlic powder, sage or paprika.

Elmer Lee Hackebeil
La Grange, TX

Three Generation Deer Sausage

30 pounds venison, trim off all fat
25 pounds Boston butts
 5 pounds pork trimmings

Cut meat in small strips. Blend in the following:

 8 teaspoons coarse black pepper
 3 teaspoons salt
 3 (4 ounce) packages Morton's sausage seasons
 3 teaspoons thyme
 3 teaspoons allspice
11 teaspoons Morton's Tender Quick salt
 3 teaspoons sage

Blend all spices with meat. Let stand in refrigerator overnight. Grind meat and let stand in refrigerator another night. Grind a second time and add one pint warm water. Let sit for 12 more hours in the refrigerator.

Stuff castings and hang to dry two or three days. Smoke-hickory chips (dampened) five to six hours or consider apple wood. Hang overnight, then freeze.

Lance Swanke
Burnsville, MN

Microwave Deer Salami or Bologna

 3 pounds lean ground deer meat
¼ cup vegetable or corn oil
 3 cups water
 2 tablespoons Morton's Tender Quick salt
½ tablespoon crushed red peppers
 2 teaspoons garlic powder
 1 teaspoon onion powder
 2 tablespoons mustard seed
 2 teaspoons ground ginger
 1 tablespoon Liquid Smoke (omit if making Bologna)
 2 cups non-fat dry milk
 2 packages Knox unflavored gelatin powder

Mix all ingredients well in plastic or glass bowl. Cover with plastic wrap and set in refrigerator until the next day.

Make four rolls of equal amounts in microwave plastic wrap.

You may double wrap if necessary. Place rolls in baking dish that will fit in your microwave. You may have to cook two at a time to allow adequate space around rolls.

Set at high temperature and cook 25 minutes, turning occasionally every seven or eight minutes, until temperature is 160 degrees in middle of roll. The complete cooking process takes about 25 minutes depending on temperature of microwave.

Take rolls out when done. Remove plastic wrap and let cool at room temperature. They will dry with a glaze to them. Re-wrap with plastic wrap and place in refrigerator. The flavor is better and it slices better when cold. Store in refrigerator. Eat within two weeks.

Andy Stitzer
Kirksville, MD

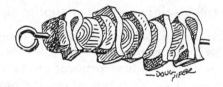

Shish Kebabs

Venison Ka-Bobs

3 pounds venison (loin or other tender cuts)
4 green peppers
4 tomatoes
4 medium onions
½ teaspoon Tabasco
⅓ cup Italian salad dressing
splash red wine

Cut venison into one inch (approximately) cubes. Cut green peppers into quarters (remove all seeds). Cut tomatoes and onions into quarters. Mix venison, vegetables, Tabasco, wine, and dressing in bowl to marinate. Let stand one to two hours. Put on skewers alternating meat, tomato, meat, pepper, meat, onion, etc. Barbecue over hot coals about 15 minutes per side, brushing occasionally with marinade. Serve with rice and enjoy.

Yield: six servings

Marty Boyajian
Torrington, CT

G Bar 7 Kabobs

1 pound venison back strap, cut in 2 inch squares
1 cup burgundy wine
1 teaspoon worcestershire sauce
1 garlic clove, chopped
1 cup salad oil
2 tablespoons ketchup
½ teaspoon sugar
½ teaspoon seasoning salt
1 teaspoon marjoram
½ teaspoon rosemary
1 teaspoon Liquid Smoke
2 pinches parsley
1 dash of lemon juice
1 chopped small jalapeño pepper (optional)

Mix ingredients to make marinade. Marinate cubed meat for three and one half hours in the refrigerator. Remove, thread cubes on skewers, alternating with assortment of vegetables: mushrooms, carrots, small potatoes, green pepper, onions, etc.

Grill kabobs about three inches from coals for approximately 12 minutes, or to doneness you prefer. Baste with marinade during cooking time, turning frequently.

Our favorite fire wood is mesquite, but oak or pecan is also good.

Gary and Linda Gallayda
Katy, TX

Venison Kabobs

2 pounds boneless venison sirloin, cut into
1½ inch cubes

Place meat in a shallow glass container and set aside.
Combine the following:

3 cups vegetable oil
¼ cup dry burgundy wine
2 tablespoons cider vinegar
1½ tablespoons Liquid Smoke
2 teaspoons salt
1 teaspoon white pepper
1 teaspoon garlic powder
1 teaspoon onion juice

Mix well and pour over meat, cover and refrigerate for 48 hours. Stirring occasionally. Remove meat from marinade (please save marinade). Alternate meat and vegetables, cherry tomatoes, mushrooms, onions and green peppers, cut into one inch pieces, on skewers. Brush with marinade. Grill over medium hot cools for 15 minutes. Turning and basting frequently with marinade. Serve with wild rice.

Yield: eight servings

John A. Davis
De Witt, AR

Steaks

Carmine's Venison Steaks

1 pound venison, cut into ¼ inch steaks, fat removed, silver skin removed
8 ounces chicken broth
1 cup white wine
juice of one lemon
6 fresh scallions, chopped
1 large yellow onion, chopped
1 cup chopped fresh parsley
2 cloves garlic, minced
2 tablespoons butter
1 tablespoon olive oil
1 cup red wine vinegar
salt and pepper to taste
1 tablespoon capers (optional)

Marinate venison by covering with water and one cup red wine vinegar for two to three hours.

Sauté the following in butter and olive oil until tender: fresh scallions, yellow onion, fresh parsley, garlic cloves.

Drain venison, wash very well, towel dry, flatten venison well with heavy object, cut into medallions and flour lightly on both sides. Sauté venison on high heat in a pan for 2 to 3 minutes on each side with 2 tablespoons butter. Remove venison from pan and add chicken broth, wine, and lemon juice. Bring to a boil, then add onion mixture and venison and cook three to five minutes or until sauce thickens. Salt and pepper to taste, add capers if desired.

Serve over white rice — makes an excellent dish.

Carmine Frattarolli
New Canaan, CT

Rouladen with Beer Sauce

1½ pounds venison round steak or similar cut
½ pound pork sausage
1 box instant stuffing mix
½ pound mushrooms, quartered
10–12 strips bacon
1 can beer
4 tablespoons flour
½ medium onion, chopped
2 beef bouillon cubes
3–4 bay leaves
salt, pepper, garlic powder to taste

Brown pork sausage in large skillet. Meanwhile, cut meat into pieces approximately 3x3 inches and about ½ inch or less in thickness. Pound with a meat tenderizer to about 5x5 inch patties. (Hint: cover with plastic wrap to avoid mess while tenderizing.) Sprinkle with salt, pepper and garlic. Prepare dressing per package instructions using slightly less water and mix in browned pork sausage. Spoon dressing mixture onto patties and roll up, tucking in ends to keep dressing from escaping. Roll bacon strips around in a spiral fashion and secure with toothpicks. Brown in skillet, rotating meat rolls two or three times. Remove from pan, add onion and brown. Add flour, one half can beer and stir until well blended. Put meat rolls back into pan, add remaining beer, bouillon cubes, bay leaves and mushrooms. Cook covered an additional hour or until tender. Serve over buttered egg noodles.

Yield: four to six servings

Mark Yarish
Albuquerque, NM

Halftime Dutch Oven Venison

2–3 pounds venison, steaks or chunks
  4 slices bacon
  6 large mushrooms, sliced
  1 large onion, sliced
  1 can cream of mushroom soup, undiluted
  ½ cup burgundy wine (optional)
    salt and ground pepper to taste

A casserole may be used, but best results will be achieved using a heavy cast iron dutch oven. In a frying pan, cook bacon and set aside. Brown venison in bacon drippings with salt and pepper. Layer meat, mushrooms and onions in a lightly greased dutch oven. Crumble bacon and spread undiluted soup on top. Add wine (or water) to frying pan and simmer a few minutes, scraping pan with a fork. Pour over all, cover, and place in a 350 degree oven just before opening kick off. Remove cover at the end of first quarter. Meal will be ready for halftime. Serve with noodles and pepper or mint jelly.

Bruce E. Czaplicki
Spring Grove, IL

Dad's Special Hayes Halycost

  4 pounds deer steak
1½ medium heads cabbage, sliced
  2 large onions
  3 cups flour
  2 tablespoons garlic salt
  1 teaspoon oregano
  1 teaspoon sweet basil
  ½ teaspoon cumin
  1 teaspoon celery salt
  2 cans sliced mushrooms
  4 ounces wine
  2 cups grated cheese
  1 cup olive oil

Mix flour, garlic salt, oregano, sweet basil, cumin and celery salt in a large bag and shake well. Place deer steaks in bag and coat meat completely. Heat oil until hot and fry steaks. When done add a little water for steam, this will help make gravy later. Add

237

sliced onions, sliced cabbage and fry until wilted, do not over-cook. Add wine and mushrooms, simmer until all is well heated. Toss and add cheese on top. You can also add tomato paste and leave out cabbage and put on noodles or spaghetti or rice. You can also use other meats such as chicken. It's great!

A Great Marinade:

1-1½ cups soy sauce
    3 cups brown sugar
    1 fresh ginger root
    6 ounces wine
    2 tablespoons almond extract
    ½ ounce lemon juice

Mix all together and shake well. Marinate your meat over night. This also makes great gravy.

Francis B. Hayes
Wolf Point, MT

Stews

Paul's Venison Stew or Is It Stew

    1 pound ground venison
    3 tablespoons shortening (Crisco)
    ½ cup diced onion
    ½ cup diced green pepper
    1 cup diced celery
    1 (15 ounce) can kidney beans
    2 cups (uncooked) broad egg noodles
    1 (16 ounce) can tomatoes
    1 (4 ounce) can button mushrooms
    1 teaspoon seasoned salt (Lawry's)
    1 teaspoon chili powder
    ½ teaspoon salt
    ⅛ teaspoon pepper
    ⅛ teaspoon ground cumin
    ⅛ teaspoon ground cinnamon

In a large skillet sauté celery in shortening for about 4 minutes. Add onions, green pepper, sauté about four to five minutes more. Add venison and cook until brown. Add all remaining ingredients and mix well. Cover tightly, bring to a boil. Reduce heat and simmer for 20 minutes. If you need a little more liquid add some beef broth or dry red wine.

Paul Pietrzak
New London, CT

Venison Stew with Mushrooms, Artichokes and Black Olives

2-2 ½ pounds trimmed shoulder/roast cut into 1 ½ inch
     chunks
   ½ cup seasoned flour (1 teaspoon salt and 1 ½
     teaspoons pepper)
   ½ cup vegetable oil
   8 ounces fresh mushrooms, sliced
   2 cups chicken broth
   1 (9 ounce) package frozen artichoke hearts
     (thawed)
   3 teaspoons lemon juice
   1 teaspoon celery seeds
   ½ teaspoon black pepper
   ½ cup half and half
   1 cup pitted black olives (ripe)
   1 cup white wine

Coat meat with seasoned flour and brown in hot oil. Drain off all but about two tablespoons pan drippings. Add mushrooms to oil drippings and cook about four minutes until lightly browned. Add broth, stirring to scrape up browned bits. Bring to a boil. Return browned meat to pot, reduce heat, cover and simmer one hour. Stir once or twice until venison is tender. Stir in artichoke hearts, lemon juice, celery seed, pepper, half and half and white wine. Bring to a boil. Reduce heat to keep warm. If too thick add more broth or more wine. Stir in olives just before serving. Serve over a bed of flat noodles.

Jack Pangburn
Westbury, NY

239

Marinade Venison Stew

    2 pounds venison stew meat, cut in strips 1 inch thick,
       1–2 inches long
1 ½ cups dry red wine
    ¾ cup sliced celery
    1 cup water
    ½ teaspoon thyme leaves (or ground thyme)
    1 bay leaf, crushed
    3 tablespoons margarine
    ¾ cup sliced carrots
    6 green onions, chopped
    1 tablespoon polyunsaturated cooking oil
       salt and pepper
       flour
    2 tablespoons sage

Place wine, carrots, celery, onions, water, oil, salt and pepper, thyme, sage and bay leaf in a stainless steel or glass bowl. Add meat. Add more water if meat is not covered. Cover and refrigerate for at least five hours, overnight is fine. Remove meat with a slotted spoon and drain vegetables, reserving marin⸱ le. Coat meat with flour, heat marinade in a large frying pan, and brown meat on all sides. Transfer browned meat to an oven-proᴏᵢ casserole. Cook vegetables, adding more marinade if necessary. Then add more marinade to pot and bring to a boil for a minute, scraping the bottom to deglaze. Pour over meat in casserole. Cover and place in a preheated 325 degree oven and bake for two hours. Add more water if it becomes dry. Serve with a salad and hot rolls.

  Yield: four servings

Elmer P. Allen
Valatie, NY

Marv's Marvelous Venison Stew

2 pounds venison, cut into ¾ inch chunks
2 tablespoons cooking oil
2½ cups hot water
2 teaspoons worcestershire sauce
2 beef bouillon cubes
1 large onion, chopped
1 garlic clove, minced
¾ teaspoon salt
½ teaspoon pepper
½ teaspoon chili powder
1 green pepper cut into ¼ inch chunks
4 medium potatoes cut into ½ inch chunks
4 sticks celery cut into ½ inch chunks
1 (14 ounce) can stewed tomatoes
1 handful frozen corn
1 handful frozen green beans
1 handful frozen peas
1 handful alphabet soup pasta
1 (22 ounce) can cream of cheddar cheese soup

Heat oil in large skillet, add meat and simmer for one hour. In a dutch oven, add hot water, worcestershire sauce, bouillon cubes, onion, garlic, salt, pepper, and chili powder. Empty skillet contents into dutch oven and bring to a boil. Add remaining ingredients to dutch oven, cover and simmer for one hour, more or less, until all ingredients are tender. Stir about every 15 minutes to keep bottom from sticking. Add more water and seasonings (such as celery salt, seasoning salt, pepper, etc.) as needed.

Note: It will taste even better if refrigerated overnight and served hot the next day.

Yield: serves eight women and/or children or four hungry hunters

Marvin C. Brenner
Houston, TX

Out of this World Venison Stew

      6 pounds venison stew meat, 1 inch cubes
      6 cans beer (Molson Golden)
 1 ¼ cups flour
      2 tablespoons salt
 3 ¼ teaspoons crushed thyme
 1 ¼ teaspoons crushed pepper
      8 tablespoons cooking oil
    30 shakes Maggi seasoning (bouillon)
      2 bay leaves
      9 unpeeled potatoes, cut into 1 inch cubes
    12 quartered carrots
      6 medium onions, cut into 1 inch pieces
      3 large whole stalks celery, cut into 1 inch length
      4 cloves minced garlic
      1 quart hot water
      2 teaspoons worcestershire sauce

In a large bowl, combine beer marinade:

 4 ½ cups beer
 1 ½ cups minced green onion
      1 cup olive oil
    ¾ cup minced green pepper
      9 tablespoons soy sauce
 1 ½ teaspoons Liquid Smoke
      6 tablespoons sugar
      3 tablespoons fresh garlic
      3 tablespoons Lawry's seasoned salt
        dash of red pepper

Marinate meat overnight in refrigerator, covered. Drain meat from marinade (let drain for one half hour) and save liquid. In a bowl (or plastic bag) combine flour, thyme, pepper and salt. Coat meat in flour mixture and brown in hot oil. Brown small amounts of meat at a time and set aside to drain. In remaining oil, add more if necessary, cook onions, celery and garlic until soft (or until onions are clear). In large pot mix hot water, Maggi, worcestershire sauce and remaining marinade juice. Add onion and celery and let come to a boil. Return meat to pot and add beer and let come to a boil. Reduce heat and simmer for at least two hours. Add potatoes, carrots and mushrooms and simmer until vegetables are soft, about 45 minutes or more. Very good with a stout warm bread and beer. Bon apetit!

Larry Aiardo
Downers Grove, IL

Venison Stew with Dumplings

1 **pound venison, soaked in salt and vinegar water**
     overnight, cut in stew-sized pieces
2 **large potatoes, cut in chunks**
1 **large Bermuda onion, sliced in thin wedges**
2 **carrots, thickly sliced**
½ **cup fresh or frozen peas**
1 **tablespoon poultry seasoning**
   salt and pepper as desired

In large skillet, brown venison to remove excess fat. Prepare vegetables and place on bottom of crock pot. Next place venison and seasoning on top of vegetables. Cover just to top of meat with water. Cook on high setting four to five hours or low setting six to eight hours or until vegetables are tender.

Add dumplings during last 20 to 25 minutes of cooking, turning crock pot on high and bringing stew to full boil.

Dumplings:

2 ¼ **cups Bisquick biscuit mix**
   ⅔ **cup milk**
     salt to taste

Mix dry ingredients, then add milk slowly, stirring until mixture is uniform (will be very thick). Drop by large spoonfuls into boiling stew. Cook covered for 15 to 25 minutes until centers are done. Do not over stir. Dumplings will thicken gravy.

Serve with fried apples or green salad.

Yield: six servings

Martha L. Sheffer
Churchville, VA

Italian Hunter's Stew*

The main reason that people do not enjoy venison, other than improper handling of game in the field, is that it is an extremely dry meat, and without exception, gamey. Regardless of the manner in which you prepare your venison, it must be de-gamed by a soaking in a mild brine solution for at least 24 hours in the refrigerator.

2 pounds venison, cut up for stew
3 tablespoons olive oil
3 tablespoons dry sherry
3 large onions, chopped in large pieces
1 pound fresh mushrooms, (or canned if fresh are unavailable)
1 (8 ounce) can tomato sauce
1 cup dry red wine
½ teaspoon of the following: marjoram, basil, oregano, thyme and parsley
4 garlic cloves, crushed
½ teaspoon pepper
water to cover meat and onions
flour to thicken liquid

A cast iron stew pot is great for this recipe. Remove venison from brine and mix dry sherry with meat. Let sit for 30 minutes. Over medium-high heat, brown venison in olive oil. Remove with slotted spoon and save oil. Sauté onions in remaining juices and oil and cook until onions are transparent. Add mushrooms (either whole or sliced) and sauté a minute or two. Return venison to pot. Add enough water to completely cover meat. Add the rest of ingredients and bring to a boil. Reduce heat to low, simmer and cook until venison shreds with a fork. (Usually four more hours). About 30 minutes before you want to eat, mix enough flour and water to add to stew to thicken and cook for 30 minutes to take out the raw taste of flour. Serve over rice. Enjoy!

*Unauthorized copying, cooking, and then eating this recipe will result in extreme heartburn. Before using this recipe, make sure that yours is an authorized copy!

Burt I. Kahn
Franklin, NC

Venison with Green Onions

1 ½ pounds venison
¼ cup dry sherry wine
¼ cup soy sauce
2 tablespoons cornstarch
4 bunches green onions or 2–3 medium leeks
  peanut oil

Sauce:
½ cup hoisin sauce
2 tablespoons dry sherry
2 teaspoons soy sauce

The venison can be steaks, chops or roasts. Remove all bones, fat, gristle and connective tissue. Cut meat into about ¾ x 1 inch chunks, then cut across the grain into ¼ inch thick slices. (Obviously, this doesn't have to be exact). Place meat in a bowl and add soy sauce, sherry and cornstarch. Mix well and allow to marinate in the refrigerator for at least one half hour or longer. Remove roots and sorry looking greens from green onions. Wash and cut into about two inch lengths, include green ends. (Can also use leeks in same general amount — clean these well as they always seem to have sand or dirt in them — leeks are milder and sweeter than green onions — both are good).

Mix sauce ingredients together. Hoisin sauce is a sort of Chinese barbecue sauce. Many brands and versions are available. I find the one produced by the Koon Chun Sauce Factory, Hong Kong, to be my favorite. Hoisin sauce should be available from a Chinese grocery or health food store.

Preferably using a wok (large skillet will work), heat about four to six tablespoons peanut oil very hot, (just starting to smoke) then add about one third of the venison and stir fry until browned. Remove first batch and fry remaining meat in one or two batches and remove. Again, heat two to four tablespoons peanut oil and add onions or leeks. Stir fry until they wilt slightly. Do not overcook! Then add sauce and bring to boil. Add venison and stir to heat through. Serve over cooked white rice. Enjoy!

Yield: serves four

Melvin R. Schaupp
Mora, MN

Venison Chasseur

5 pounds venison, cubed (haunch is best for this)
¼ pound butter or margarine
3 tablespoons olive oil
⅓ cup hot sherry
2 pounds pearl onions
1½ pounds large fresh mushrooms
3 tablespoons tomato paste
2 shallots, chopped
1 clove garlic, pressed
2 tablespoons flour
3 tablespoons beef stock
2 cups red wine
   salt to taste
   freshly ground pepper to taste
4 sprigs parsley*
2 sprigs thyme*
2 sprigs tarragon*
6 shoots chives*

Cut rump or haunch of venison into large cubes and brown in hot butter and oil. Pour hot sherry over venison. Remove venison to heated bowl. Brown onions in pan, add mushrooms and cook until golden brown. Remove onions and mushrooms to warmed bowl with venison.

Add tomato paste, garlic, shallots, meat glaze and flour to pan. Stir until smooth. Add stock and bring to boil. Add one cup red wine. Season. Add venison, parsley, thyme, tarragon and chives.

Cover and simmer very slowly for one and half hours. Add onions and mushrooms and one cup red wine. Continue simmering for 45 minutes longer. Sprinkle with chopped parsley. Serve with wild rice.

*Herbs may be of the dried-in-the-jar variety.

D. F. O'Donnell
New Bern, NC

Venison Goulash

2 pounds boneless, lean venison (cut into 2 inch cubes)
   pepper
3 tablespoons butter or margarine
3 yellow onions, peeled and sliced
2 small carrots, sliced
2 red bell peppers, chopped
2 green bell peppers, chopped
1 clove garlic, pressed
2 tablespoons Hungarian paprika (more if desired)
1 tablespoon tomato paste
2 tablespoons flour
1 ½ cups beef broth
 ½ teaspoon pepper
1 cup dairy sour cream
 ½ teaspoon pepper

Sprinkle venison with pepper. Heat butter in large skillet. Brown venison quickly on all sides, remove. Add carrots, onions, peppers and garlic to skillet. Cook over moderate heat, stirring until vegetables are soft. Stir in paprika, cook a few minutes longer then add flour and tomato paste, stir to blend. Stir in broth and bring to a boil. Add venison and one half teaspoon black pepper. Cover and cook slowly about three hours. Add sour cream just prior to serving. Heat through, but don't boil. Serve over hot cooked noodles or rice.

   Yield: serves four persons

Patricia Maurer
Dumont, NJ

Green Chili Stew

1 ½ pounds venison or elk, cut in ⅔ inch pieces
 4 ounces green chilies, chopped
 2 onions, chopped
 2 pounds tomatoes, canned, chopped
 2 cloves garlic, crushed
 2 bell peppers, chopped
 2 tablespoons flour
 3 tablespoons cooking oil
 1 teaspoon cumin
 2 teaspoons oregano

1 teaspoon salt, optional
½ teaspoon black pepper
2 bay leaves
½ cup hot water

In a ten inch dutch oven or stew pot sauté onions and bell peppers in one tablespoon hot cooking oil until soft. Mix half the chilies, all tomatoes, garlic, herbs and seasonings in a separate bowl. Remove softened onions and bell peppers from dutch oven and mix with other ingredients in bowl. Brown flour in remaining hot cooking oil in dutch oven and add meat. Stir meat until it browns, then add hot water and bay leaves. Cover and cook until tender. Remove bay leaves, add ingredients from bowl, and cook about a half hour. While stew is cooking sample the liquid, and add more chilies if necessary for desired piquancy.

Yield: about four pints

Jack K. McPardee
Albuquerque, NM

American Hunter Stew

1 ½ pounds cubed venison stew meat
 1 pound cubed squirrel or rabbit
 2 cups finely chopped onions
 ½ cup diced celery
 1 cup finely chopped carrots
 2 cups diced potatoes
 ½ cup parsnips (optional)
1 ½ cups diced fresh tomatoes
1 ½ cups all purpose flour, approximately (to dredge meat)
 1 cup dry sherry or marsala wine
 ½ teaspoon thyme leaves
3 ½ cups water
 ½ cup canola or other quality oil for cooking
 2 tablespoons gravy enhancer (Gravy Master)
 4 tablespoons ketchup
   salt and pepper to taste

In a large stainless steel pot or cast iron dutch oven, over medium heat, sauté onions, carrots and celery in two tablespoons oil. Once onions become transparent, remove mixture from pot and set aside. Reduce heat to low.

Add remaining oil to pot and while waiting for it to warm up to temperature, generously flour stew meat.

Return temperature to medium and sauté all meat until it is evenly browned. Quickly add five to six tablespoons of your left-over flour, sprinkling over meat and stirring until all oil is absorbed. This is the thickening agent.

Once mixture begins to bubble, allow to cook for three to four minutes, stirring constantly.

Carefully add wine, deglazing the pot and stirring as you do. Next add water, tomatoes, onions, celery and carrot mixture and mix thoroughly,

Reduce heat to low. Simmer for about one hour, stirring from time to time to prevent sticking.

Now add potatoes, parsnips, ketchup, gravy enhancer and thyme. Stir well and continue to simmer until potatoes are done. They should drop off easily when speared with a fork.

Salt and pepper to taste.

Yield: serves six to eight people

Brian V. Cannavaro
Kalispell, MT

Sam's Spicy Stew
Grandfather Samuel Zimmaro
of Philadelphia's Recipe

2-2½ pounds venison, cubed (may use rabbit, squirrel, quail)
   1 (13 ounce) jar/can brown gravy
   1 large onion, diced
   3 cloves garlic, minced
   1 pound mushrooms, sliced
 2-3 large hot cherry peppers, sliced
   2 (4 ounce) cans hot pepper juice, to taste
   2 (4 ounce) cans water
     pinch of salt
     black or white pepper to taste
   2 tablespoons oil
     carrots, potatoes and celery, diced (optional)

In oil, brown game on both sides over low flame with garlic, onions, salt and pepper. When browned, add peppers, mushrooms, hot pepper juice and gravy. Let simmer for about five minutes. Add water (and optional vegetables, if desired) and continue to simmer on low flame for approximately 30 to 45 minutes or until game is tender, stirring occasionally.

As a hearty stew, try omitting potatoes and serve over rice or noodles.

Serve with a hearty loaf of Italian bread for dipping ... our favorite!

Branden Peacock
Cherry Hill, NJ

Al's Venison

¾ cup tomato juice
1½ cups water
2 beef bouillon cubes, dissolved
1½ cups chopped onion
¾ teaspoon paprika
2 teaspoons salt
pepper to suit
3 pounds venison stew meat
½ cup olive oil
flour

Dredge venison in flour and brown on all sides in fry pan with olive oil. Put all ingredients in pressure cooker. Cook for 25 minutes at 15 pounds pressure. Let pressure drop of its own accord. Serve with noodles

Yield: five to six servings

Albert Janwich
Matawan, NJ

Spicy Hearty Venison Stew

1 pound venison, cut into 1 inch cubes
2 tablespoons olive oil
3 cloves garlic, minced
1 tablespoon worcestershire
½ teaspoon Tabasco
1 can chicken broth
1 (28 ounce) can tomatoes, cut into chunks with liquid
3 medium onions, cut into wedges
2 medium carrots, cut into bite size chunks
½ large bell pepper, diced
8 medium mushrooms, cut into quarters
1 small rutabaga or parsnip, diced
¼ teaspoon gumbo filé
2 medium bay leaves
   salt and pepper to taste

Brown venison in dutch oven with olive oil, Tabasco, worcestershire and garlic. When browned, add vegetables and other ingredients. Bring to a boil then reduce heat and simmer for 45 minutes to one hour.

Serve in bowls over steamed rice or buttered noodles. This is an excellent pick-me-up, warming meal, for cold Montana day or at camp.

Yield: four to six

John W. Townsend
Trout Creek, MT

Czech Flavored Deer Stew

2 pounds cubed deer meat
1 large onion
1 tablespoon oil
1 tablespoon catsup
2 beef bouillon cubes, dissolved
1 large carrot, sliced
2 cut up potatoes (optional, can use rice or noodles)
1 tablespoon instant coffee
2 tablespoons flour
   water to cover
   salt and pepper
   dash of parsley (optional)

Have deer meat at room temperature, simmer onion in heavy stew pan with oil. Add meat and cut up vegetables.

Cover with a heavy lid and simmer one hour or until meat is tender. Can be served over noodles or rice, omitting potatoes of course.

Last 15 minutes add coffee and flour mixture with enough water to make a nice gravy.

Virginia N. Strohm
Lititz, PA

A Party Stew

- 10 pounds venison, cubed
- 4 pounds potatoes
- 2 pounds onions
- 2 pounds carrots
- 1 stalk celery
- 2 pounds turnips (white or yellow)
- 2 large cans tomato soup
- 2 large cans beef broth
- 4–5 bay leaves
- 1 tablespoon thyme
- 1 tablespoon marjoram
- 1 tablespoon garlic salt
- 1 teaspoon black pepper
- ⅓ cup brown sugar
- 2 cups red wine
- ¼ cup worcestershire

Dredge venison in flour and brown in skillet. Add browned meat to large stew pot (you may need two pots). Cover with water and add onions cut in slices. Allow meat and onions to simmer for about two hours. Add carrots, turnips, celery, potatoes, tomato soup, beef broth, crumbled bay leaves and other spices, brown sugar, wine, and worcestershire sauce. Add additional water if needed and continue to simmer at low heat for two or more hours.

This recipe should serve about forty people. Most stew recipes call for meat and vegetables plus spices and seasonings; this recipe makes a delicious stew. You might want to add some of your own ingredients or omit some mentioned here. You can substitute any wild game meat in place of venison if you like.

Gene Prickette
Waco, TX

Venison Burgundy Stew

2 pounds venison stew meat
8 ounces burgundy wine
4 large potatoes
1 large white or yellow onion
3 bay leaves
  garlic to taste
4-6 ounces catsup

Cut venison to bite size pieces, put in stew pot with wine, bay leaves, garlic and catsup. Simmer for one half hour. Add thinly sliced potatoes and onion, simmer for another one half hour.
  Serve with a fresh salad and enjoy!

Jack Seebacher
Johnstown, PA

Deer Ragout

2½ pounds deer (possibly leg) cut into 1 inch cubes
1¾ cups red wine
  1 small onion, chopped
  2 carrots, sliced
  1 rib celery, chopped
  1 clove garlic, chopped
    sprig of thyme
  1 bay leaf
  6 tablespoons butter
    flour
½ pound fresh mushrooms, sliced
  2 tablespoons brandy
    salt and peppercorns

Marinate venison 48 hours in the refrigerator in red wine, onion, carrot, celery, thyme, bay leaf, a pinch of salt and some peppercorns. Melt four tablespoons of butter, drain venison almost dry, roll carefully in flour and brown in butter over high heat. Add marinate, season with salt and peppercorns (careful now!) and simmer, covered, for at least two hours over medium heat. Sauté mushrooms in remaining butter. When meat is tender to the fork, remove it from pan juices and filter juices through strainer. Pour strained sauce over meat, add mushrooms and brandy and reheat until bubbly. Season to taste if necessary with additional salt and pepper.

Yield: serves four

Luigi Farina
Brooklyn, NY

Hunter's Stew Wellington

3 pounds venison, cubed and lightly floured
½ cup oil, may add more if needed (to brown venison)
½ stick butter
4 slices bacon, minced
4 cloves garlic, minced or crushed
1 teaspoon rosemary
4 fresh basil leaves or ½ teaspoon dried
2 apples, minced, red or golden delicious
2 stalks celery
1 large onion, minced
4 large carrots, diced
2 tablespoons Gravy Master
5 cups apple cider or apple juice
¾ cup sour cream
1 sheet Pepperidge Farm pastry

Brown meat in oil and remove meat and add bacon to brown. Add meat to bacon and drippings with garlic, butter, rosemary, basil, celery, carrots, onion, apple juice and Gravy Master. Mix and cook over medium to low heat for two and one half hours, until carrots are tender (may thicken with two tablespoons corn starch and six tablespoons water). Add sour cream and mix well. Season with salt and pepper. Put all above into baking dish and cover top with pastry sheet rolled out to cover baking dish. Prick pastry with fork. Bake one half hour or longer till crust is lightly browned.

Jack Stroming
Pompano Beach, FL

255

Microwave Venison Stew

  2 pounds venison stew meat
  4 tablespoons flour
  2 tablespoons butter or margarine
  1 cup chopped carrots
  1 cup chopped parsnips
  1 medium onion
  1 (4 ounce) can mushrooms
  1 (8 ounce) can tomato sauce
  1 (10¾ ounce) can cream of mushroom soup
1½ cups water
  1 tablespoon salt
  ½ teaspoon Ragin' Cajun spices
  ¼ teaspoon pepper

Coat meat with flour, place butter and meat in a two quart glass dish with lid. Microwave on high for 15 minutes or until meat is brown. Stir in remaining ingredients and cover. Cook on medium low for 20 minutes. Stirring twice. Cool for another 15 minutes or until meat and vegetables are tender.

Serve with fresh baked bread.

Ken Murkett
Norwich, CT

Venison, Moose, Caribou Delight

1½ pounds meat, trimmed and cut into 1 inch cubes
  ¼ cup flour
    salt and pepper
  ½ cup chopped onions
  ½ cup green peppers
  1 small can mushrooms, drained
1½ cups plum sauce
  3 tablespoons oil
  ½ cup water
  1 cup red cooking wine

Put oil in fry pan, drop meat in oil and stir until well covered with oil, flour and fry until well browned. Add onions, green pepper, mushrooms, salt and pepper to taste, water, plum sauce and wine. Simmer until meat is tender.

Serve over rice or with boiled potatoes and vegetables.

This is also good with game birds.

Bill Armour
Haines, AK

Shotgun Stew

1 pound ground venison
5 diced potatoes
½ teaspoon salt
¼ teaspoon cayenne pepper
1 (16 ounce) can stewing tomatoes
½ cup vegetables (okra, corn, peas, beans, can be fresh,
    frozen or leftovers)
1 (6 ounce) can tomato paste
1 slice of bacon

Brown venison with bacon, breaking meat into BB-sized pieces.
In separate pot, barely cover potatoes with water. Boil for 20
minutes. Add meat and remaining ingredients. Simmer until
vegetables are tender.

Serve with corn bread and pass the hot sauce!

Winnie Alphonse
Forked River, NJ

Venison Stew, Home Style

2 pounds venison chuck or rear quarter, cut into one
    and a half inch cubes
2 medium potatoes
1 cup celery
2 medium size carrots
2 medium size onions
2 cloves garlic
1 quart soup, broth or water

Cut potatoes, carrots and onions into one inch cubes. Put in cold
water and set aside. Slice garlic and put in iron skillet or dutch
oven and brown in small amount of fat or oil. Add venison and
braise for 10 to 15 minutes on low heat or until brown. Add one
quart soup, broth or water and cook for 30 to 45 minutes on
low heat. Add onions, potatoes and carrots to meat and cook
till tender, about 45 minutes. Can be thickened with two tablespoons flour or cornstarch and water mixture. One ounce burgundy wine can be added just prior to serving.

This is a proven recipe for 30 or more years.

Yield: serves six to eight hungry people

Earl Conrad
Glasford, IL

Venison and Lentil Stew

2-3 pounds bite size pieces of venison
  5 tablespoons oil
    flour for coating venison
  2 cup lentils, washed and drained
  2 cans rotel tomatoes, chopped
  1 onion, chopped
  ½ cup soy sauce
    salt and pepper

Coat venison with flour and brown in hot oil in large dutch oven. Remove venison and stir in chopped onions. Cook onions for three to five minutes. Return venison to dutch oven along with tomatoes and soy sauce. Add three and one half cups water, cover and simmer for two to three hours or until meat is tender. Salt and pepper to taste. Serve alone or over rice.

Jim Doescher
Panama City, FL

Quick Venison Stew

1 quart canned venison or canned bear
1 can cream of mushroom soup
1 can beef consommé
2 cups frozen mixed vegetables, can substitute 2 cups leftovers
1 (16 ounce) can sliced potatoes, can substitute 2 cups boiled or sliced leftovers
1 small jar pearl onions or 1 small sweet Spanish onion, diced

Combine all ingredients with undiluted soup and consommé. Cover pot and simmer 30 minutes over low heat. Season and serve.

Yield: five servings

Charles J. Neuendorf
Loyal, WI

Kentucky Oven Venison Stew

2-3 pounds venison stew or roast meat cut into chunks
    with all fat removed
  8 potatoes
12 carrots
  5 onions
  4 stalks celery
  2 large green peppers
  1 can zesty tomato soup
  1 can tomato bisque or 2 cans zesty or tomato soup
  1 can cream of mushroom soup
  1 can golden mushroom soup
    seasoned salt
    pepper

Place meat in roasting pan, season with seasoned salt and pepper. Cut up potatoes, carrots, onions, celery and green peppers in chunks and place all over meat. Cover with zesty tomato soup, tomato bisque, cream of mushroom and golden mushroom over the top and smooth out over meat. May add a little water or wine, just a little to get it started (not much). Cover and bake slowly until done. You may need to check halfway through to mix a little, but leave meat on the bottom. Bake at 300 to 325 degrees for two and a half to three hours.

Serve with French bread and salad.

Betty A. King
Berry, Ky

— DOUG PIPER

Stroganoff

Venison Stroganoff

1 pound venison, cut into cubes
¼ cup flour
1 teaspoon salt
⅛ teaspoon pepper
   dash of seasoned salt
2 tablespoons bacon fat, olive oil or vegetable oil
1 large onion, chopped
4 cloves garlic, minced
½ pound fresh mushrooms, sliced
3 tablespoons parsley, chopped — reserve 1 tablespoon
   for garnish
1 green pepper, diced
10 ounces beef broth
1 tablespoon worcestershire sauce
   dash of Tabasco
1 cup sour cream

Combine flour and seasoning, roll meat in mixture. Heat fry pan and add fat, when hot add meat and brown on all sides. Add onion and garlic, sauté two minutes. Add broth, worcestershire and Tabasco and bring to a boil. Cover and simmer until green peppers are tender, about 15 to 20 minutes. Stir in sour cream. Heat at low simmer, do not boil. Sprinkle with reserved parsley. Serve over buttered egg noodles.

Mary E. Carvalho
Cranford, NJ

Venison Stroganoff #2

I use packaged dry mix to make stroganoff. We have found that it works very well with venison that has been tenderized like a cube steak. If venison has a strong wild scent to it, place meat in a shallow pan with one half water and one half apple vinegar. Let it set two or three hours. Rinse meat well and cut it into small pieces. Proceed as package directions state, but simmer for one hour. Mushrooms may be added for flavor. Serve over noodles or rice.

Sarah J. Rockhold
Belen, NM

Venison Stroganoff #3

1 pound steak, cut in very thin strips or 1 pound
    ground venison
¼ cup butter
2 cloves garlic, minced
1 large onion, chopped
1 beef bouillon cube
¼ teaspoon black pepper
1 (8 ounce) can cream of mushroom soup
2 tablespoons catsup
2 tablespoons flour
2 tablespoons minced parsley
1 cup sour cream
    hot cooked noddles or rice

Brown venison in butter. Add garlic and onion and cook until tender. Add beef bouillon, pepper, mushrooms, mushroom soup and catsup. Mix together, cover and cook on low heat for 20 minutes.

Mix together flour, parsley and sour cream. Add four tablespoons hot liquid from meat dish. Stir and pour sour cream mixture into cooking pan with hot meat. Heat thoroughly. Serve over hot cooked noodles or rice.

Gordon F. Shiflet
Frazeysburg, OH

261

Venison Stroganoff #4

2 pounds venison tenderloin, cut ino ¾ inch cubes
1 (8 ounce) package cream cheese
2 cups chopped onions
1 (10½ ounce) can mushroom soup, fresh mushrooms
    can be added if desired
1 (10½ ounce) can onion soup
1 cup sweet vermouth
¼ cup wine vinegar
1 teaspoon salt
½ teaspoon each: pepper, tarragon leaves, marjoram
    leaves, bon appetit, rosemary leaves, sweet basil
    leaves and parsley flakes
½ cup flour
1 cube butter

Combine one half cup flour, salt and pepper and coat meat. Melt one half cube butter in skillet, brown meat on both sides. Add cream cheese to meat and mix well. Add mushroom soup (fresh mushrooms) and onion soup. Add onions prepared in separate pan with one half cube butter. Add all other ingredients and simmer for two hours. Serve with domestic and wild rice mix.

Gene Southwell
Prineville, OR

Ground Venison Stroganoff

1 pound ground venison
1 yellow onion, sliced
1 (10 ounce) can mushroom soup
½ teaspoon garlic salt
1 (2½ ounce) jar sliced mushrooms
4 tablespoons catsup
1 tablespoon worcestershire sauce
1 (8 ounce) carton sour cream

Brown ground venison. Add onion and cook five minutes. Add mushroom soup, garlic salt, mushrooms, catsup and worcestershire sauce and cook for 10 minutes. Stir in sour cream and warm through. Serve over cooked noodles.

Berneta Austenfeld
Emporia, KS

262

Hunting Camp Venison Stroganoff

1 ½ pounds venison ham steak, sliced thin approx-
      imately ⅛ inch thick and 1 ½ inches long
 ¼ cup cooking oil
 1 cup mushrooms, sliced (fresh if available)
 1 cup onion, chopped
 1 cup cream of mushroom soup, undiluted
 1 cup flour, seasoned with salt and pepper
 1 package beef flavor instant broth or beef bouillon
      cube
 1 cup water
      splash red wine (if desired)
      garlic salt (or powder), salt and pepper to taste
 ½ –1 cup sour cream

Place seasoned flour in a bag and shake meat until each piece
is coated. Save flour for thickening if needed. Brown venison in
a dutch oven with a small amount of oil. Remove meat and sauté
chopped onion and mushrooms in remaining oil. Return meat
to dutch oven and add mushroom soup, beef flavor packet (or
dissolved bouillon cube), water and seasoning and bring to a boil.
Stir to blend all ingredients. Boil for three to five minutes, reduce
heat to just under a boil, add a splash of red wine and additional
water as required for a consistency that will cook without sticking. Cook covered, stirring occasionally, for about one hour or
until meat is tender. Remove from heat, stir in sour cream. Serve
on toast points.

Note: This can be served on rice or noodles, but for some
reason it tastes much better on toast. Enlarge the recipe into a
big pot size for leftovers or make it ahead for it seems to be even
better the next day.

Yield: feeds four hungry hunters

W. Raymond Seal
Sumter, SC

Roasts

Yankee Venison Roast

The evening prior to dinner have venison roast (2 pounds or so) defrosted, cleaned and trimmed. Place venison in a regular size cooking bag and place in a 9x9 inch or larger roasting pan. Next, in a bowl mix the following to make venison marinade.

½ teaspoon thyme
2 cloves garlic
½ cup orange juice
1 tablespoon worcestershire sauce
2 tablespoons each, steak sauce and lemon juice
1 bay leaf
1 medium onion, chopped (save ½ for later)
½ cup rosé wine
1 tablespoon parsley
½ teaspoon season salt
½ teaspoon black pepper (lemon pepper)

Pour marinade over roast and turn several times to coat thoroughly. Sprinkle generously with salt and lemon pepper. Seal cooking bag and refrigerate roast in roasting pan until the next morning. Next morning turn venison roast over to thoroughly marinate venison on the other side. Once again refrigerate until two hours prior to dinner. Approximately two hours before dinner time preheat oven to 325 degrees. Allow 45 minutes cooking time per pound of deer meat. (Two pounds or so equals one and a half to one three quarters hours cooking time required). At the same time remove marinated venison roast from the refrigerator and add:

4 ounces fresh mushrooms, sliced
1 large bell pepper, sliced
4 fresh sweet carrots, chopped
2 stalks fresh celery, chopped
½ teaspoon salt
½ medium onion saved from marinade

In a jar add two tablespoons corn starch and one half cup water. Shake until dissolved. Pour over venison roast and bake for one and a half to one three quarters hours. Serve chunks of delicious venison roast and vegetables along with or over your favorite rice.

Steve Loder
Lansdale, PA

Camp Roast Venison

    2-3 pounds rump roast
      2 garlic cloves, slivered
      1 large sweet onion, sliced thinly
      3 Jonathan apples, cored, sliced, not peeled
 1-12 whole peeled carrots and whole peeled potatoes,
          quartered (depending on size of pan)
      2 (10¾ ounce) cans Campbell's golden mushroom soup
        garlic/parsley/salt to taste
        lemon pepper to taste
      2 tablespoons worcestershire sauce
      6 drops Tabasco
      1 bay leaf

Trim all possible fat from venison. Place slivers of garlic evenly in slits in meat. Place in roasting pan according to size of roast and quantity of carrots and potatoes to be cooked. Empty soup into pot over medium heat. Add worcestershire, Tabasco, salt, pepper and bay leaf. Simmer until gently blended. Place carrots and potatoes around meat. Place apple and onion slices on top of meat and vegetables. Pour heated mushroom soup mix over the assemblage in roasting pan. A variation of this for camp would be to use a Dutch oven with a self basting lid. Dig a pit and fill with hot coals. Work dutch oven into a hollow in coals with a shovel. Pull coals up over the top of pot leaving bail standing upright. Shovel dirt over the top of pit, being careful not to dislodge the lid and also to leave bail sticking up where it will be easy to locate. We have fixed the above recipe in camp in this manner at breakfast and returned from a hard day's hunt that evening to a fine pot roast dinner. Works better than the crock pot back home.

Cook in the oven back home at 425 degrees for approximately one hour until done.

Gravy may be served over vegetables and/or bread slices.

Yield: serves four to six, depending on their appetite

Cliff Keeler
Camdenton, MO

265

Venison Roast Sauerbraten

    4–5 pound venison roast (tied as with a roast beef)
      1 tablespoon salt
      ½ teaspoon pepper
      2 onions, sliced
      1 carrot, sliced
      1 stalk celery, chopped
      4 cloves
      4 peppercorns
      1 pint red wine vinegar
      2 bay leaves
      8 tablespoons butter
      5 tablespoons flour
      1 tablespoon sugar
  15–20 gingersnaps, crushed

Season roast with salt and pepper. Place in glass, enamel or earthenware bowl. Combine onions, carrot, celery, cloves, peppercorns, vinegar and bay leaves and two and one half pints water or enough to cover meat. Cover and put in refrigerator for four days. Turn meat if necessary to marinate entire roast.

On the fifth day, remove from refrigerator, drain meat, sauté in three tablespoons butter in enamel, glass or earthenware until seared on all sides. Add marinade liquid and bring to a boil, then lower heat and let simmer about three hours. Melt remaining five tablespoons butter in a pan. Stir in flour smoothly, add sugar, blend and let brown to a nice dark color. Add to simmering meat mixture. Cover and continue cooking until meat is tender, about one hour. Remove meat to a warmed serving platter. Stir crushed gingersnaps into pot of juice and cook until thickened. Pour gravy over meat.

I usually serve this with cold beer and raisin-pumpernickel bread and it is always a big hit.

Yield: serves eight or more

Daniel A. Cea
Peekskill, NY

Smoked Venison and Ham

1 (5–7 pounds) venison hindquarter roast
1 (8–10 pounds) fresh uncooked ham
1 can sliced pineapple
1 gallon apple juice
1½ gallons good red wine
1 (20 pound) bag charcoal (have extra on hand)
6–8 chunks hickory
3–4 large onions
10 garlic cloves
1 can Tony's Creole seasoning or equivalent
1 Mr. Meat smoker or equivalent

To prepare venison, make sure meat is free of all fat and membrane. Make small deep cuts in meat and stuff with onion and garlic. Sprinkle generously all over with Tony's Creole seasoning. Let this chill overnight, then let it stand at room temperature for at least one hour before cooking.

Note: Season to taste, but venison takes a lot more seasoning than beef or other meat.

To prepare ham, make small deep cuts in meat and stuff with onion and garlic. Sprinkle all over with Tony's Creole seasoning. Chill overnight, then let stand at room temperature for at least one hour.

Line bottom of smoker pan with foil and fill with heaping amount of charcoal and light. Fill water pan with apple juice, wine, hickory chunks and water. Place venison roast on bottom rack. Place ham on top rack, place pineapple slices on top with toothpicks. Place lid on and let it cook for 10 to 12 hours.

Periodically check water and charcoal. Keep water in pan at all times. Service water and charcoal pans through access door because removing lid will let heat escape and meat will take longer to cook.

About two hours before meat is cooked, take hickory chunks out of water pan and place in charcoal.

Note: Do not expect any leftovers!

Clyde J. LaPorte
Denham Springs, LA

Marinated Venison or Elk Roast
with Sweet Vadalia Onions and
Morel Bourgionne Gravy

A lot of deer taken in my part of the country tend to be gamey or tough depending upon the age of the animal and its eating habits. The brining process I use will make roast more palatable to those without an acquired taste for wild game. This brine also works well on duck and partridge, if you substitute chicken base for beef base.

Brine Marinade:

1½ gallons water
⅛ cup balsamic vinegar
¼ cup burgundy
¼ cup beef base
¼ cup sugar
¼ cup crushed juniper berries
2 large vidalia onions, sliced thick (6 slices per onion)

Roast and Gravy:

4–6 pounds venison roast (preferably from the 'round' with some fat left on)
3 garlic cloves
¼ cup burgundy
2 tablespoons beef base
sliced onions from brine
6–8 morel mushrooms
2 teaspoons sugar
4 cups water
1 teaspoon celery seed
5 sticks butter (four are for roux)

Put roast in a large stainless steel pot or suitable tupperware container. Combine all ingredients of marinade except onions and mix thoroughly until sugar, salt and beef base are dissolved.

Pour over roast and add onion slices. If roast is not completely covered by liquid, it must be turned over every 12 hours. Marinate roast for 48 hours prior to cooking, occasionally stirring marinade to prevent settling. The roast's exterior will appear whitish after awhile. This is nothing to worry about, as a brine of this type will actually begin to "cook" the roast.

Remove from marinade two hours before cooking and pat dry

with a clean towel. Save onion slices and discard the marinade. Place roast in a baking pan fat side up. Let meat get to room temperature.

Peel garlic, slice cloves in half, and place each piece in a slit in the fat side of roast, equally spread apart and far enough in so garlic is level with top of meat. Lay onions over roast and secure them with tooth picks. There should be enough slices to completely cover the roast. Place any extras in the bottom of pan.

Add about three cups water to pan and one tablespoon beef base. Melt two tablespoons butter and baste onions.

Preheat oven to 400 degrees. Place roast in oven uncovered and cook for about 45 minutes to an hour, or until internal temperature is about 125 degrees (since oven temperatures vary). The roast will be a perfect medium-rare. It is always a good idea to use a meat thermometer when cooking roasts. Occasionally baste onions with pan drippings and keep about two cups liquid in pan while cooking by adding more water.

When roast is done, turn oven off and pour pan drippings into a two quart stock pot. Keep roast warm while making gravy.

For the gravy, add 1 tablespoon beef base and enough water to make about one quart liquid. Add burgundy, sugar and celery seed. Wash and slice morels and add to liquid. Bring to a full boil and remove any 'foam' on surface. If sauce tastes bland, add a little more beef base.

Melt butter and whisk enough flour for a batter consistency. Add this roux to sauce while whisking constantly to prevent lumping. Bring back to a full boil. When gravy is thick, remove from heat.

To serve, remove toothpicks, onions and garlic. Slice thin with browned onions on top and drizzle gravy over onions.

Henry J. Homan
New London, NH

Chapter 7
Fish Recipes

Grilled Trout

    1 teaspoon lemon juice
    ½ cup white wine
    ¼ teaspoon fresh ground pepper
    2 teaspoons butter or margarine
    ¼ teaspoon paprika
    ¼ teaspoon garlic powder
    ¼ teaspoon dry mustard
    ¼ teaspoon marjoram
    ¼ teaspoon basil
  2-4 trout
      paprika
      non stick cooking spray

Melt butter. Combine with other ingredients. Microwave one and a half minutes.

Spray outer skin of trout with cooking spray. Dust with paprika. Baste inside of trout with sauce, using enough to moisten very well (some sauce should run off trout). Wrap each trout in foil. Grill three to four minutes per side or until center bone lifts out easily.

Serve remaining sauce as a warm accompaniment.

Suzy Stefani
Rillton, PA

Baked Crappie Fillets — ala Italian

16 crappie fillets
½ stick oleo, melted
2 thin slices red sweet onion, chopped
   pinch of sage
   pinch of thyme
1 drop Tabasco
   parsley flakes
   garlic, parsley, salt
   lemon pepper
   parmesan cheese

Place crappie fillets flat in a large pyrex or ceramic baking dish. They may touch, but not overlap each other. Place butter in small pan (such as single poached egg pan) and turn heat up to melt butter. Be careful not to scorch it. Place chopped onion, sage, thyme and Tabasco in butter and simmer until onion pieces start turning translucent. Pour evenly over the fillets in baking dish. Salt and pepper to taste. Then lightly sprinkle parmesan cheese and parsley flakes evenly over fillets. Bake in oven at 350 degrees until white and flaky, approximately eight to ten minutes. If not a carousel microwave, be sure to turn every two minutes.

This makes a nice alternative to fried fish.

Yield: serves up to four persons (as long as they only eat their share)

Cliff Keeler
Camdenton, MO

Deep Fried Fish

Take Ritz or Club crackers and roll with rolling pin until very fine. Put this in a dish and set aside. Beat together 2 eggs and 2 cups milk and set aside. Mix together 2 cups flour and 2 tablespoons salt. You now have 3 dishes setting in a row. Take your damp fish and roll in flour, then into milk and egg and then in cracker crumbs. Now place into hot oil (375 degrees) until golden brown.

This is great for walleye!!

David E. Zuercher
Orrville, OH

273

Pickled Fish and Cream

   large fish fillets
   white vinegar
1 cup sugar
⅛ cup salt
2 tablespoons pickling spices wrapped in a cheesecloth
1 medium onion, sliced thin
   sour cream
   quart jar

Cut fillets into bite sized pieces. Fill quart jar about one half full of vinegar and add sugar, salt and spices. Shake well until salt and sugar are dissolved.

Begin filling jar by alternating chunks of fish with onions until full. Make sure all fish is covered. Cap and refrigerate for seven to ten days.

Remove from refrigerator and drain in a colander. Remove spices. Place fish and onions in a large bowl and add enough sour cream to completely cover it, gently mix together and return to jar. Recap and store in refrigerator. It will keep as long as sour cream is good.

Fix a day or two ahead of time for a party. Enjoy!

Tom Fisher
Homerville, OH

Cajun Crawfish Etouffee

1 pound crawfish, or shrimp may be used
2 sticks margarine
3 large onions, chopped
1 large bell pepper, chopped
1 clove garlic, chopped fine
1 (6 ounce) can tomato sauce
1 (10 ounce) can rotel tomatoes with chili
½ bunch green onions, chopped
½ teaspoon cayenne pepper
   salt to taste
½ teaspoon black pepper
   crawfish fat if available

Sauté onions, bell pepper and garlic in margarine until onions are clear. Add crawfish fat if available. Mash rotel tomatoes, add along with chopped green onions and tomato sauce. Cook down for about 30 to 40 minutes. Add crawfish tails and cook for about 20 minutes. Add seasonings to taste and cook for 10 more minutes. Serve over rice. *"C'est si bon."*

Yield: serves four persons

Carl J. Bourque
Prairieville, LA

Cajun Fish Fry

Use this recipe on whole scaled fish, fillets of bass and catfish. It brings out the real flavor and is inexpensive.

    2 cups yellow corn meal
 1 ½ teaspoons garlic powder
    1 teaspoon cayenne pepper, use creole seasoning if
        available
 1 ½ teaspoons salt

Place fish in a bowl of tap water. Mix remaining ingredients in a covered 8x10 tupperware bowl, drop in four or five fish at a time, shake for about 10 seconds until fish is well coated. Cook in hot oil for four to five minutes, don't overcook. This will be some of the best fish you have ever tasted.

Yield: will batter about 25 whole bream

Carl J. Bourque
Prairieville, LA

Baked Fish

  10 fish fillets (bass, catfish, red fish, etc.)
   1 cup milk
   2 teaspoons salt
     Italian bread crumbs
 ¼ stick butter

Add milk and salt into a bowl. Dip fish fillets into milk and then into Italian bread crumbs that have been placed in tupperware bowl for shaking. Place fillets on a cookie sheet, drip on melted butter and bake at 500 degrees for about 10 to 15 minutes.

Yield: five servings

Carl J. Bourque
Prairieville, LA

How to Cook a Bluegill

I used to live in southern Ohio and while there I enjoyed catching bluegill on very light fly fishing tackle. We used to do bank fishing while camping in reclaimed coal strip mines. The bluegill is fun to catch, because it will strike at anything, but the question of what to do with the catch led to the development of this recipe. Most fishermen regard the bluegill as too small to bother cooking, but it is really quite easy to cook and very delicious. It is an extremely simple, delicious meal and an important part of the ritual of our weekend fishing trips.

3-4 (6 inch) very fresh bluegill per person (uncleaned)
  1 egg
  ½ bottle of beer (use a light flavor, not a heavy bock or dark beer)
  1 (9½ ounce) box cracker meal
  butter or margarine
  vegetable oil
  1 (3 ounce) jar of capers
  ½ lemon per person
3-4 cherry tomatoes per person
  1 green onion per person

Fillet fish. Use a very sharp flexible knife and begin cutting behind gill structures. Keep knife under meat and on top of ribs while sliding it towards tail. Do not separate fillet from tail. Instead flip fillet past tail and continue cutting away from head, but holding knife under meat and separating skin. Two easy cuts per fillet. No gutting. No scaling. All the offal in one easily-disposed-of piece.

In a bowl, make an egg wash using whole egg and one half bottle of beer. Whip with a fork until thoroughly blended.

Empty box of cracker meal onto a plate, a sheet of foil, wax paper or a torn open paper bag.

Grease a skillet with 50/50 mixture of butter or margarine and oil. This is not deep frying, use just a little more than is required to coat the bottom.

Dip each fillet in egg wash, dredge in cracker meal and drop into hot greased skillet. Brown lightly on both sides and serve.

Garnish with a few capers (drained and chopped), green onions, (chopped) and cherry tomatoes (chopped). Serve with lemon juice, salt, and pepper.

James Speed Hensinger
Aurora, CO

Microwave Nuked Trout

2 trout, one pound each
8 ounces sliced almonds
2 lemons
  chopped tomato
  basil
1 teaspoon garlic powder
1 small chopped onion
2 tablespoons butter
1 ounce dry sherry
  salt and pepper to taste

Blanch almonds in a little butter. Set aside. Place trout in glass baking dish. Squeeze one half a lemon on inside of trout, followed by one half the sherry. Dust inside with basil and garlic powder, sprinkle in diced onion. Close trout, squeeze the rest of lemon and sherry over trout then sprinkle on almonds. Equally space butter around fish. Cover with plastic wrap and poke a hole in top to allow moisture to escape. Place in microwave on high for 10 to 11 minutes.

Remove from microwave and allow to stand for two minutes. Uncover and garnish with chopped tomatoes.

Fish and vegetables are excellent when cooked in the microwave. I avoid meat and fowl. My personal preference is to allow meat and fowl to absorb and maintain their own juices while cooking at a slower pace.

Edd Rankin
Colorado Spring, CO

Trout Almandine

4 clean trout
1 lemon
  dry sherry
  onion powder
  basil
¼ pound butter or margarine
¼ cup sliced almonds

Wash trout in cold water. Place in Pyrex baking dish. Dust inside of fish with onion powder, garlic powder and basil. Lightly squeeze lemon inside trout. Sprinkle sherry and additional lemon over outside of fish. Section butter into four pieces and place evenly in dish.

Toast almonds in 400 degree oven for 10 minutes or until light brown. Do not burn. Sprinkle almonds over trout. Cover dish with plastic wrap, pole a hole in plastic and microwave on high power for approximately 11 minutes. Note: check your microwave instruction book. If it is less than 700 watts, adjust to prescribed additional cooking time.

For a conventional oven, *do not cover with plastic wrap*. Cover with foil and bake for 25 minutes at 375 degrees or until trout is flaky. Uncover fish for last five minutes so that they will brown.

Edd Rankin
Colorado Springs, CO

Salmon and Dill Gravlax with Mustard Sauce

2–3 pounds skinless salmon fillets
  1 cup dried dill
2½ tablespoons salt
  5 teaspoons sugar
  ¼ teaspoon each black pepper and allspice

Remove bones from fillets with tweezers. Sprinkle some of the mixed dried ingredients in the bottom of a glass tray, place salmon fillets tightly into glass tray, add more of dried ingredients, then salmon, alternate until you have used all salmon and dried ingredients. Cover loosely with plastic wrap. Place a piece of wood (plywood) cut to fit inside the glass tray on top of fillets. Place a brick or heavy juice bottle (about five pounds in weight) onto plywood to compress fillets. Refrigerate for four days, letting fish to steep in own juices, turning fish once per day. Scrape off with dull knife and slice thinly.

Mustard Sauce:

   2 tablespoons dried Dijon mustard
   1 tablespoon sugar
1½ tablespoons wine vinegar
   ½ teaspoon salt
   ½ teaspoon dried dill
   ⅓ cup salad oil

Beat the above with a fork, makes two thirds cup.

Place gravlax slices on your favorite cracker with mustard sauce.

For variety, use Lapsang Souchong tea leaves (not in a tea bag) instead of dill. This makes a gravlax that tastes smoked.

Avi J. Friedman, courtesy
Leonard Guralnick
Baltimore, MD

Pickled Salmon

4–5 pounds salmon fillets

Brine fish in 100% saturated salt solution using Kosher salt for one and a half to one and three quarter hours. Rinse in cold water, skin fillets and cut into chunks as desired.

Pickling solution:

   1 pint water
   1 pint vinegar
   1 pint light wine or sherry, can use less, and this is
       optional
   ⅓ cup brown sugar
   2 tablespoons pickling spices

Boil pickling solution ingredients and strain off spices. Using a one gallon jar, pack fish in jars with onion slices, lemon slices, carrots, green peppers, cauliflower, broccoli or whatever you want. Refrigerate for one week before eating. Keeps a long time in the refrigerator.

Avi J. Friedman, courtesy
Thom Wischer
Baltimore, MD

279

Baked Rainbow Trout

whole rainbow trout (fresh is best)
Dijon style mustard
strawberry preserves
butter

Clean trout (heads on or off as desired). Coat inside of cavity
with Dijon mustard. Add one or two pats butter, fill cavity with
strawberry preserves. Wrap tightly in aluminum foil. Place in
preheated 450 degree oven and bake approximately 10 minutes
per inch of thickness.

Very good served with wild rice and steamed vegetables.

Terry G. Box
Fayetteville, AR

Baked Stuffed Trout

1 pound trout, cleaned and boned
2 tablespoons chopped shallots
2 tablespoons chopped parsley
2 tablespoons chopped chives
2 tablespoons chopped basil
1 teaspoon grated lemon rind
1 cup butter
2 tablespoons lemon juice
1 teaspoon salt
1 teaspoon pepper

Mix shallots, parsley, chives, basil and lemon rind and cream
with butter. Add lemon juice, salt and pepper. Stuff trout with
mixture. Wrap in foil and place on a buttered baking dish, bake
at 350 degrees for 20 minutes.

Yield: serves two people

Betty A. King
Berry, KY

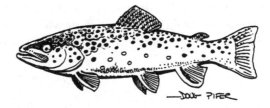

280

Beer Batter Fish

1 cup pancake flour
1 cup beer, can use your flat beer
1 teaspoon lemon and pepper seasoning salt

Blend together. Cut fish fillets in two to three inch chunks and stir into mixture. Let stand for one half hour. At meal time heat one inch oil to very, very hot in a fry pan. Put in fillets and turn until dark brown.

Note: To check temperature of oil, touch it with a wooden match. If it ignites in four or five seconds oil is hot enough.

Leon Gretsch
Big Fork, MN

Jim's Mustard Baked Fish

3 pounds whole fish (red snapper, redfish, etc.)
¼ cup Italian salad dressing
¼ cup mayonnaise
½ stick butter-margarine
2 teaspoons Tony's seasoning or your own seasoning
   salt and pepper
   dash worcestershire sauce
2 tablespoons wine vinegar
1½ tablespoons prepared mustard
1 stalk celery, thin sliced
½ medium onion, chopped
¼ bell pepper, chopped

Wash fish well, pat dry, sprinkle liberally with Tony's seasoning inside and out, both sides, and set aside.

Combine all ingredients except vegetables and fish, stir well until blended over low fire, bring to a boil, reduce heat and simmer for seven minutes. Add vegetables and continue to cook for another 10 to 12 minutes, until vegetables are wilted. Place fish in baking dish, pour mixture over fish, cover with foil, and bake at 350 degrees for one hour. May bake on low rack if preferred.

James D. Sandefur
Oakdale, LA

Fried Bluegill

bluegill
1 cup flour
2 tablespoons lemon and pepper seasoning
½ teaspoon garlic salt
¼ teaspoon season salt

Fillet bluegill. Let stand in water 24 hours. Rinse thoroughly and drain. Combine above ingredients, dredge fillets in flour mixture and fry until crispy on the outside and flaky on the inside. Time will depend on type of pan used.

Larry E. Slightom
Tolland, CT

Smoked Trout

trout
pickling salt

Use only fresh caught trout for smoking. Remove head by cutting just back of pectoral fins, then make a slit along entire bottom side of fish and remove entrails. Remove other fins; you may leave tail or remove it as you desire. Leave skin on fish. From slit made along bottom of trout cut on through fish by the backbone to skin along back, but do not cut through skin.

Prepare brine, the amount depending on how many trout you are going to smoke, by mixing one and one half cups pickling or canning salt to each gallon fresh, clear, cool water. Use only a glass, crockery or plastic container for entire process. Completely cover fish with brine, using a heavy plate to hold fish under brine if necessary. Keep fish in brine for about two hours and try to keep the temperature between 35 to 45 degrees. Refrigerator if weather is warm.

After two hours in brine remove fish and drain, rinse well and drain again for a few minutes. Now dredge and roll trout in pickling salt and layer in container mentioned above. Place a layer of fish in container, add a layer of salt, layer of fish, layer of salt, staggering position of fish. Larger fish will need about 10 hours to dry cure while smaller fish require about eight hours. Then thoroughly rinse meat several times to remove all salt possible. Next lay fish in a warm, dry place for about four hours to dry. During drying a "pellicle" of firmness of the meat will form.

The actual smoking process is next. They may be either cool or hot smoked. To hot smoke, place trout skin side-down on grid in your electric or charcoal smoker/cooker, using fairly low heat and smoke/cook until meat is done but not dried out. Hot smoked trout should be eaten within a couple of weeks and should be kept refrigerated.

There are two methods of cool smoking trout. The first takes one day. String fish on heavy thread, string or clean wire so they do not touch. Place in a smoke house and for full flavor use a mixture of apple, pear and hickory wood chips and smoke for about eight hours. Fast smoked trout may be frozen or refrigerated. Slow smoking takes about a week. String fish or place on racks in your smoke house and keep a slow, easy smoke going constantly for about a week, making sure that temperature inside smoke house or smoker does not rise above 70 degrees, regardless of temperature outside. Store smoked fish in cheesecloth or "breathable" fabric bags and hang in a cool, dry location. Trout smoked by slow process needs no refrigeration and can be eaten as is or may be heated and further cooked before eating.

Jerry Ponder
Fairdealing, MO

— DOUG PIFCC

Sturgeon Jerky

Skin, clean and remove head. Cut part way through, all around, in front of tail. Twist tail and pull to remove cord. Cut into five inch long slabs. Stand slab upright and with a long, thin knife cut down one side of center and around cavity. Turn this slice down and carefully cut remaining red and yellow meat away. Next cut lengthwise into strips as thin as possible, approximately one eighth inch strips.

Marinade:

> **1 cup Chung King soy sauce**
> **4 tablespoons granulated sugar**
> **1 teaspoon ground pepper**

Mix ingredients in a large frying pan and heat fast, continue stirring until mixture starts bubbling. Remove from stove and let cool a little. Add sturgeon strips and let them soak for 20 minutes. Stir occasionally to make sure all strips are coated evenly. Next place strips on cake cooling racks; place foil under racks to catch drippings. Sprinkle ground pepper on strips, using just enough to lightly cover completely. Place racks in oven, dry at 160 degrees for approximately five hours. After drying, put strips in an airtight container and store at room temperature. Amounts can be scaled up or down depending on how may racks your oven can hold.

Steve Dypvik
La Jolla, CA

Steelhead on the Grill

One or more steelhead or salmon fillets with skin left on
butter or margarine
salt and pepper
lemon, optional

When cleaning fish, leave skin on fillet. Rinse fillet off and lay it skin side down on your pre-heated gas or charcoal grill.

Spread some butter or margarine on fish. Salt and pepper to taste and add lemon if desired. Close lid. Check in 15 minutes. Edges will brown when fish is well cooked. Slip spatula under meat and lift off skin to serve.

Stuart Grell
Lafayette, IN

Hot and Sour Sturgeon Soup

1 pound sturgeon fillets, sliced ½ inch thick (trimmed
     white meat only — see author's illustration)
6½ cups water
2 tablespoons chicken bouillon
¼ cup white vinegar
1 large yellow onion, sliced lengthwise
¼ teaspoon ground black pepper
6-8 ounces canned sliced mushrooms, drained
1 tablespoon soy sauce
2 cloves garlic, minced
½ teaspoon dried crushed red pepper
2 tablespoons cornstarch
2 tablespoons cold water
1 egg, beaten
1 green onion, chopped

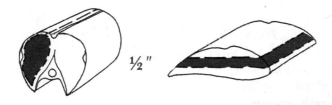

½ "

In a dutch oven or large saucepan put in water, yellow onion
slices, vinegar, pepper and bouillon. Bring to a boil and add fish
fillets. Simmer, covered, for six minutes. Take fish out and add
mushrooms, soy sauce, garlic and red pepper to soup. Bring back
to a boil, cover and simmer for 15 minutes. Cut fish fillets into
one half inch cubes and add to soup. Mix cornstarch and two
tablespoons water in a small bowl. Bring soup back to a boil and
add this mixture, stirring until soup thickens, about one minute.
Add beaten egg, turn stove off and stir one half minute or more
then sprinkle green onion on top and serve. Good luck!

Steve Dypvik
La Jolla, CA

Pickled Fish

2 quarts cubed fish
1 cup pickling salt
3 quarts cold water
1½ cups sugar
2 teaspoons pickling spice
3 medium onions, sliced
    white vinegar to cover

Put fish, salt and water in a gallon crock or glass jar and place in refrigerator for 48 hours. Remove and wash fish well in cold water, cut in bite-size pieces and wash again, drain well.

Put sugar, spices and onions in a jar and add fish, cover with vinegar. Let stand 48 hours in the refrigerator. Now it is ready to eat. It will keep up to six months in the refrigerator. I put mine in pint jars as it is easier to store.

Rupe Knapp
Everly, IA

Ketchikan Barbecue Salmon

2 or more large king salmon, fresh
1 quart honey
1 pint soy sauce
6 fresh lemons
1 cup sherry wine
½ cup olive oil
2 tablespoons rosemary
1 tablespoon dill weed
2 tablespoons powdered ginger
1 tablespoon thyme
1 tablespoon marjoram

Place all but salmon into large pot and heat until honey is more fluid. Squeeze in lemon juice. Stir all ingredients until thoroughly blended. Remove from flame. Keep warm and well-blended. Thoroughly scale and wash fish. Cut into steaks by placing knife at each backbone joint and severing between each vertebra. Rinse each steak and drip dry. Dip into sauce and place on barbecue grill. Cook 12 inches above pre-arrange bed of hot coals. Baste as necessary. Cook approximately four to six minutes on each side.

Serve with green salad and chilled white wine.
Yield: serves 15 to 20 people

Gorden K. Holcomb
Garden Grove, CA

Paté of Salmon

1 pound salmon fillets
1 (6 ounce) can mixed tiny and broken shrimp, drained
1 (6 ounce) can crab meat
4 egg whites, chilled
1 cup heavy cream, chilled
4 tablespoons tomato paste
⅛ teaspoon nutmeg, freshly grated
1½ teaspoons salt
1 teaspoon white pepper
1 teaspoon tarragon leaves, crushed
1 teaspoon rosemary leaves, crushed
  butter
¼ pound boiled ham, thinly sliced
1 package Knorr white sauce mix
2¼ cups milk

In a food processor, grind salmon fillets, shrimp and crab meat to a paste. With machine running, gradually add chilled egg whites and cream. Add tomato paste, nutmeg, salt, pepper, tarragon, and rosemary. Mix until well-blended. Cover and refrigerate while you line the mold.

Preheat oven to 350 degrees. Line the bottom and sides of a greased 9x5 loaf pan with ham slices, reserving one to two slices for the top. Spoon cold paté mixture into loaf pan and cover with remaining slices. Place a piece of wax paper loosely over top of pan. Place pan into a large baking dish and fill dish with enough hot water to reach halfway up the sides of the pan. Bake one hour, or until a knife comes cleanly out of center of loaf. Remove from hot water and let stand for 20 minutes. Carefully run knife around the sides of pan to loosen and un-mold onto platter. Prepare white sauce mix with milk and serve over sliced paté.

Gary D. Wear
Hastings, MI

A Light Coating for Deep Frying Panfish

¾ cup flour
½ cup corn meal
2 teaspoons paprika
½ teaspoon ground black pepper
2 tablespoons chili powder
1 teaspoon salt

Mix above ingredients together. Put in plastic bag and add a few fish fillets. Shake well until fish is well coated. Remove fillets from bag and deep fry.

Gary Straub
West Bend, WI

Beer Batter Fish

Cut any fresh white-fleshed fish into one-inch squares. Place flour in a bowl (amount depends on how many fish you are preparing). Add garlic powder, basil, oregano, salt, pepper and spike. Mix well and then add beer and mix until smooth and the same texture as pancake batter. Deep fry until they float, and enjoy!

James Marchini
Copper Center, AK

How to Fry Fish

While most people who do any amount of reading have learned that eating fish has definite health benefits, most of us have been led to believe that fried fish is unhealthy. The fish is good for us, but most oils used in frying are not. Unsaturated oils are better, and olive oil is the best: we have used this method for may years. Cholesterol levels are safe, and it is simple and tasty. We use a black iron skillet, with just enough virgin olive oil in the pan to prevent the fish from sticking. Skin fillet and cut into serving size pieces. Then immerse into beaten whole eggs, making sure that the whole piece is covered. Each piece is then rolled in cracker meal, (we prefer Italian style, which is pre-seasoned). Heat oil until a small drop of water spatters, then place the fish in the pan, with space between each piece.

The cracker meal turns crispy brown, and adds flavor. Once the fish pieces are well browned, they are turned to brown the opposite side, and then they are done. We believe fish should be cooked just until they are white through, and flake easily. Overcooking turns them tough and many times increases any "fishy" odor which may be present.

A crisp green salad and steamed rice makes a simple, delicious and filling meal with the fish, and almost any white fleshed fish may be used. We have even prepared the dark meats this way along with a number of the tuna family and had excellent results.

The combination of oil, egg and cracker meal accomplishes the following: the hot oil cooks the egg immediately thus preventing penetrating the flesh. The cracker meal turns crispy brown, and adds flavor.

Charlie Davis
Hunting Beach, CA

PoPo's Fish

4-6 fish fillets (perch, bass, catfish, snapper or turbot)
  1 cup cheese chunks
  1 tablespoon butter
  ½ cup white wine or cream
  ½ cup chopped onion
  1 small can sliced water chestnuts
    parsley to taste

Put fillets into a greased casserole. Roll each fillet around a cheese chunk. Pour melted butter, parsley, onions, chestnuts, wine or cream over rolls.

Bake at 300 degrees for 30 minutes. Remove and put remaining cheese on top, put back into oven long enough to melt cheese.

Edie Fitch
Janesville, CA

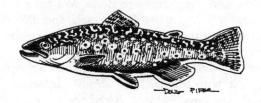

Jersey Clam Pie

½ cup chopped onion
6 tablespoons butter
½ cup flour
3 cups clam liquor (juice from 1 dozen clams)
4 cups chopped clams, chowder size
5 ounces frozen peas
1 can chopped pimentos
2 cups chopped potatoes

Prepare pastry. Cook onion in butter until tender. Cook potatoes until tender, then add pepper to taste. Blend flour with one teaspoon salt and then add all other ingredients.
Cook at 450 degrees for 20 to 25 minutes.

Robert M. McCorristin
Millville, NJ

Trout Loaf

6–7 medium trout
1½ cups cracker crumbs
1 cup milk
1 teaspoon salt
¼ teaspoon pepper
2 tablespoons chopped onion
2 eggs, beaten
catsup

Steam trout for five minutes. When cool, pick bones out and remove skin. Combine all ingredients, make into a loaf, place in greased loaf pan, spread catsup on top and bake at 350 degrees for one hour.

Wanda V. Richardson
Coolville, OH

Oven Smoked Salmon

salmon
table salt
Wright's condensed Liquid Smoke

Fillet salmon; leave skin on. Soak for one hour in salt water to remove blood. Remove from the soak and pat dry with paper towel. Cut in two and one half to three inch pieces. Place on wire racks, skin side down, with pan underneath to catch drippings.

Sprinkle liberally with table salt. Wait one hour. Brush liberally with Liquid Smoke and wait one more hour. Repeat process two more times (six hours in all). Excess liquid will drip into pan underneath. Drain off liquid and bake in oven at lowest temperature (200 degrees) for one and a half to two hours depending on thickness of salmon.

Fish may be frozen or canned. To freeze, place in a Seal-a-Meal bag to prevent drying out. To can, process at 90 minutes for every 10 pounds and add 1 teaspoon olive oil to all salmon except king. King salmon makes its own oil. No oil is needed for freezing.

Skin may be removed after baking. Its purpose is to hold the fish together.

This recipe takes a bit of time but is well worth it when salmon season is long gone.

Mrs. C. R. Woodall
Eagle, AK

Lake Erie Perch Stir Fry

12 fillets Lake Erie perch, boned and dredged in corn starch
1-5 cloves garlic, or to taste
1 (8 ounce) can sliced bamboo shoots
1 (8 ounce) can sliced water chestnuts
¼ pound pea pods, cleaned and sliced once
2 cups fresh bean sprouts
½ cup white wine
soy sauce
corn starch
olive oil

Heat wok. Add about one fourth cup olive oil and coat sides. Cut up garlic and add to oil, browning lightly. Immediately add perch fillets. As fillets start to cook break up into pieces with stirring utensil. After four or five minutes add bamboo shoots, water chestnuts and pea pods. Cook about two minutes, add wine and soy sauce to taste. Finally, add bean sprouts and cook until they are still slightly crunchy. Serve over rice.

This dish must be stirred constantly while cooking.

Yield: four good-sized servings

Helen M. Hurtuk
Bedford, OH

Mayonnaise Baked Fish

Best Foods mayonnaise
garlic salt
your our favorite fish fillet, one half inch thick
oyster sauce, if desired
foil
cookie sheet

Put foil on cookie sheet and spread mayonnaise about one eighth inch thick on foil the size of fish. Sprinkle lightly with garlic salt. Put fillet on top of mayonnaise and another layer of mayonnaise on top of fish with more garlic salt. Put in oven and bake until golden brown, about 10 to 15 minutes.

Allen Chang
Wahiawa, HI

Smoking Fish with Elderwood Chips

1 cup kosher salt
1 cup rock salt
6 cloves garlic
2 tablespoons lemon juice
3 slices fresh ginger, chopped
½ pound brown sugar
1 pint honey
elderwood chips for smoking
5-25 pounds frozen fish fillet, salmon, tuna or halibut

Dissolve salt and spices in warm water and add frozen fish fillets and soak for three hours, stir occasionally. Meanwhile, heat honey in saucepan and add brown sugar when honey is warm. Rinse and dry fish and brush lightly with warm brown sugar and honey mix. Smoke with elderwood for three or four hours. Reapply honey mixture as needed to keep fish moist when done.

R. G. Graig
Escondido, CA

Fish Sausage

20 pounds fish fillets, any kind (we use suckers)
 6 pounds bacon
 ¼ pound soda crackers, rolled or crushed
 8 ounce package pork sausage seasoning
 2 cups powdered milk
 2 cups water

Grind fish through a meat grinder, mix and combine all ingredients. Feed a little bacon in as you grind ingredients the second time. Shape into rolls or patties and freeze. Fry or put into sausage casings and smoke. A great way to get the most out of good tasting fish that has a lot of bones.

Louis Buch
New London, WI

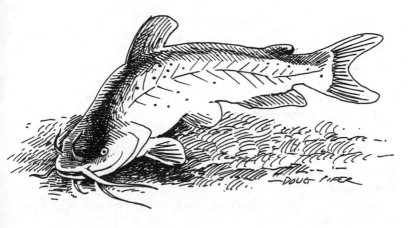

Coquilles St. Jacques

3 pounds small to medium bay scallops
1 tablespoon minced shallot or onions
1 ¼ cups flour
4 egg yolks
1 pound fresh mushrooms
2 cups white wine
1 stick butter
1 cup heavy cream or whipping cream
1 cup bread crumbs

Boil together shallots and wine. Add scallops and cook until scallops are done, about three minutes (do not overcook).

Remove scallops and reserve liquid. Over high heat, cook liquid until reduced to one cup. In a saucepan, melt butter and add flour and cook until flour is done but not brown.

After a few minutes of cooking, add reserved scallop liquid to melted butter and flour mixture. Simmer for 15 minutes. Mix heavy cream with egg yolk and add to mixture. Heat for one more minute. Add cheese and stir until melted.

Sauté mushrooms over high heat in a small amount of butter, drain and add to sauce. Drain scallops well and add to sauce.

Divide mixture into scallop shells, sprinkle bread crumbs over top and put into very hot oven until bread crumbs begin to brown.

Yield: serves six

Dan Dobbins
Columbia, SC

She-Crab Soup

¼ pound butter
½ cup flour
1 pound crab meat
1 pint whole milk
1 pint half-and-half
1 teaspoon Old Bay seasoning (or any seafood seasoning)

Combine butter and flour, cooking over low heat for three to four minutes.

Add milk gradually, stirring constantly, then add seasonings and crab meat.

Simmer on low heat for about 30 minutes until soup is desired consistency. Remove from heat and add sherry and half-and-half. If desired, garnish with crumbled egg yolks.

Dan Dobbins
Columbia, SC

Male (left) and female Blue Crab

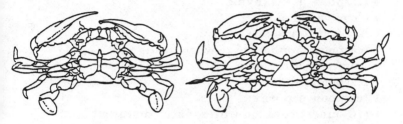

Seafood Quiche

½ cup mayonnaise
2 tablespoons flour
4 eggs, beaten
½ cup milk
4 ounces swiss cheese, grated
4 ounces sharp cheddar cheese, grated
4 strips crumbled, cooked bacon
1 small cup drained mushrooms
½ cup sour cream
1 teaspoon salt
1 teaspoon worcestershire
⅓ cup green onions, chopped
1 (6 ounce) can crab meat or 6 ounces fresh crab meat
1 (4½ ounce) can shrimp or 1 pound fresh shrimp, cooked

Mix all ingredients and pour into a pre-cooked 10 inch pie shell. Sprinkle top liberally with grated parmesan cheese and bake in a 350 degree oven until golden brown on top (about 40 to 45 minutes).

Dan Dobbins
Columbia, SC

Shrimp Gumbo

3 pounds medium to large shrimp, peeled and
   de-veined
4 quarts water
2 ounces shrimp or crab boil (¼ cup)
1 cup each diced celery, onions, bell pepper
6 tablespoons butter
1 (28 ounce) can tomatoes
1 teaspoon dried thyme
1 clove garlic, minced
1 bay leaf (optional)
1 teaspoon gumbo filé powder (optional)
   worcestershire sauce
1 teaspoon salt
1 teaspoon pepper
1 (10 ounce) package frozen okra, defrosted
¼ cup rice

In a large pot, bring four quarts water to a hard boil. Tie shrimp boil into cheesecloth bag and place in boiling water. Add shrimp and return to a boil for approximately three minutes until done. Drain shrimp and reserve two cups stock. Chill shrimp with ice to stop cooking process. Put butter into a dutch oven or heavy pot and cook onion, bell pepper and celery until tender. Add shrimp stock, tomatoes, thyme, garlic, bay leaf, worcestershire sauce, filé powder, salt and pepper and simmer for 45 minutes. Then add shrimp, okra and rice and simmer for 30 minutes until rice is done.

Yield: serves six

Dan Dobbins
Columbia, SC

Seafood Gumbo

2 pounds peeled shrimp
1 pound fish fillets, chopped
1 pound peeled crawfish
2 pints oysters
1 pound crab meat
1 cup olive oil
2 cups flour
3 cups chopped onion
1 cup chopped bell pepper
1 cup chopped green onions
1 cup fresh parsley
4 tablespoons worcestershire
1 tablespoon chopped garlic
3 tablespoons hot sauce
2 quarts cold water
2 tablespoons salt

In a large pot, combine olive oil and flour, mix into a roux. Add onions, bell pepper, green onions, parsley and chopped garlic. Cook together until vegetables are almost done. Add cold water and stir over heat until well mixed. Add remaining ingredients and simmer for several hours. Serve over rice.

Dan Dobbins
Columbia, SC

297

CHAPTER 8
MISCELLANEOUS RECIPES

—DOUG PIPER

The Berries of Death

This isn't really a game recipe but after the hunt, you might find it appropriate.

½ pint raspberries, blueberries or blackberries
1 fifth, quart or litre of vodka (depending on your
politics)

Pour out and save about a cup vodka. Put berries in bottle and top it off with the saved cup of vodka. Put bottle in the refrigerator for a week or so, and give it a shake every couple days. After a week or so, transfer to the freezer compartment. Serve ice cold as a cordial.

Tom H. Nagel
Columbus, OH

No-Bread Stuffing for Game Birds or Poultry

1 sweet potato, cooked firm
1 onion, chopped
1 celery stalk, chopped
1 apple, peeled and diced
1 carrot, shredded
¾ cup walnuts, finely chopped
1 egg, beaten
season to taste, salt and pepper
brown sugar, poultry seasonings

Combine sautéd onion and celery with diced potato. Add remaining ingredients and blend. If stuffing seems too soft or wet, adjust with oat or cornmeal, if too dry, adjust with milk or another egg. Stuff, truss, and roast bird as usual. Cook extra stuffing in ovenware at the same time and baste it with pan drippings for flavor.

This recipe is an outgrowth of stuffing ducks with cut up raw vegetables. Roasting the bird and the vegetables together makes a tasty combination.

This is a kitchen tested recipe. Other combinations of vegetables can be substituted, however, for individual tastes. If you are tired of traditional bread stuffing, I am certain that you will enjoy this variation.

Lawrence C. Ransom
Tucson, AZ

Shish Kebab in the Field

1 pound meat from any four-legged animal (preferably
    lamb or beef) cut into 1 ½ inch cubes
3 medium tomatoes
3 bell peppers
2 onions, white medium
    salt and pepper to taste
1 medium lemon (may substitute oil/vinegar salad
    dressing)

After cutting meat into cubes, place meat and one sliced onion
into a container. Squeeze lemon onto meat and mix, this will
serve to soften meat's fibers, especially if it's wild game. Add salt
and pepper to taste. Let mix sit and marinate for two hours.

After meat has marinated, find some sturdy dry sticks to use
as skewers. You should skewer tomatoes, peppers and remaining onions separately since they'll all cook at different rates.

Place skewers onto "Y" shaped branched forks and above
flames. Keep an eye on the cooking so nothing burns.

When everything is cooked, remove from skewers. Make pita
bread sandwiches. Enjoy.

V. Tarbassian
Framingham, MA

Larry's Venison and Fish Batter

1 cup Drakes batter mix
1 egg
¼ teaspoon pepper
½ teaspoon salt
1 teaspoon garlic powder
3 tablespoons vinegar

Heat grease in deep kettle to almost smoking, we use a wood
match to tell us when our grease is just right. A match tossed
in grease should light in five seconds if grease is hot enough.
If match does not light, remove and try a new match in a few
minutes. Keep grease hot so venison and fish will cook quickly
and not soak up grease. Slice venison in steak or tenderloin cuts
to no more than three eighths inch thick. Thin batter mix with
water to water-like consistency. Dip steak or fish in batter and
cook until golden brown.

Even folks who don't like venison will love this recipe, and you'll
find no better fish batter.

Larry W. Carson
McClure, OH

Polish Pigeon's Stuffed Cabbage

1 good firm head of cabbage
1 medium onion, finely chopped
1 tablespoon butter
1 pound ground venison
½ pound ground pork
1 slice of white bread
½ teaspoon marjoram
2 eggs, beaten
1 cup mushrooms, frozen
½ cup barley (cooked according to instructions)
   salt and pepper to taste
   thin sliced bacon

Cut cabbage in half, boil in salted water until limp, cool and drain. Brown onions in butter, do not burn. Mash frozen mushrooms to a paste. Soak bread in milk, then mash out excess milk.

Mix all ingredients together and spread evenly on cabbage leaves. I use about one and a half tablespoons per leaf. Roll tightly, and pack tightly in a roaster that you have buttered or line the bottom with thin slices of bacon. Add one half cup water and simmer covered until almost dry, about 45 minutes.

Marion A. Koszewski
Breaksville, OH

Hobert's Mulligan

5 pounds wild game (venison, dove, squirrel or duck)
1 pound chopped onions
1 pound chopped bell peppers
1 bunch chopped celery
½ pint cooking oil
½ pound oleo
2 pounds long grain rice
6 tablespoons worcestershire sauce
2 tablespoons Accent salt
2 tablespoons seasoning salt
4–5 bay leaves
   garlic, salt and black pepper to taste

Cover meat with water, bring to a rolling boil. Skim if needed. Add salts and black pepper. Boil one hour, add one half mixed vegetables, bay leaves and cooking oil. Boil until meat is almost done. Add remaining vegetables, garlic and worcestershire sauce. Boil until meat is done. Add more water if needed but not too much.

Bring rice to a rolling boil and rinse in cold water. Add rice and oleo to other ingredients. Cook until rice is done, stirring constantly to prevent rice from sticking.

Yield: serves about 10 people

Hobert Stamper
Heidelberg, MS

Polish Hunter's Stew "Bigos"

In ancient Poland up to the first world war some families had huge estates. One family owned over 80,000 hectares. The forests contained some of Europe's best hunting: deer, hares, bear, wolves, boars, partridges, pheasants, mountain cocks (average 15 pounds), heath cocks, hazel hens, quail, moose, lynx, beaver, and herds of European bison.

Each manor house had a large cooking staff and butchers. Hunting parties were arranged, some parties had 75 hunters. Game was brought back to the manor house, trophies were mounted and the meat was prepared for the hunters and their families. Some of these feasts took six hours to consume.

One of the most popular meals was "Bigos," Hunter's Stew. Sometimes it was strictly made from leftover meat and other times it was made beginning to end from scratch. It was served before the soup with a pitcher of crystal clear gold flecked vodka from Gdansk.

This is great prepared the day before then re-heated.

> **any kind of game cut into cubes off bone**
> 1 **good sized head of cabbage**
> 2 **onions, finely chopped**
> 2 **sour apples, finely diced**
> ½ **cup uncooked barley**
> ¼ **teaspoon caraway seeds**
> 2 **bay leaves**
>   **salt and pepper**
> 4 **cups stock (chicken or beef)**
> 1 **can sauerkraut (well drained)**
> 1 **cup white wine**
> ½ **pound fresh Polish sausage**
> ½ **pound smoked Polish sausage, sliced thin**
>   **plenty of sweet butter (unsalted)**

I use bear (precooked, otherwise it's tough), venison, pheasant, rabbit, wild pig (or pork neck bones), whole cornish game hens, or dove.

If you don't have enough game meat substitute domestic meats such as roast beef, pork chops, chicken, veal or cornish hens.

Slice or chop cabbage thinly, sprinkle with salt and let it stand 15 minutes, then press out moisture. Mix all ingredients together except sausage. Spread one tablespoon butter in a large roaster, put a layer of mixture over butter, then another tablespoon butter, then another layer of mixture. Add fresh sausage, another layer of mixture, more butter, until it is all in roaster. Now add stock and wine. Preheat oven to 275 degrees, cover tightly and roast for one hour, then check for moisture, if needed add more stock and wine. Slice smoked sausage, add to roaster and stir well. Return to oven for one and a half hours longer, checking moisture occasionally.

In a saucepan melt two tablespoons butter and mix in one tablespoon flour. Make sure it's smooth, and mix thoroughly with meat and cabbage. Bake for another 15 minutes. This is ideal for a large gathering and don't forget the vodka! Nazdrowie!

Marion A. Koszewski
Breaksville, OH

Wild Game Oven Bag

1 wild turkey, quartered
1 small venison roast, about 2 pounds
2 rabbits, quartered
4-6 quail breasts
2 yellow onions, peeled and wedged
6 small Idaho potatoes, peeled
1 tablespoon flour
1 teaspoon each: salt, pepper and sage
1 large (turkey size) baking bag
1 large oven roaster

Coat inside of baking bag with flour, salt, pepper and sage. Load in meats, onion and potatoes randomly. Bake at 350 degrees until done, approximately two hours.

Served hot, this is an effective recipe for introducing "wild" game to friends and relatives that are skeptical about the taste of wild meat.

Garland L. Hunter
Dallas, TX

DOUG PIFER

Oven Salami

5 pounds lean hamburger
3 teaspoons garlic salt
4 ½ teaspoons mustard seed
2 teaspoons Liquid Smoke
5 heaping teaspoons Morton's Tender Quick salt
4 ½ teaspoons pepper

Mix in large bowl. Divide into three equal parts and place in double plastic bags. Place in the refrigerator for three days, mixing each day. On third day roll into rolls and place on cookie sheet. Bake in oven for eight hours at 200 degrees, turning every two hours.

Paul Dever
Diamondville, WY

Wild Game Pot Roast

3-5 pounds trimmed and boned game meat
2 large cans rotel tomatoes
1 large sweet onion
5-6 potatoes
1 teaspoon seasoned salt
1 teaspoon ground black pepper
1 cup dry red wine

Place meat into a heavy, deep roasting pan. Cover meat with tomatoes, cut onions and potatoes into about six pieces and put into pan with all other ingredients. Slowly pour wine over meat. Cover tightly with foil and cook slowly over charcoal using indirect heat and a kettle type grill. You can also use your oven if you must! Cook slowly at about 250 degrees for three hours. Remove from pan, ladle sauce over potatoes, meat and bread . . . enjoy!

Barry A. Hall
Chicago Hgts, IL

Van Metre's Jalapeño Cornbread Casserole

1–1½ pounds lean ground venison
  2 cups cornmeal (yellow or white)
1½ cups milk
  2 eggs
  1 (15 ounce) can cream style corn
  1 (15 ounce) can western style pinto beans
  1 teaspoon salt
  ½ teaspoon soda
  2 tablespoons vegetable oil
  1 cup chopped onion
  ½ sweet green bell pepper, chopped (optional)
    garlic, chopped (optional)
4–6 jalapeño peppers
  ½ pound grated cheddar cheese

In a large bowl combine cornmeal, milk, eggs, corn, beans, salt, soda and oil and mix well. Mixture will be thin. In a large skillet cook ground venison and drain. To make filling, in a large bowl combine meat, onion, green bell pepper, garlic, jalapeño peppers and grated cheese. Pour one half batter into a well greased and floured 12 inch cast iron skillet. Spread filling evenly over batter. Pour remaining batter over filling. Bake at 350 degrees for one hour or until firm.

Note: You may use jalapeño beans and less jalapeño peppers. Serve with a lettuce and tomato salad for a complete meal. Try it, you'll like it!

Milton E. Van Metre
Corpus Christi, TX

Bwana Eddie's Buffalo Burritos
Smothered with Chili Verde

Shredded Buffalo Filling:
- 1 pound boneless buffalo chuck
- 1 cup water
- 6 peppercorns
- ¼ medium onion
- 1 garlic clove
- 1 tablespoon olive oil
- ½ medium chopped onion
- 1 small can tomatoes, peeled, chopped (½ pound)
- ¼ teaspoon ground cumin
- 1 teaspoon ground black pepper
- salt
- 8 flour tortillas

Place meat in a large saucepan, add water, peppercorns, one fourth onion and salt to taste. Cover and simmer on low to medium heat for about one and a half hours, or until meat is tender. Cool meat in stock. Save one half stock.

Shred buffalo with fingers or two forks. Make a paste by mashing garlic clove with one fourth teaspoon salt.

Heat oil in a large skillet and add garlic paste and remaining onion. Cook until onion is soft. Add green chilies and tomatoes to onion and garlic and sauté for about four minutes. Place meat, cumin and ground pepper in skillet. Heat and stir until mixture is heated thoroughly. Add reserved stock and salt, if needed, and stir. Keep warm until ready for use.

Note: For dryer mixture reduce stock to one third.

Chili Verde:
- 1 pound lean diced pork
- ½ diced onion
- 1 (8 ounce) can jalapeño chilies
- 2 cloves garlic, minced
- 2 tablespoons vegetable oil
- 2 small tomatoes, peeled and chopped
- 1 (8 ounce) can stewed tomatoes
- 2 teaspoons all purpose flour
- 2 tablespoons cumin

Garnishes:
   sour cream
   shredded cheese
   sliced avocado
   diced ripe olives

Cut pork into one inch cubes. Add oil to dutch oven and heat. Add pork and cook until brown. Add onion and garlic, cooking until tender. Add flour. Cook and stir until thoroughly mixed (about two minutes or longer).

Add cumin, jalapeños, stewed tomatoes and peeled tomatoes, breaking up tomatoes with a fork. Add salt and pepper to taste.

Heat flour tortillas and place on a warm plate. Place four tablespoons buffalo mixture in center of tortilla and roll up. Smother with chili verde and garnishes.

Yield: serves six, or four hearty eaters

Edd Rankin
Colorado Springs, CO

Barbecue Armadillo

1 armadillo, dressed
1 (15 ounce) can tomato sauce
1 cup barbecue sauce
¼ cup dark molasses
¼ cup hot barbecue sauce
1 diced onion
2 tablespoons vinegar
1 teaspoon salt

Pressure cook or pot boil armadillo until meat falls from bones, using as little water as possible. Remove bones and break meat into small pieces. Drain broth, set aside. Add remaining ingredients to meat and simmer 30 minutes. Stir often. If too thick, add some reserved broth.

Frances Gwaltney
Hiawassee, GA

—DOUG PIFER

Pintler Wilderness Stew

1 pound any type wild game meat, preferably
sirloin tips, cut into ½ inch cubes
½ - ¾ package onion soup mix
1 can golden mushroom soup
1 small can mushrooms pieces
½ can water chestnuts, sliced
½ cup dry vermouth
tarragon spice (optional)

Cook in a 350 degree oven for one to one and a half hours. Serve over Chinese noddles, egg noddles or rice.

To make your own Chinese noodles, boil spaghetti per instructions. Pat dry on paper towel. Cut into one half or three quarter inch lengths. Dust lightly with corn starch. Deep fry in vegetable oil until golden brown. Drain on paper towel before serving. Chinese noodles can also be made by using cooked spaetzele (German noodle) dough and following above instructions.

C. Ray Fischer
Philipsburg, MT

Wild Snapper Stew and Roux

1-1½ pounds snapper turtle meat (stew-sized chunks)
1 can golden mushroom soup
1 (12 ounce) package fresh mushrooms, sliced
1 small red pepper, diced
1 medium onion, diced
1 cup white wine
½ pound margarine
½ cup fresh parsley or 2 tablespoons dried
1 large can cream corn
1 box frozen peas
flour
water

Dredge meat in flour, brown in frying pan with one stick margarine. While you are doing that, brown onion, mushrooms and red pepper in margarine in a two quart saucepan. Add meat, golden mushroom soup, wine and parsley to vegetables, saving meat drippings. Cook at a simmer, stirring occasionally, and keep adding water if it gets too thick. This should cook for about one and a half hours.

To meat drippings, add remaining margarine with one half cup flour to make your roux, stirring often. This should brown up nicely in about one half hour. Now add this to your meat and vegetables and let it simmer until meat is tender (this should not take longer than an hour). Now add your corn and thawed peas. Simmer to heat peas and corn, stirring often. Serve with or over rice or egg noodles.

John Mazzariello
Rutland, VT

Wild Gumbo

 1 large mallard duck, cleaned and dressed
 2 squirrels, cleaned and dressed
 3 pounds raw shrimp, shelled, de-veined
 2 pounds kielbasa sausage, cut in small pieces
1 ½ gallons water (24 cups)
 1 large green pepper, chopped and seeded
 5 large jalapeños, minced
 1 head garlic, peeled and minced
1 ½ tablespoons filé powder
 2 teaspoons salt
 1 (12 ounce) can beer
 1 pound cup okra
 1 cup oil
 1 pound flour (4 cups)

Simmer duck, sausage and squirrels in water until tender with scallions, jalapeños, garlic, filé and beer. You will need a pot with a capacity of at least three gallons (12 quarts). After about one and a half hours, remove duck and squirrels, bone, and return meat to pot. Add okra and, stirring, return to simmer. Meanwhile, heat oil in a heavy skillet. Add flour and brown, stirring constantly, and simmer 15 to 20 minutes, or more. Turn off heat and let stand uncovered for 30 minutes. Do not stir. Serve in bowls over mounds of hot cooked rice.

Yield: about 30 servings

Mr. Sandy Kirby
Mt. Airy, MD

Baked Elephant's Foot

This is an old family recipe. I do not know how it got its name.

2½ pounds meat (venison, small game, fowl, beef, pork,
    chicken or a mixture), de-boned if preferred
  6 medium raw potatoes, peeled and diced
  3 medium onions, peeled and diced
  1 medium carrot, peeled and diced
  1 (15 ounce) can vegetables (corn, peas, limas, green
    beans or a mixture)
  2 stalks celery, cut fine

Cook meat, remove from roaster, de-bone if preferred. Place
potatoes on bottom of roaster. Mix carrots, onions, vegetables
and celery and layer on top of potatoes. Season with salt and
pepper to taste. Pour broth from meat over vegetables (if you
do not have enough broth to cover add one bouillon cube and
one cup water). Place meat on top and bake in 350 degree oven
for 45 minutes until potatoes are tender. For a change you can
substitute the cup water and bouillon cube with a 15 ounce can
stewed tomatoes.

Homer A. Kretzer
Gibsonia, PA

Leftover Wild Game Casserole

  1 pound game meat
  1 pound pork shoulder
  3 tablespoons butter
  1 medium onion
    salt and pepper to taste
1½ cups whole corn (canned or frozen)
  ⅓ cup cream
  1 teaspoon corn starch

Potato Topping:
  5 medium potatoes
  2 tablespoons butter
  2 egg yolks
    salt and pepper

Heat butter in a large frying pan over medium heat. Sauté onions until transparent. In a meat grinder or processor, mix game meat and pork. Add spices and meat to onions in skillet and fry until cooked. Spread mixture in bottom of a baking dish. Put corn, cream, and corn starch in skillet, bring to a boil until thick. Pour over meat.

Boil peeled potatoes in salted water. Mash potatoes with butter, egg yolks, salt and pepper, spread over mixture in baking dish. Bake at 400 degrees for about 20 minutes or until top starts to brown. Cut in squares and serve with a salad on the side.

Edd Rankin
Colorado Springs, CO

Alligator Jerky

Cut alligator tail into long strips one inch wide and one quarter inch thick or less.

Prepare "jerky salt mix" either with your favorite or mine:

1 part garlic salt
**1 part black or other pepper (swamp folk mostly use
    Tony Chachere's creole seasoning, Opelousas, LA)**

Sprinkle a thin layer of "jerky salt mix" on cutting board and lay alligator strips on salt mix. Sprinkle a layer of salt mix on top of alligator, so both sides are completely salted. Stick a toothpick through one end of each meat strip and suspend strips from oven or smoker rack after shaking off excess salt.

Heat or smoke around 120 degrees until dry (about four hours). Leave longer for super dry.

Store jerky in airtight containers, such as jars, and it will keep forever.

Try it, you'll like it.

Jim Esterly
Start, LA

313

Slow-Cooked Rattlesnake

6–8 pieces rattlesnake
½ cup lime juice
½ cup vegetable oil
1 cup flour
1 teaspoon seasoning salt (to taste)
1 cup chicken bouillon
½ cup chopped celery

Cut off rattlesnake head and skin. Remove entrails and cut into three inch sections. Wash in salt water and drain. Mix lime juice and oil and pour over snake pieces. Cover and let marinate in refrigerator overnight. Drain and pat dry. Roll in flour and seasoning salt. Brown in lightly oiled frying pan. Place celery in bottom of slow cooker and add meat. Pour bouillon over meat and cook on low 6 to 8 hours. Baste occasionally during cooking. Juice can be thickened slightly and used for gravy.

Benice Anderson
Richmond, MO

Sausage with Kraut

2 rings fresh sausage
1 (3 ounce) can chicken or beef broth
1 (28 ounce) can tomatoes, un-drained
1 bag sauerkraut, un-drained
1 (4 ounce) can mushrooms, drained
3 small onions, quartered
3 small potatoes, quartered
1 green pepper, chopped
1 bay leaf
3 peppercorns

In a large pot combine and simmer until potatoes and green pepper are firm. Then put in two rings fresh sausage. Cook until done.

Rodney Patuszwsk
Detroit, MI

Sauces

Barbecue Sauce for Rabbit, Squirrel or Ribs

1-2 cloves garlic, minced
2 tablespoons onion
2 tablespoons celery
2 tablespoons minced green pepper
½ cup catsup
2 tablespoons honey
2 tablespoons soy sauce
¼ teaspoon dry mustard
¼ teaspoon fresh ground pepper
¼ teaspoon basil or tarragon
¼ cup white wine

Combine above ingredients. Microwave for two minutes. Broil in oven, smoke or grill pieces of squirrel, rabbit or sections of venison or wild boar ribs.

Suzy Stefani
Rillton, PA

Tangy Wine Sauce for Venison Steak

½ teaspoon garlic powder
¼ teaspoon each: oregano, basil, marjoram, and fresh black pepper
¼ cup red wine
¼ cup catsup
1 teaspoon Dijon mustard
1 teaspoon worcestershire sauce

Combine all ingredients. Microwave one and a half minutes. Use as a basting and/or sauce as a warm accompaniment.

Suzy Stefani
Rillton, PA

Wine Sauce for Venison Roast or Steaks

1 clove garlic, minced
1 teaspoon minced onion
¼ teaspoon each: basil, oregano, marjoram and fresh
   ground black pepper
½ cup red wine

Combine above ingredients and microwave for one and a half minutes. Use one half as a marinade. Use reserve as basting and warm any remaining sauce and serve on the side with meat. Grill steaks in oven or on grill. Roasts may be smoked or cooked on grill or oven.

Suzy Stefani
Rillton, PA

Orange Honey Glaze for Grouse, Turkey or Pheasant

1 (6 ounce) can orange juice
¼ cup honey
2 tablespoons brandy
¼ teaspoon each: nutmeg, ground cloves, ginger, and
   dry mustard
1 orange, peeled and finely chopped

Combine above ingredients and microwave for two minutes.
   Use half of sauce for marinade. Smoke meat over sweet wood fire or roast in oven until internal temperature reaches 185 degrees. Baste with remaining sauce. Any leftover sauce may be reheated and served as a side dish with meat.

Suzy Stefani
Rillton, PA

Cranberry Glaze for Grouse, Pheasant or Turkey

¼ cup honey
1 small can jellied cranberry sauce
1 (6 ounce) can orange juice
2 tablespoons brandy, ginger brandy or ¼ teaspoon
   ginger

Melt cranberry sauce and honey for two minutes in microwave. Whisk in remaining ingredients. Microwave one and a half minutes more. Use one half as marinade. Smoke your choice of meat over sweet wood fire or roast in oven until internal temperature reaches 185. Baste frequently with remaining sauce. Warm unused sauce and serve with meat.

Suzy Stefani
Rillton, PA

Barbecue Backstrap

A tenderloin and backstrap marinade for deer and elk.

    1 cup teriyaki marinade and sauce
    1 cup olive oil
    ¼ cup parsley flakes
    2 teaspoons curry powder
    1 teaspoon black pepper
    1 small lemon, just the juice

Combine and mix ingredients. Make enough marinade to cover meat. Marinate approximately one half hour for every inch of meat thickness. Turn meat over one time while marinating.

Thaw out meat completely prior to marinating. Remove any connecting tissue. Do not cut tenderloin or backstrap into steaks or slices . . . leave whole or cut into length you wish to cook.

Place on a preheated barbecue grill on medium high if using gas or, if using standard grill, when coals begin to turn white. Cook with lid on barbecue grill approximately 10 minutes per side or until meat is still slightly pink and moist on the inside. Dip meat in marinade every time you turn it to cook the opposite side. Some flames can be expected from olive oil but they will not burn long nor hurt meat. Remove meat immediately when finished. Slice into one quarter inch thick steaks and serve.

Vernon E. Lovejoy
Lakewood, CO

Wild Game Barbecue Sauce

Great for any wild game or country style ribs. Cut large cuts of meat into one inch cubes or use strips of meat from small game, cut-up chicken, or wild fowl, three or four pounds. Combine the following:

- **3 tablespoons brown sugar**
- **2 tablespoons Liquid Smoke**
- **2 teaspoons garlic powder**
- **2 tablespoons chili powder**
- **2 tablespoons worcestershire sauce**
- **1 cup white or red wine**
- **1 can rotel hot chili peppers/tomatoes, diced**
- **1 cup catsup**
- **2 cups stewed tomatoes**
- **1 medium onion, minced**
- **2 tablespoons horseradish**
- **1 teaspoon dry mustard**

Prepare sauce the night before, cover and refrigerate.

Brush meat with vinegar, then dredge in flour and brown in a large cast iron skillet, oven-proof or dutch oven. Pour off grease. Pour sauce over meat and cook two hours at 350 degrees or until meat is fork tender. Add water if more liquid is needed during cooking to keep meat slightly covered.

Recipe may be prepared at campsite using dutch oven or iron skillet buried in coals.

Yield: serves four to six

Lee Jamerson
Topeka, KA

Venison Marinade

2 pounds venison steak
2 ounces soy sauce
2 ounces sweet vermouth
4 cloves fresh garlic, grated
1 medium onion, diced

Soak venison for one to three hours in refrigerator, stirring occasionally. Soaking time will depend on thickness of steaks. For a one half inch cut, one and a half hours is ideal. Broil in oven or over charcoal for extra marinade and flavor; baste while cooking.

Ron Walden
Bow, WA

Moose Marinade

Can also be used for elk, venison, caribou, lamb and beef.

½ bottle Heineken beer (or your favorite)
1 dash each: basil leaf, ginger, oregano and parsley
    flakes
3 dashes pepper
3 dashes seasoning salt or salt substitute
3 tablespoons Heinz 57 sauce
3 tablespoons red wine vinegar
3 tablespoons Durkee hot sauce
5 tablespoons worcestershire sauce

Mix ingredients in mixing bowl and marinade meat for at least four hours in refrigerator, uncovered.

Moose tastes best to me when steaks are grilled on a barbecue and marinade is lightly basted over steaks.

Mark T. Zack
Henderson, NV

A Good Marinating Sauce

1 can tomato paste
4 tablespoons chopped green pepper,
2 tablespoon Karo syrup

Simmer above on low heat for one half hour, remove from heat and add 1–1½ ounces Everclear (190 proof grain alcohol). Marinate game overnight, put it on before cooking, or use it as a sauce.

Casey Sidaway
Phoenix, AZ

Porcupine Sweet Sauce

The first time I had porcupine on my menu, comments and facial expressions were suitable for most comic books. The porcupine however, was the first to be eaten. This recipe is very sweet and will get people who aren't fond of game to sit up and clean their plates. Though not a must, I bone all meat before cooking. It makes eating easier and reduces slugs or shot pellets from people's plates.

1 teaspoon ground cinnamon
½ teaspoon nutmeg
3 tablespoons butter
⅛ cup lemon juice
¾ cup brown sugar
3–5 pounds game meat
1 cup apple juice

Combine above ingredients in a small pot. Mix well while heating on medium heat. Pour over game meat, cover with foil and bake at 350 until done. Baking pan should be no larger than is needed to hold meat.

When you are cleaning a pheasant, dove, squirrel or rabbit, always save heart and gizzards. Combine these items with scraps of other meats you are preparing. These items marinaded overnight in this sauce and simmered until done make great appetizers.

Mr. and Mrs. Steven Fairbrother
Turner Falls, MA

320

Scrap Sauce

1 pound game meat
½ bottle barbecue sauce
2 ounces worcestershire sauce
4 ounces soy sauce
2 ounces teriyaki sauce
⅛ teaspoon white pepper
⅛ teaspoon garlic powder (optional)

Drain sauce before serving. Sauce may taste bitter if sampled before cooking, but the finished product is what counts.

Mr. and Mrs. Steven Fairbrother
Turner Falls, MA

Just for Catfish and Bass

Fillet fish and warm deep frier to 400 degrees. Cut fillets into one inch squares. If fish seems dry place in an eggwash and then put in a bag with the following:

1½ pounds fish
1 cup flour
1 tablespoon Mrs. Dash seasoning
1 tablespoon sweet basil
1 teaspoon parsley flakes
½ teaspoon of white pepper

This is not a batter; shake bag until outside of fish is powdered only. A light coating is all you need. Deep fry until golden brown. It must be good, even our kids like it!

Mr. and Mrs. Steven Fairbrother
Turners Falls, MA

Sauce for Venison

No marinating needed.

½ **cup diced celery**
½ **cup catsup**
½ **cup water**
 1 **small onion, minced**
 1 **tablespoon brown sugar**
½ **tablespoon lemon juice**
 1 **tablespoon vinegar**
 1 **tablespoon worcestershire sauce**
 1 **teaspoon salt**
½ **teaspoon garlic salt**

Combine all ingredients and pour over meat. Let simmer for one and a half hours. Great for venison steaks and chops.

H. J. Townsend
Janesville, WI

Venison Gravy

½ **cup cooked venison roast**
3-4 **tablespoons Puritan oil**
2-3 **tablespoons flour**
 1 **(8 ounce) glass milk**
   salt to taste
   dash of pepper

Chop one half cup cooked venison roast that has been prepared in crock pot. Brown flour in Puritan oil at medium high heat. Add milk, salt and pepper. Mix in chopped venison. Stir constantly to prevent lumping. Cook until mixture thickens. Serve over home made biscuits or toasted loaf of bread.

   Yield: three to four servings

Peggy Ivy
Paducah, KY

Venison Shish-Kabob Marinade

½ teaspoon ground oregano
2 teaspoons brown sugar
1 teaspoon dry mustard
½ teaspoon ground ginger
½ teaspoon salt
2 tablespoons vegetable oil
1 tablespoon white vinegar
6 tablespoons soy sauce
¾ cup water

Mix dry spices with vinegar to a paste. Add remaining ingredients and stir well for a good mixture. Cube meat approximately one and a half inches. Remove all excess fat. Marinade for up to eight hours in refrigerator. Broil on skewers with desired vegetables no longer than six minutes per side.

Bud Sherry
Cornell, WI

Tomato Juice and Mushroom Sauce for Deer

8 slices deer meat, pounded to ¼ inch thickness
2 small onions
½ teaspoon garlic powder
1 tablespoon worcestershire sauce
1 (4 ounce) can mushrooms, with juice
1 cup flour
　　salt and pepper to taste
¼ cup Crisco
1½ pints tomato juice

Brown floured meat and diced onions in oil in a ten inch skillet. Mix tomato juice, worcestershire sauce and garlic powder together and pour over browned meat, add mushrooms, simmer for 45 minutes to one hour.
　Yield: serves four

Mrs. Dorothy V. Harry
Waiterville, WV

Marinade for Game Steaks

Score steaks in crisscross pattern with sharp knife.
  Mix marinade in a glass or plastic bowl.

¼ cup soy sauce
¾ cup vegetable oil
½ cup finely chopped green onion
 3 tablespoons honey
 2 tablespoons wine vinegar
1 ½ teaspoons ground ginger
 1 teaspoon garlic powder
 2 teaspoons meat tenderizer

Marinate meat in the refrigerator for 24 hours. Broil under flame
or on outdoor barbecue grill.

Jannie Vaught
Sheridan, WY

Marinade for Fish

Generally, fish has almost no fat or oils, and this limits cooking
to either frying in deep fat, with or without batter, or in a frying
pan. Some fish lend themselves to baking, steaming or boiling,
but when cooked on grills over live coals or gas, most fish stick
to grill, or fall apart when it is time to turn them. These prob-
lems can be corrected with marinades, which will firm the flesh
and add wonderful flavors. Oil based salad dressing makes an
inexpensive marinade, needs no advance preparation, is easily
available and one which we use regularly on many species of fish.
We have tried many flavors, but our favorite is Italian dressing.
We place serving sized pieces fillets or chunks, in a plastic bag,
then pour in enough Wishbone to cover exposed fish, and roll
fish pieces around until they are all in contact with dressing.
Depending upon thickness and size of pieces, we leave them in
bag, refrigerated, for a half hour to 45 minutes, turning them
at least once. Cook them on grill until done, turning them only
once. We baste thick pieces once with leftover dressing. This is
one possible salad dressing marinade, and others we have tried
work well too.

Charlie Davis
Huntington Beach, CA

Linguine with Shark Sauce

1 ½ pounds shark in bite size pieces, 1x1 inch
 1 pound linguine pasta
 3 cans tomato sauce
 2 tablespoons fresh garlic, crushed
 1 small to medium yellow onion, finely diced
 1 tablespoon dry sweet basil leaves, crushed
 1 teaspoon salt
 ½ teaspoon crushed red pepper, optional
 1 tablespoon sugar
 ⅓ cup olive oil
 ¼ cup red wine, optional

Heat olive oil in large saucepan and sauté onion, garlic, basil, and red pepper until brown. Stir in tomato sauce, wine, sugar and salt and simmer for 30 minutes on low heat, covered. Turn off heat and add shark meat, mix gently and let stand uncovered for one hour. This cooks the shark without disintegrating the fish. Re-heat slowly, uncovered, for 10 minutes while cooking pasta (follow directions on package). Serve shark sauce over pasta along with Italian dressed salad with a light cabernet or chianti wine.

Yield: serves four to six people

Tom Ceglia
Durango, CO

Venison Spaghetti Sauce

1 ½ pounds ground venison
 6 stalks celery
 1 large onion
 1 (6 ounce) can tomato paste
 3 (8 ounce) cans tomato sauce
 1 can cream of mushroom soup
 ½ teaspoon oregano
 1 clove garlic, crushed and minced
   salt
   pepper
 ½ pound fresh mushrooms or 1 large can mushrooms

Brown ground venison in a frying pan and drain. Sauté celery, onion, and mushrooms, if fresh, until tender. Add remaining ingredients, stir and simmer over low heat for two to three hours, stirring occasionally. Serve over spaghetti noodles with garlic bread.

Or, make the same recipe by reducing venison to one pound, omit oregano, use ½ teaspoon garlic powder for the clove of garlic and add 1 (15 ounce) can tomatoes. Reduce cooking time to one hour. Cook the same as above.

Dan Dobbins
Columbia, SC

Side Dishes

Steve and Buddy's Base Camp Pork and Beans

1 (10 ounce) can pork and beans
4-6 slices bacon
  1 tablespoon mustard
  1 small handful brown sugar or ¼ cup maple syrup, molasses or honey
  1 small onion, cut up (or more to your taste)

Put beans in a pot and simmer over coals or on the stove. Add bacon, mustard, brown sugar (or syrup, molasses or honey) and onion. Let this simmer until it thickens and bacon is done. Sure improves a can of beans.

Stephen G. Roberts
Wasilla, AK

Bwana Eddie's Jungle Green

1 pound chopped spinach or broccoli
1 pound mozzarella cheese, shredded
1 teaspoon garlic powder
1 teaspoon onion powder
1 medium chicken or duck egg
¼ teaspoon black pepper
¾ cup light cream
1 tablespoon butter

Cook vegetables of choice. Frozen vegetables are very convenient.

Rinse with cold water and drain. Melt butter in small saucepan and mix with vegetables. In separate bowl, beat eggs with a whisk while adding cream. Add garlic powder, onion powder, pepper and shredded mozzarella cheese to eggs and cream. Mix thoroughly by hand. Add your spinach or broccoli to mixture. Place in individual ceramic or Pyrex dishes and bake at 375 degrees for approximately 15 minutes or until mixture starts to bubble and lightly brown on top. Jungle Green is an excellent entree when served with a fresh green salad.

Yield: eight side dishes or four as entree

Edd Rankin
Colorado Springs, CO

Cowboy Beans

1 pound ground beef
2 tablespoons minced onion
1 teaspoon salt
dash of black pepper

Brown the meat in a large skillet. Combine above and season with celery salt and seasoning salt to taste. Add above ingredients to a large pot and stir in the following:

¼ cup firmly packed brown sugar
¼ cup molasses
¼ cup vinegar
¼ teaspoon dry mustard
½ teaspoon garlic powder
1 can kidney beans
1 can lima beans
1 can baked beans
5 slices of bacon, cut up and cooked
2 cups sliced onions, sauteed

Simmer over a low flame for about one hour or until all flavors are absorbed.

Joseph V. Stefko
Greensburg, PA

Tortelini Ala Bwana

1 (12 ounce) package tortelini, cheese or meat
1 (8 ounce) carton whipping cream
1 ounce dry sherry
⅛ teaspoon nutmeg
3 tablespoons butter
1 ounce oil

Bring water to a boil with salt and oil. Drop tortelini into boiling water. Cook to desired texture. In a saucepan, mix butter, cream, sherry and nutmeg. Cook on low heat and when sauce begins to thicken add cooked tortelini and gently mix together.

Serve as a side dish or main entree. This is an excellent addition to fish or fowl dishes.

Edd Rankin
Colorado Springs, CO

Breakfast in an Orange Skin

Cut off the top third of an orange and eat the orange with a spoon, leaving some pulp inside. Crack an egg into the orange, set it upright in coals of your campfire, and in a few minutes you'll have a cooked egg with a delicious, different taste. Children love this breakfast and it takes very little time to prepare.

Edd Rankin
Colorado Springs, CO

Part III
The Complete Hunter

CHAPTER 9

SAFETY AND ETHICAL CONSIDERATIONS

—DOUG PIFER

afety is the primary consideration for every hunter. Safety first of all involves your firearm. Know how it works, the proper ammunition it uses, and learn to shoot it properly. Observe all the gun safety rules, keeping your muzzle in a safe direction at all times. Carry and use only the proper ammunition, maintain your firearm and keep it clean. Establish zones of fire when hunting with others. In short, follow all the gun safety rules printed at the beginning of this book.

Safety Afield

Safety also involves yourself and your fellow hunters. Don't hunt under adverse conditions such as when overly tired, cold, hungry or if you are otherwise stressed. At such times your reflexes, judgment and physical performance can endanger your safety and that of other hunters.

General outdoor safety includes preparing for adverse weather conditions and avoiding outdoor mishaps like becoming lost, falling, hypothermia and drowning. Use common sense, prepare yourself ahead of time and exercise care in using such outdoor equipment as stoves, hatchets, and knives. On major big game hunts camping and horseback riding bring hazards of their own. Prepare yourself by taking a short shakedown trip in advance.

Finally, exercise care while field dressing and packing out game animals. Wear orange clothing and keep it visible even if you remove your coat. Accidents often occur during dusk or twilight conditions. Carry and use a flashlight so you won't be mistaken for game or suffer from a fall.

The Ethical Hunter

This cookbook is testimony to the responsible NRA member who doesn't just shoot game and leave it in the field. In short, consuming wild game is ethical, safe, responsible hunting.

Responsiblities to Other Hunters

Try to pass on responsible hunting behavior to fellow hunters. Educate new hunters in hunting ethics whenever you can, and don't hunt with a companion who refuses to hunt responsibly.

Responsiblities to the Game

A responsible hunter will pass up a shot that might be less than lethal. By so doing you avoid shots that may simply wound an animal or ruin the meat. A carelessly gutshot animal often escapes to die later unretrieved, or the meat is often contaminated by internal body fluids. Furthermore, an animal that is wounded and later retrieved is likely to be tough and strong tasting because of the buildup of lactic acid and other elements due to stress and trauma.

Responsible hunting is more than knowing and following game laws. Identifying your target is more than just knowing whether you're shooting a buck or a doe, the sex and species of duck coming in, or the difference between a turkey hen or gobbler. Is there anything beyond your target? Should you wait for a better shot?

333

Responsibilities to Yourself

Safe hunting means unloading your firearm and putting it in a safe place while you field dress your deer. Continue to wear blaze orange, and be careful to wrap some of it around your deer or turkey as you take it out of the woods. Otherwise you might be mistakenly shot at by another hunter.

Responsibility to the Public

Ethical hunting means respecting the nonhunting public. Dispose of gut piles and inedible parts of carcasses discreetly, and don't display dead game in public view.

Responsibilty to Landowners

Respect private and public property. Respect yourself and behave as a lady or gentleman. Be careful to ask permission to hunt and offer the landowner a share of your game. Respect the game and don't overshoot our favorite hunting spots.

—DOUG PIFER

Pass Along the Tradition

Sharing wild game with family and friends is a great tradition and fulfills a hunter's role in game management. By so doing, you realize that hunting isn't a spectator sport. Hunters don't watch nature from the sidelines or on television. They are part of it.

Finally, hunting involves American family life. Most hunters grow up eating wild game at the family table. Often this is the best way to favorably introduce women and children to hunting. Helping to prepare game and sharing it with the family involves your children in hunting's heritage. When and if they choose to hunt and pass the bounty along to their children, they'll be responsible, ethical and safe.

Appendix

—DOUG PIFER

THE NRA AND HUNTING

The National Rifle Association of America encourages and supports sport hunting through a wide variety of programs and services.

The NRA Hunter Services Division assists state and provincial hunter education programs with support materials and training programs for professional and volunteer staff. NRA Hunter Clinics, offered by an NRA sponsored event or a trained instructor, answer the demand for advanced education by emphasizing skills, responsibility, and safety as applied to hunting techniques and game species. The NRA Youth Hunter Education Challenge uses hunting simulated events to give young hunters a chance to apply basic skills learned in the classroom on local, state and national level. The NRA Hunter Recognition Program offers awards to hunters for big game hunting achievement. Financial support for wildlife management and shooting sports research is available through the NRA Grants-in-Aid Program.

The NRA Institute for Legislative Action protects the legal rights of hunters. NRA Publications provides a variety of printed material on firearms, equipment and techniques for hunters, including *American Hunter* magazine, the largest periodical in the U. S. devoted to hunting. Junior programs encourage young people to participate in hunting. Special insurance benefits are available to NRA hunting members, and hunters can further benefit by joining an NRA hunting club or by affiliating an existing club with the NRA. The NRA works with other hunting organizations to sustain a positive image of hunting as a traditional form of recreation, to combat anti-hunting efforts, and to promote a life-long interest in hunting.

For further information, contact the National Rifle Association of America, Hunter Services Division, 1600 Rhode Island Avenue, N.W., Washington, D.C. 20036–3268. Telephone (202) 828–6029.

To join NRA today, or for additional information regarding membership, please call 1–800–368–5714. Your membership dues can be charged to VISA or MasterCard.

NRA Materials for the Hunter

The following are materials available from the NRA Sales Department and can help you prepare your next hunting trip.

Description	Item No.	Unit Price
The Hunter's Guide	HE5N5090	$ 8.95 each
NRA Hunter Skills Series		
Student Manual		
Upland Bird Hunting	HS5N5476	$ 5.00 each
Bowhunting	HS5N5261	$ 5.00 each
Muzzleloader Hunting	HS5N5145	$ 5.00 each
Whitetail Deer Hunting	HS5N5047	$ 5.00 each
Western Big Game Hunting	HS5N5207	$ 5.00 each
Waterfowl Hunting	HS5N5083	$ 5.00 each
Wild Turkey Hunting	HS5N5707	$ 5.00 each
Hardbound Version		
Upland Bird Hunting	HS5N5501	$14.95 each
Bowhunting	HS5N5449	$14.95 each
Muzzleloader Hunting	HS5N5172	$14.95 each
Whitetail Deer Hunting	HS5N5261	$14.95 each
Western Big Game Hunting	HS5N5243	$14.95 each
Waterfowl Hunting	HS5N5136	$14.95 each
Wild Turkey Hunting	HS5N5734	$14.95 each
NRA Members' Wild Game Cookbook	HS5N5805	$12.95 each
Life Size Game Targets*		
Brochure	HS3N0017	NC
Package containing one each:		
Whitetail Deer, Turkey,		
Duck, Rabbit, Groundhog,		
Mule Deer Black Bear,		
Pronghorn, Javelina,		
Coyote, Red Fox, Pheasant,		
and Squirrel	HS5N1023	$ 7.00

*Note: Various package quantities are available.

NRA Hunter Clinic Program
Brochure — Keeping the
Tradition Alive and Flourishing! HS3N0053 N/C
NRA Hunter Clinic Instructor
Certification Order Form HS3N8037 N/C
Other Brochures
NRA Hunter Recognition Awards HI3N0106 N/C
Wild Game From Field to Table HI3N0080 N/C
Hunting and Wildlife
Management HE3N0140 N/C
Landowner Relations HE3N0033 N/C
Responsible Hunting HE3N0024 N/C
Hypothermia HE3N0079 N/C
Fitness and Nutrition HE3N0097 N/C
Water Safety HE3N0051 N/C
Tree Stand Safety HE3N0015 N/C
Turkey Hunting Safety HE3N0113 N/C
Hunting's Future? It's Up to You HE3N0159 N/C
Eye and Ear Care HE3N0042 N/C
NRA and Hunting HI3N0115 N/C

NRA Hunter Clinic Video Collection
(VHS) Brochure/Order Form HI3N5003 N/C

NRA Hunter Services
Materials Price List HI3N8091 N/C

NRA Standard Order Form XS7N8000 N/C

ORDERING INFORMATION

- Use the NRA Standard Order Form to order items listed. Prices are subject to change without notice.
- Prices do not include shipping and handling charges. Certain state sales taxes are applicable.
- Order forms and current prices are available from NRA Sales Department, P.O. Box 5000, Kearneysville, WV 25430-5000 or call **toll free 1-800-336-7402**. Hours: 9:00 a.m. to 5:00 p.m. Eastern time.

THE NRA HUNTER SKILLS SERIES

The NRA Hunter Skills Series is a developing library of books on hunting, shooting, and related activities. It supports the NRA Hunter Clinic Program, a national network of seminars conducted by the NRA Hunter Services Division and volunteer hunter clinic instructors.

The hunter training manuals are developed by NRA staff, with the assistance of noted hunting experts, hunter educators, experienced outdoor writers, and representatives of hunting/conservation organizations. The publications are available in student (bound) and instructor (loose leaf) editions.

The program is planned to include clinics and support material on hunting whitetail deer, waterfowl, wild turkey, small game, predators, upland game, western big game, and others. It will also address marksmanship and hunting with rifle, shotgun, muzzleloader, handgun, and archery equipment.

For more information about the NRA Hunter Clinic Program and its training materials, contact the National Rifle Association of America, Hunter Services Division, 1600 Rhode Island Avenue, N.W., Washington D.C. 20036-3268. Telephone(202) 828-6029.

NRA Big Game Hunter Awards

L et the NRA Big Game Hunter Awards Program help preserve the excitement and memories of some of your best hunts. This program emphasizes the hunter's skills and quality of the hunt — not trophy size. The minimum requirements for all 14 categories of North American big game that are accepted for these awards are listed in the chart below. The program recognizes achievement in four different hunting methods:

> **Modern Firearm — Long Gun**
> **Modern Firearm — Handgun**
> **Muzzleloading Firearm**
> **Bow and Arrow**

Beautifully designed certificates mounted on walnut plaques are personalized with the hunt method, hunter's name, animal category and the year and the state or province of the hunt.

Requirements

Category	Index for Determining Status	Minimum Requirements
Black Bear	Greatest width plus	16 inches
Cougar	length of skull	12 inches
Grizzly and Brown Bear	without jaw	18 inches
Elk	Minimum numbers	5
Mule Deer	of points on at least	4
Black-tailed Deer	one side of rack	3
Whitetail Deer		4
Coues Whitetail Deer		3
Moose	Greatest spread	40 inches
Caribou	Maximum inside spread	30 inches
Pronghorn	Length of longest horn	11 inches
Rocky Mountain Goat		8 inches
Native Wild Sheep	Extent of curl	¾
Wild Turkey	Beard length	8 inches

For more information on the NRA Big Game Hunter Awards refer to the NRA Hunter Recognition Program brochure (HI3N0106) or contact the National Rifle Association of America, Hunter Services Division, 1600 Rhode Island Avenue, N.W., Washington D.C. 20036-3268. Telephone (202) 828-6029.

Index

WEIGHTS AND MEASURES TABLE

Equivalents:

4	cups	=	1	quart	=	950 ml
2	pints	=	1	quart	=	950 ml
16	ounces	=	1	pint	=	500 ml
2	cups	=	1	pint	=	500 ml
2	cups	=	16	fluid ounces	=	500 ml
16	tablespoons	=	1	cup	=	240 ml
8	liquid ounces	=	1	cup	=	240 ml
4	tablespoons	=	¼	cup	=	60 ml
¼	cup	=	2	liquid ounces	=	60 ml
1	liquid ounce	=	2	tablespoons	=	30 ml
3	teaspoons	=	1	tablespoon	=	15 ml
1	cc	=			=	1 ml